How It Looks Going Back
Growing Up in the Montana Woods

Doris Knowles Pulis

RIVERBEND
PUBLISHING

Author's Note

This book is a collection of memories. Therefore there are bound to be inaccuracies and for these I sincerely apologize. The people about whom I have written are portrayed as accurately as possible, according to my recollections and those of my parents and my sister. In a few instances I have compacted or rearranged events to keep a pace enjoyable for the reader. It has been my intention above all to recreate the Yaak Valley and the people we knew there, and to share our memories with others who might have treasured the experience as much as we did.

D.K.P.
October 2009

Cover design by DD Dowden
Text design by Barbara Fifer

RIVERBEND
PUBLISHING
P.O. BOX 5833
HELENA, MT 59604
1-866-787-2363
www.riverbendpublishing.com

To my heroes:
Mom, Dad, Bob and Steve

Acknowledgments

For an inexperienced writer, making the commitment to write a book takes little more than a mountain of naive enthusiasm. Seeing the task to its end can only happen with the help and guidance of others. I would like to thank Myrna Chaney for seeing something in my childhood memories worth setting down on paper. I could not have completed the task had it not been for Lucia Work, who made me take my writing seriously, lent me her eyes as an editor, her shoulder and good council as a mentor and friend, and her courage whenever I began to doubt my own. To my mother, Marilyn Knowles, I would like to express my profound admiration for her ability to reach into her head and pull out details from fifty-odd years ago. During the writing of this book, I have been grateful every day for her patience with my endless phone calls and questions. To my daughter, Anne, I owe many thanks for her heartless criticism, her energetic research skills and for getting me back on track time and again when I was lost in adjectives and nostalgia. To my son, Chris, who provided me with priceless tech support and regular, generous doses of a novice writer's most basic sustenance, praise, I also owe my heartfelt thanks. To my husband, Cal, for putting up with midnight weirdness and the disaster of a computer crash, for accompanying me on research trips and then spending long, lonely days without a wife, for listening to forty-five years of Yaak stories, I owe, and have already given, a lifetime of love.

Contents

Introduction

Roughly 35 miles south of the Canadian border, between the towns of Troy, Montana, and Bonners Ferry, Idaho, the Yaak River flows out of the Purcell Mountains into the Kootenai River. The Yaak pierces the larger Kootenai at right angles, the central thrust of its current carrying across the hundred yards to the Kootenai's opposite bank. Fittingly, the name, "Yaak," is derived from a Native American word for "arrow."

The Yaak River begins its course in British Columbia. On the map, it appears as a tiny line wandering southwest across the upper left-hand corner of Montana. Alternately rushing over stony grades, then drifting lazily, the river cuts a narrow valley through mountains forested with larch, spruce, pine and fir. This valley, with its creeks and waterfalls, low-lying, swampy stands of cedar trees and rocky, ragged meadows, is a place caught in a pocket of time.

The Kootenai Indians once had hunting trails along the Yaak River and up into Canada. In the late 1800's a few miners and trappers began to set up permanent camps in the area. The 1910 fires destroyed much of the main mining settlement at Sylvanite but brought men who fought the fires, liked the country and stayed. By the 1940's, some thirty-five to forty families lived in the valley, many on land they had homesteaded. Some were immigrants, some were Forest Service employees, a few were loggers. Most were a hard working bunch who loved the secret and beautiful place they called home. Well past the middle of the twentieth century, these hardy folks did without running water and electricity and regularly got snowed in during the winter. To them, "The Yaak," as they called this place that was too far from everywhere, with its legendary snowfalls, notoriously short summers and a treacherous road that discouraged all but the most determined traveler, was the center of the world.

My family happened to drive down through the Yaak Valley in the summer of 1949, from Canada, where we had been vacationing. My mother and dad, with my three-year-old younger sister and me, age eight, were on our way back home to San Diego, California. Dad had heard about the fishing in the Yaak River and wanted to give it a try. Purely by chance, we came across a homestead, 160 acres with a lake and a log cabin, for sale. On a whim, my parents, city dwellers their whole lives, decided to buy the place and move up there.

It was an outrageous idea, particularly to anyone who knew my parents. My mother was born and raised in Chicago; her family were well-to-do in the 1920's. She grew up in a large house—the first "all electric" home in the city—with every possible convenience. In Mom's childhood, summers were for going to the beach and winters were for trips to New York, to go shopping and see plays. In her teens she learned to jitterbug in the ballrooms of the big Chicago hotels and helped her mother give fancy dinner parties. She loved art and was a natural portraitist, which earned her a scholarship to the Chicago Art Institute. When the Depression came in the Thirties, the family wealth—mostly real estate investments—was lost. Mom's parents were too old to start again and died within six months of each other. In January of 1939, she came out west. She stopped in the town of Fallbrook, California and took a job waiting tables at the El Real Hotel.

My father couldn't get over the injustice of the Depression. Even years later, his eyes would tear up when he recalled that terrible time, seeing people subsist on potato peelings. When hard times hit Salt Lake City, Dad's parents lost their livelihood—a lumberyard—and ultimately their health. By the time Dad turned fifteen, both his parents were gone.

He was the youngest child in a family of six boys and a girl. Dad's mother was a gentle Mormon lady who nurtured a love of music in all her children and wanted nothing more for her sons than that they grow up to be church-going gentlemen. But Dad's father stressed education as a priority and insisted upon naming his youngest son Darwin Emerson. Dad, blessed with the brain of a scholar, but bringing up the rear in the family, had to leave school when his parents died. His brothers scattered to find work, his sister went to live with an aunt and Dad lied about his age and joined the Civilian Conservation Corps. During the next half-dozen years he had thirteen jobs. And he spent every spare minute trying to catch up with what he imagined must be the educated world, always miles ahead of him. He read anything he could get his hands on, a disorganized conglomeration of subjects: he made his way through Courant's *Methods of Mathematical Physics, The Wealth of Nations* by Adam Smith, Frank Dawson Adams' *The Birth and Development of the Geological Sciences,* the philosophies of Heidegger and Hegel, Marx and Kant, essays by Thoreau and Emerson, anything he could get by Dickens, Poe, or Kipling and a hodgepodge of others from Fitzgerald to Jack London to Booth Tarkington. He owned two copies of his favorite, *Science and the Modern World* by Alfred North Whitehead. Sometime during those years he decided his mother's Mormon faith was a fairy tale.

He drifted south and wound up in Fallbrook, where he found a grocery store sitting empty. He managed to get it going. He was his own janitor, stock boy, clerk, butcher and bookkeeper. One day a tall young woman in slacks came in. She stood in front of the glass meat case and frowned at the steaks. His beef prices were too high, she said. She told him she knew what she was talking about because she had just come from Chicago, the stockyard city. She bought a lamb chop. After she left he had to polish her fingerprints off the glass.

Dad's sister, Melba, was horrified when barely six weeks after "that girl from Chicago" walked into Dad's store, and the two of them ran off to Yuma and got married.

Having grown up with snowy winters, both my parents loved Southern California. Not long before Pearl Harbor, they sold the store and moved to San Diego. Dad went to work in a defense plant where they were building the B-24 bombers. He became a foreman in the wing section. My sister and I were born. When the war was over and the whole country was high on optimism, Dad started a business selling new Chevrolets. After years of scrambling for pennies, suddenly there was plenty of money. We had a new car, a new house, even a television set, with an antenna in the back yard on a fifty-foot mast, so we could get good reception from Los Angeles.

In later years, if you asked my parents about their reasons for moving to Montana, they would grin at each other, painfully, as if remembering a joke, one that was on them. But at the time, they had their reasons. To me, Montana is where I wallowed in childhood. I was part of a family that most of the time was the only thing that really mattered to any of us. It was a cozy, scary, painful, hilarious, dangerous, interesting and grand time, and the most fun I ever had.

CHAPTER 1

The Initial
Escapade

It started out as a fishing trip in June of 1949. We were going camping in Canada. Dad knew a lot of people through his car business in San Diego and a friend of his had a friend who knew about a tiny lake in British Columbia, Puntzi Lake, near the town of Redstone. We had never heard of anyone going on a camping vacation. It was Dad's idea.

He got us outfitted with army surplus gear. We had a six-by-nine canvas tent, four sleeping bags with air mattresses, a folding camp table and four stools, a gas cook stove and lantern, and a set of tin cooking utensils, including plates and silverware that fit inside a single, large pot.

We had a car-top carrier that fastened with suction cups to Dad's brand new, ice green, four-door deluxe Fleetline Chevrolet demonstrator. We loaded everything up and set out on Highway 395—my parents, Dar and Marilyn Knowles, my younger sister Barbara Jean, known to us all as "Bob" and me, Doris Ann, called "Dee." We drove the two thousand miles from San Diego to Puntzi Lake, stopping wherever we found good fishing, and camping wherever we wanted, beside a creek or in a pretty spot in the woods. The world my sister and I knew, open sky and sunny beaches, disappeared.

North of the Canadian border the road turned to gravel. We were climbing one minute, deep in a canyon the next, lost among dark trees. We crossed and re-crossed rivers on narrow, creaking log bridges. Towns were tiny and few. On our few stops, I saw native men and women wrapped in blankets, with long black braids and moccasins on their feet. I was old enough to be in awe of these silent, black-eyed people who stood by the doors of shops and watched my sister and me, both of us no doubt appearing outlandishly blond and pale. Tall, lanky Mom, the Chicago native, stood out like a sore thumb with her brown

5

hair in a citified pageboy and her mascara-ed eyelashes. She grabbed our hands and held us tightly against her whenever she guided us in or out of a general store or a café or a gas station privy.

The first thing we noticed about Puntzi Lake was the mosquitoes. They swarmed all over, biting in two or three places at once. Citronella was the repellent we used, and Mom slathered us with it. After a few days we got used to having the wretched pests around.

Puntzi Lake Lodge was situated in a meadow about a hundred yards back from the edge of the lake. It was a cavernous, darkish log building with a kitchen and a long dining table in the front, and a rock fireplace at the far end. A ladder went up the outside of the building to the sleeping loft, but after checking out the ladder and the loft, Dad suggested that we sleep in our tent. So we pitched camp on the meadow grass beside the lodge and there we stayed for the next couple of weeks.

The fishing was wonderful. Mom and Dad spent all day, every day, along the shore of the lake with their fly rods, whooping with laughter whenever a fish flashed into the air on the end of one of their lines. They fished until their arms were tired.

We ate all our meals in the lodge kitchen. Mr. Kingswood, the lodge owner, and his son did the cooking. For dinner we usually had fish—great, heaping platters of fried trout. And we learned to eat them as our hosts did, like corn on the cob, head in one hand, tail in the other. We put the bones on newspapers under the table for the cats. Dessert was always a surprise. One night we might have biscuits layered with canned peaches and chocolate pudding, another night, pancakes smothered in strawberry jam with thick, straight cream poured over the top.

The night before we were to leave the lodge, Dad mentioned that there was a river in Montana he had heard about and he would like to try the fishing there on the way home. The next morning we packed our gear into our scratched-up, squeaky, left-listing Chevy and headed for the trout stream in Montana, a river with the odd, Tibetan-sounding name of "Yaak."

We came across the Canadian border into Montana near the town of Rexford. From there we crossed the Kootenai River on a rickety wooden bridge, then traveled west into the mountains for about thirty miles, over a terrible road. Several times we stopped so Dad could roll rocks out of the way of our low-riding car. Where the road was narrow and there was a steep drop-off on one side, Mom got behind the wheel and Dad walked ahead to guide us. We were determined to get to this Yaak River, wherever it was, and we pushed on until we saw a Forest Service sign that said we were there. We found a shady spot along the bank of the North Fork of the Yaak River for our camp.

The river was rocky, some thirty feet across and flowing gently, perfectly clear and cold. Spruce, pine and fir trees grew to the edge of the water on both banks. We were deep in the mountains; "a perfect spot," Mom said. She began to unpack as cheerfully as if she were moving into a new house. That's when she discovered something was missing from her "kitchen." We had left our tin plates back at Puntzi Lake Lodge.

It was a minor oversight. But it changed our lives.

There's no doubt about it, I was one reason we moved to Montana. I was a scrawny kid and wouldn't thrive. My little sister was bouncing with health but I saddled my parents with a chronic worry. I wouldn't eat and had dark circles under my eyes. During polio season—all summer—my parents were told to keep me indoors, away from other kids. According to the doctors, I was allergic to everything in California.

But it is also true that in addition to loving the outdoors, both my parents had peculiarities that might explain "what got into them," as Aunt Melba put it, when they turned their backs on sunny San Diego, all their family and friends and a perfectly fine business, and moved to a cabin in the wilderness.

Mom was born with a reckless streak and the heart of a gypsy. She was game for anything. In her twenties, a life that challenged her strong body and made her heart pound, intrigued her. She couldn't help it, she wanted to try something that was the complete opposite of her childhood.

Dad had his bugaboo: the Depression. But when it was over, he thought the world was going haywire all over again, with the pendulum swinging too far the other way and everybody obsessed with making money. With a talent for business, especially the automobile business, that he considered almost perverse, he saw a danger of getting too caught up in it himself. He thought a man mustn't let the pursuit of wealth take over his life. He wanted to find a way to live that wasn't going to cost somebody else. Besides that, he had painful memories of a childhood jerked away too soon. He had something else in mind for his own daughters.

Tin plates were pretty much a necessity in that time before paper dishes were common. If we'd had something else to use, we would have no doubt camped and fished our way down the Yaak River to the south end of the valley as planned, returned to the paved road—good old Highway 2—and driven on home to California. As it turned out, Dad decided to walk back up the road to a mailbox we had passed and see if he could find someone around. I went with him.

The name "Shultz" was painted on the mailbox and a rough pair of ruts turned off the main road there, leading north. We followed the ruts about a quarter of a mile along a zig-zagging rail fence with cattle grazing inside it. We came to a log barn and then to a substantial log house. In spite of the warm day—it must have been in the 80's—there was smoke rising from the chimney.

Mrs. Shultz was a stocky, gray-headed lady, dressed in a house dress and bedroom slippers, busy at a contraption I later learned was a milk separator, when we knocked at her door. She sized up Dad's sturdy shoulders, energetic hazel eyes, wild, wavy hair and strong, under-bite jaw and decided we were okay. She invited us to sit down, out on the porch. Supper was cooking on the stove; she said, and the kitchen was too warm for comfort. She had some plates to lend us—yellow china with flowers—and she wrapped up a chunk of homemade butter in a piece of waxed paper to send along. She asked Dad lots of questions about where we were from, what he did for a living and what we were doing way up here so far from home. Dad told her we were on a fishing trip. She said she couldn't imagine anybody driving such a long way just to go fishing. She passed along some of the local gossip, as if we might know some of the folks involved, and as we left she mentioned that there was a small private lake nearby that we could fish in, if we wanted.

The weather stayed nice and the fish in the river were plentiful, but small. After a couple of days Dad went back to the Shultz place to inquire about the lake Mrs. Shultz had mentioned. This time Mr. Shultz was home. He gave Dad directions to a caretaker's cabin where we could ask permission to fish in the lake. Standing in the doorway as Dad left, he called out, "That lake place is up for sale. In case you're interested."

The caretaker's name was Mrs. Wheeler. She was a fragile-looking lady of about seventy and the mother of the owner of the lake, a man by the name of Ted Miller. Mrs. Wheeler's little cabin was on the West Fork road, right beside the Yaak River. She was living there alone, waiting for her son's property to sell, she told us, at which time she planned to join him in Seattle. Although she was too old to stay alone any longer, she explained, she wasn't looking forward to leaving. The Yaak Valley had been her home for many years. Her son had owned the lake property for a couple of years but his wife's health had not been good, and so now they must all move to the city.

Mrs. Wheeler apologized for her own cabin, which was a simple two rooms, mostly bare, built of rough-sawn lumber. It was a temporary situation, she explained. And then, with Bob and me listening in utter fascination, she told how her log home of fifteen years had burned down the previous winter, how she had actually been awakened in the middle of the night by the sound of flames roaring overhead—a chimney fire, as it turned out—and had barely gotten out alive. The local folks had pitched in and put up the present building to get her by until she left for Seattle.

Bob and I went outside to view the big black patch next to the cabin, where Mrs. Wheeler's house had once stood. We'd never seen the remains of a burned-down house. It was spooky and interesting. To top it off, Mrs. Wheeler said she had lost a diamond ring in that fire. Bob and I were still busy searching through the rubble for the ring, black to the knees and elbows, when Mom and Dad came out a half-hour later. Mrs. Wheeler had given them directions to the lake and a warning not to try to drive our car over the road into the place.

We parked on the main road and set out on foot, carrying fishing gear and a picnic lunch. Above the jack pines crowding close on both sides of us, mountains and sky were all we could see. The road itself was a mass of rocks. Dad said he was sure we would have broken the oil pan if we had tried to drive in. After about a half-mile we came out of the trees and there was the place, in front of us.

It was a lake about twenty acres in size, roughly pear-shaped, with a log house on the far side. To the right of the house, a creek flowed into the lake from the northeast. A stand of big tamaracks loomed close behind the house.

The lake matched the sky: blue beneath blue. The air smelled of sun and pine. The dust from the road settled into our footsteps as we all stood there and looked.

In quiet voices, Mom and Dad exchanged comments about how picturesque it was, how magical, how peaceful. Then, after a few more minutes of looking and admiring, I noticed that both of them had stopped talking. Their eyes were fixed on the surface of the water.

First came Dad's whisper:

"My god. Look at the fish jumping!"

Mom whispered back, "It looks like the water's boiling!"

Without further ado, my parents abandoned their children and their lunch and moved with measured stealth toward the lake, rigging up their rods as they went. Bob and I were used to this behavior. When both your parents were afflicted, you learned to live with it. We wandered on around the edge of the lake and decided to explore the house.

It was built of tamarack logs, all around eighteen inches in diameter, with white plaster chinking and a shake roof. There was a long porch across the front. I went up the steps to the door, which was locked. I peeked in a window and as I leaned against it, it turned out to be unlatched so I just pushed it open and climbed inside. Bob followed.

The floors were varnished hardwood. There was a living room about twelve feet by fourteen, with a twelve-foot-square bedroom on each side of it, all three rooms with windows facing the lake. A pot-belly stove stood against the chimney in the rear wall of the living room. To the left of the stove was an opening that went through to the kitchen, also a room about twelve feet square. All the ceilings seemed low, even to me. There was a back door going out of the kitchen on the east side, a small back porch, then a path that led off toward the creek. At the end of the

The home on the lake.

porch, beneath the overhanging eve, an outside stairway led up into the attic. We climbed up there: log rafters, big, open space all the way to the roof, window in each end—and then we came down and went out to the outbuildings. There were three, a chicken house, a large open-ended shed which we guessed was the garage, both built of small diameter lodgepole logs, and, sitting primly between the two, a very nice little privy, which we used, and which seemed quite modern if such a thing is possible, because it was newly built of regular lumber, and had shiny hinges on the door.

We walked down the path to the creek, a distance of about forty feet. The creek was noisy for its size, only about three feet across and maybe a foot deep, but the water—ice-cold like the Yaak River—raced over rocks as it tumbled down the slope to the lake.

Back inside the house, we looked around again. There were odds and ends that were curiosities to city kids like us: the pump beside the kitchen sink, which we tried, but it didn't work; a couple of kerosene lamps with glass chimneys; two wood-burning stoves, one, a black-and-chrome monster in the kitchen, the other, the potbelly heating stove in the living room; a wind-up record player with a stack of about fifty records stored inside; a contraption that we thought must be an army cot in one of the bedrooms; a copper boiler and wash plunger; and in the attic, a large, black, empty trunk with leather straps and brass hinges and two huge mousetraps that we later learned were for catching pack rats.

Meanwhile, Mom and Dad had worked their way around the lake and were approaching the mouth of the creek. We could hear their voices through the open windows:

"A royal coachman? How about a black gnat?"

"I dunno. Maybe I'll try a wet fly."

Actually, it didn't matter. Anything worked. Both their creels were bulging. Dad said he hadn't seen fishing like this since he was a kid. There would definitely be fish-on-the-cob for dinner that night.

Later, back at camp, as I lay in my sleeping bag watching the half-lit shapes of my parents in front of the fire, their red cigarette points glowing as they smoked and talked, wisps of their conversation drifted near. I heard phrases like, "three thousand dollars," and "decent school system," and I knew that an idea was being born. Serious things were afoot, things they weren't ready to mention to my sister and me.

In Bonners Ferry, Idaho, we stayed for a few days in a motel as the details of the property purchase fell into place. Mom and Dad told us about it in bits and pieces, with growing excitement, on the drive back home to California. We were moving. It was going to be a wonderful adventure. Would we like living up there in the woods? Having our very own lake? We had no idea. But, of course, we answered, "Yes!"

The move. It all happened so fast.

We now drove a truck, a 1937 International ton-and-a-half stakeside delivery truck, yellow, with the words 'Cliquot Club' and an Eskimo face on both doors. Everything we had was loaded onto that truck and by the trip's end our powerful old warhorse of a rig with her big, gnarly tires that could climb rocks and churn through all kinds of muck, had become part of the family. Dad had to have nick-names for everything and everybody—"Dee" and "Bob" for us girls, and Mom was never called Marilyn, always "Tweet" or "Butch." Now he christened our truck "Jenny."

There was hardly room in the cab for the four of us to sit comfortably. Bob rode on a four-by-four block placed on the floor between Mom's legs. And except for a rainy spell when I was squeezed in between Dad and Mom, straddling the gear shift, I was ensconced in my mother's wingback chair, situated back on the truck bed behind the cab, surrounded and hemmed in by all our stuff.

And that was the size of my world then. I couldn't think about what was ahead. I couldn't possibly have imagined. From early dawn until dusk, I felt the wind in my hair and watched the other world, the great outer space that wasn't any business of mine, go on by, like pictures in a book. I read signs. Reading had become my thing recently, so I tried not to let a sign escape.

Lone Pine—Pop. 345

Fresh Peaches

Creeks Motel—Modern Cabins—Hot Water

I sang, shouted songs as loud as I could. "Ragtime Cowboy Joe." "Ghost Riders in the Sky." But the rushing air and Jenny's motor drowned me out. I made up a rhyme:

I'm going far away, I don't know where. I'm flying off in a wingback chair!

Every so often I'd peek into the cab through the rear window and knock, so they would remember I was back there.

My World. Population 4.

In Bishop, California we got stranded for a week. Jenny boiled over in her first attempt to negotiate the pass north of town, and ended up getting a new water pump. Bob had her fourth birthday and got a pair of cowboy boots.

On Thursday, September 8, 1949, at around noon, we arrived at the Yaak Post Office, which was also the home of Icie Betzer, the postmistress. We had come into the valley this time from the southwest, over the main Yaak Road. There were now sixty miles between us and the nearest town of any size, Bonners Ferry, Idaho.

And not easy miles.

A short distance north of Bonners Ferry, Highway 2 descended into the dark, narrow Moyie Gorge and crossed the Moyie River on a spindly bridge that seemed to hang in mid-air between the sheer walls of Moyie Canyon. Out of the gorge, the highway wound another twenty miles with the wild, turquoise water of the Kootenai River far down on the right. Not long after crossing into Montana, there was a turnoff on the left side of the highway. A narrow gravel road led northeast, into the mountains. A sign there said "Yaak River Road."

Dad stopped by the turnoff and I was made to abandon my truck-bed chair and was taken into the cab for safety, stuffed in between the rest of my family with the gear shift vibrating against my ankle bones. We started once again and bumped along over the narrow, mostly second-gear road, climbing steadily through trees and more trees until we emerged high on the side of a mountain. Far below us on the right was the Yaak River, threading its way through the bottom of a deep canyon. Dad shifted into low and we held our breath as we climbed higher yet, up the steep canyon wall. We crept along the narrow rocky shelf praying we wouldn't meet another car. Once over that summit—later we would learn that this was the notorious stretch known as Stonechest Grade—we could all breathe again, but Dad paid close attention throughout the remaining thirty miles of curves and potholes that made up the Yaak Road.

The "town" of Yaak consisted altogether of Icie Betzer's post office/gas station. With the flag pole out front, the Betzer place was in plain sight from the main road, through a scattering of trees and off to the right about a hundred yards. The Betzer house was plain and solid-looking, built of logs, as were the few other buildings we had passed on our way into the valley. The Yaak River, about forty feet wide there, drifted slowly by, close behind the Betzer barn. Across the river a wide meadow stretched to timbered foothills with tiers of timbered mountains beyond. This central part of the valley was flat and open, with grass meadow and cattail swamp along much of the river.

And there was the smallest sense that you were finally "here" in this place called Yaak. Maybe it was only because a short distance upstream from the Betzer place there was a regular sort of intersection on the main Yaak Road. You could make a right turn there and cross the river on a substantial bridge. We would come to know the road across the river as the South Fork road. In the summer months, if you were adventurous enough to try it, and had a tough vehicle to drive, it was open all the way to the town of Libby.

We rolled into the Betzer yard churning a cloud of dust behind us. We stopped by the gas pumps. There were two, the kind with glass measuring tanks on top. Other than the flagpole and the gas pumps, the Betzer place was like most of the other farms in the valley: log barn with gaping hay mow, various outbuildings, privy out back, a barking dog, chickens, cats, cows and, that time of year, something we newcomers ought to have noticed but didn't, firewood. It was piled everywhere, split and stacked between trees, piled to the eves on the porch and head-high against the side of the barn. A pile of uncut logs lay at the edge of the yard, axe and crosscut saw resting against a sawbuck.

We were hot and dusty. Dad climbed out and got the canvas water bag that dangled behind the cab. We were having a cool drink of water when a middle-aged woman in a house dress and apron came walking out of the house.

"Hi, folks," she called out, as we untangled ourselves and climbed out of the truck. She reached for a big pair of stained floppy leather mitts hanging by the gas pump and pulled them on. She began pumping gasoline up into the glass pump top with a back-and-forth handle on the side of the pump. Before Dad could move a step to help her, she had unscrewed Jenny's gas cap and was filling the tank. To our surprise, she said, "You must be the Knowleses!"

She was a lively, talkative lady with thick glasses and short gray hair. While the gas gurgled, she introduced herself. "I'm Icie. Betzer. I run the post office," she said, gesturing toward the house. "I thought you folks'd try to get here during the summer!"

Before we could figure out exactly what she meant by that, she went on to say that she knew we were from California, knew we were the new owners of the Miller place, even knew that Dad—she gave him a quizzical look—was a car salesman. Then she smiled at Mom. "I heard about your pretty smile, too," she said.

We hadn't expected so much news to be out ahead of us and Icie explained, "Well, Rosy Schultz knew, and that's all it takes. We have a Grapevine in this valley that's better than a daily paper!" She cackled. "And probably about as accurate!"

Mom apologized and said if it was all right, we were needing to use her privy as soon as possible and Icie said, "Well, sure you do!" She handed the gas over to Dad and showed us out there. It was wallpapered and there was a regular toilet seat over the hole. Afterwards we all went trooping into the tiny Yaak Post Office.

The post office occupied every inch of an eight-foot-square room built into the front of the Betzer house. There was a Dutch door between the office and the kitchen. The top half of the door stood open during working hours, and there were a couple of benches along one wall.

The first fall we lived in the Yaak, I got lost. I was going to get the mail and tried a shortcut. I left the road and walked through the trees, and somehow got turned around. Suddenly there was the river, in front of me. It was impossible. For a few minutes I was sick with panic. Then reason took over and I walked away from the river, back to the road. I felt too silly about it to tell anybody.

Icie Betzer had been the Yaak postmistress since 1920. She was a widow and had lived in the Yaak Valley since 1912. Her husband, Ed, had passed away three years before. She now had a friend, a man named George Lang, who helped around the place and who, she carefully explained to Mom, "lived in the back of the house."

Icie wore a green eyeshade when acting in her official capacity. She put it on and sat down behind a little desk and we arranged for our mail. She told us our address would be Route 1, Yaak, Montana. She said we needed to put our name on the mailbox at the turnoff to our road, and Lang Wallace, the mail carrier, would deliver every Tuesday and Friday. We could order groceries from two stores in Troy, Weidners' Grocery and Kenslers Market. Send an order down on Tuesday and it came up on Friday with the bill, which you paid the next Tuesday. It was okay to send cash but any change went against your next bill. And don't order perishables in this hot weather, she said; by the time they got all the way up to our end of the valley, they would spoil in the back of Lang's truck.

"You have neighbors up your way," Icie said. "The Binders are less than a mile from you folks. Then there's Schultzes, three, maybe four miles. Phillipses are on up a little further on the Rexford road towards Dodge Summit."

Dad paid for the gas, and Mom bought stamps and gave Icie some letters to mail with our new address on the envelopes. We were anxious to get going. Icie said she didn't blame us a bit, and warned us that the road could get kind of rough way up there in our end of the valley. We still had eleven miles to go to reach our new home.

About a mile past the post office we came to the Yaak School. School was in session. We stopped in the middle of the road to have a look. I had persuaded Dad to let me climb back into my open-air perch for a while, so I had a good view.

It was just another log cabin in the woods, with big windows across the front. There was a wood shed out behind it and two privies, one on each side, farther out in the woods. Kind of disappointing, I thought. I would be starting there the following week, third grade. I started to feel pretty cocky.

What the heck, I thought, all eight grades in one little old cabin? There weren't even any monkey bars or swings. This was nothing compared to the acre of glass and concrete that was my old school. I'd show these kids a thing or two. I was from California.

A girl in a red dress appeared in one of the windows, looking out at us in our truck. Pretty soon a whole line of kids' faces appeared in the windows. Up front, Mom and Dad chattered back and forth, smiling and pointing at the privies, having a great time. Meanwhile, I realized, every kid in the place was gawking at me on my silly-looking throne in the back of the truck. What a sight we must have been! I knocked on the top of the cab and mouthed, "Let's go!" through the rear window. Dad understood the situation immediately. He gunned the motor. Jenny, while idling innocently in the middle of the road, had somehow manufactured a smoky and thunderous backfire and chose that moment to blow it out her tailpipe like a huge fart. We were thrust forward by the force of the thing but not fast enough. Laughter rippled out of the school windows straight across to my blushing red ears. I sank as deep as I could get into the stuffing of Mom's wingback chair. We thundered off down the road, enveloped in smoke, Jenny letting off a half-dozen minor, fart-like explosions as we went.

Icie was right; the farther up the road we went, the rougher it became. But the last bit of our ride, over our own rocky road into our house, nearly shook me and the rest of the load loose from the truck. This was the road we had walked over before. Dad stopped after only a few yards and had me get up front in the cab again.

Then we were driving into the yard of our new home for the first time. It all looked just the same, tall trees, blue lake, snug house, tumbling creek. Mom had a set of door keys but I remembered the unlatched window. I was the first one in.

CHAPTER 2

The Honeymoon

I heard it several times in the weeks preceding our move: there would be a lot of things for all of us to get used to. Not having electricity or plumbing, at all, that was the main thing. This was no camping trip. This was the way it was going to be, every day from now on.

But that first night in "The Yaak," as the locals called the valley, we weren't much concerned with plumbing or electricity; we were high on excitement and the novelty of the place. Mom and Dad could hardly tear themselves away from the living room windows and the view out across the lake—our lake!—long enough to do some basic unpacking. Mom finally got the floors swept, and dusted some cupboards while Bob and I helped Dad start unloading the truck. We had sandwiches for dinner and drank one of our last quarts of grocery store milk and then Dad got the antique Victrola going. Rudy Vallee came on, singing, "Tiptoe Through the Tulips." Mom and Dad danced like a pair of honeymooners, in and out between bedsteads and boxes and the odds and ends that were piled all over the house.

By evening the beds were made up, a bucket of water had been carried up from the creek, and an armload of firewood brought in from a small woodpile Dad had discovered in one corner of the garage. We found the camping coffee pot, a few groceries were stowed away and both lamps had been filled with kerosene and lit.

A log house is at its best just at dusk, softly flame-lit, as with our two kerosene lamps. We sat around on boxes and admired the place, our new home, stout, solid logs, warm and shadowy, quiet.

"It's a well-built little cabin," Dad announced solemnly, and we all felt good because we knew he would know. My parents were deep in the moment; they stared at each other and laughed and said, "What in the world are we doing *here?*" and laughed again. Outside, the lake, quiet as glass, gleamed in its darkening bed in the mountains. The trees around the house grew larger and loomed close. Then it got darker, and darker yet. No lights anywhere, not a single one for miles. "Blackout dark," Mom called it, remembering San Diego during the war.

At bedtime Mom gave Bob and me a flashlight to keep in our room

Mom, Marilyn Knowles.

and told us to come and get her if we had to go out to the privy during the night. We vowed we wouldn't have to go, no matter what.

The temperature was every *bit* as comfortable as California, Mom said, as she and Dad climbed into bed. All the windows in the house and the bedroom doors were wide open, and after a while a breeze came across the lake and wafted through the rooms, across our beds, and stirred the tamaracks behind the house.

"Oh! Isn't that wonderful?" Mom sang out, loud enough for us all to hear, and I called back, "Yes! It's wonderful!"

I was wide awake, my head full of this new place that was turning out to be like a perpetual summer vacation. I lay listening to my parents' murmuring talk and soft laughter. They were wondering if the fish were still biting like back in June. "We'll find out first thing tomorrow," Dad said.

In the black dark I muttered to Bob, two feet away in her twin bed that matched mine, "It's just like camping, huh!"

"No," she muttered back sounding mournful, "It's too big."

I fell asleep thinking about that.

Mom had her work cut out for her. She had to learn how to cook on the wood stove.

At first, the stove owned the kitchen.

Be gone, Mortals! roared the firebox. *How dare you try to cook on me!*

The lids clattered, the damper squeaked, the door to the firebox popped open all by itself. The warming oven door was hard to lift and once you got it to a certain height it fell open and pinched your fin-

Dad, Dar Knowles.

gers. It was a dirty and dangerous beast that belched sparks and smoke and ashes, sometimes right in your face. There were no end of hot, sharp corners and unyielding edges that always seemed to be in the way. The big iron body clanked menacingly as it heated up.

Stay back! I need the whole room! Any minute I may explode!

It could gobble up armloads of kindling without producing any heat at all, but would instead generate a houseful of smoke. Food was either burned, raw, dried-out or not hot enough. We used lots of ketchup. During one of Mom's earliest efforts at fire building, the short section of stovepipe going from the stove into the brick chimney suddenly got very hot. Scary, cherry-red hot.

"Go get Dad," she ordered.

He came and quickly closed all the drafts and turned the damper in the chimney closed, and Bob and I were told to get outside. Minutes later Dad came out and looked up at the chimney—shades of Mrs. Wheeler's catastrophe racing through all our heads. There were no sparks, thank heavens. We all went back inside and the stovepipe slowly faded to its normal black. The cooling firebox ticked evilly.

Huh-huh! Had you going for a minute there, didn't I?

But gradually Mom took control. As far as she was concerned, cooking was one of those areas where there was no room for compromise or foolishness and she was going to be in charge, cantankerous stove or not. She learned how to split kindling on the edge of the kitchen wood box, using a small razor-edged hatchet, and how to get a hot blaze going on the first try. She learned how to control the heat of the fire once it got going, using the coarser-cut "holding wood." She fine-tuned this by the use of the drafts and the damper. And one of the round stove-lids had two removable sections, a three-inch round in the middle, then a doughnut-shaped circle that enlarged the hole another two inches. Mom used all these options and sometimes took out the whole stove lid and set the bottom of a pot right down in the fire. She learned how to gauge the

Bob (Barbara Jean) and Dee (Doris Ann) Knowles.

temperature of the oven with her hand, and keep an even heat going all day long. Every so often the stove would have to be shut down and the ashes under the firebox cleaned out; she learned to do that too.

There were still periodic catastrophes—cookies burned; pans got ruined; there was one spectacular grease fire that happened during the frying of a big mess of fish. Dad jumped up and managed to pitch the flaming pan out into the yard. One chilly morning, Mom lifted a stove lid to start the fire and a mouse ran right up her arm. After that, she said, she could survive anything. But eventually the stove lost its roar and purred like a kitten. Mom learned to handle it as easily as she had once used a gas range.

Besides being used for cooking, the big stove was usually crowded with works-in-progress that went into the managing of our back-country household. We didn't have the counter space for a dishpan next to the sink where the water pump was, so the stove became the dishwashing center, with one pan for washing and another for rinsing. Mom threw in a couple handfuls of Tide and then let the dishes soak in the soapy water. When she had accumulated a pan full, she washed them and piled them into the rinse pan where she scalded them with boiling water. On laundry days the wash boiler full of clothes took up most of the stove top. In later months I was to discover that I was one of those unlucky kids whose feet are permanently cold in the wintertime. When I'd come in from outside, frozen solid, Mom would pull a chair over, open the oven door, put a couple of magazines down for padding and let me roast my toes. I grew very fond of that stove.

One of the first things Dad tackled was the kitchen pump. He spent a couple of days taking it apart, cleaning all the joints and the pipeline. For most of a morning he had Mom pouring water into it to prime it, while he pumped and pumped, and finally, here came the water, gushing into the sink with every stroke of the handle, crystal clear as the creek, and so cold it made your hands ache. Pumping wasn't as easy as turning a tap, but it sure beat carrying water up from the creek by the bucketful.

We spent the next several days ironing out other major wrinkles. We civilized our privy as much as possible. It wasn't as pretty as Icie Betzer's, but Mom cleared out spider webs and swept it out good and put a bathroom rug on the floor. We kept a can of lye in there to sprinkle in after you used it, and Dad made a lid for the hole to keep the stink down. But it was still a privy, and not a place you wanted to spend any more time than you had to. Dad was a fanatic about hand-washing so we hung a basin on the wall above the kitchen sink and we all had to use it every single time, or else.

We had no refrigerator, of course. What we had was a window on the north wall of the kitchen with a wide sill that extended about a foot outside. The outside box was framed in and covered with screen wire and accessible from the kitchen by simply opening the window. Eggs and lettuce, butter and jam, things like that, stayed cool. In addition, in the shady ell between the kitchen and Bob's and my bedroom, was an outdoor cooler, a phone-booth-sized storage pantry with screened-in sides, designed mainly for hanging dressed game like deer or other big pieces of meat.

But at that time of year, early September, nothing except the water in our creek was really cold. A few weeks after our arrival, Mom started buying milk from our neighbors, the Binders, who had cows. Bob and I got our first taste of whole milk, right out of the cow, *un-cold*, and just about gagged. So Dad found a three-gallon lard can with a tight-fitting lid and tied it down in the creek to use as a cooler. It was colder there, but not cold enough. The milk crisis continued for years.

Garbage disposal was another thing that took some adjusting. Everybody in the Yaak had a can pile. Someplace out behind an outbuilding where it didn't show, you would dump cans, glass jars and bottles and other things that wouldn't burn. Our can pile had already been started out behind the garage. Just about everything else had to be burned. Mom was amazed at the things that could be consumed in the kitchen stove: coffee grounds, potato peelings, left-over Cream of Wheat. Once in a while Dad would have to take something out in the woods, like a loaf of moldy bread, and leave it there. For whoever might be waiting around.

I started school. In the midst of our moving drudgery, Mom had kept all my school clothes carefully folded away in a suitcase under my bed. For my first day, she got out my red plaid skirt and white blouse and my pair of red-and-blue felt embroidered suspenders. They were stylish for girls back home in California. With my curly brown hair and those suspenders, Mom said, I looked just like Heidi.

Looking like Heidi (Shirley Temple) was not what I had in mind. I wouldn't have minded looking like Dorothy (Judy Garland), but my real choice was to somehow be transformed into my stunning, twelve-year-old cousin, Anne, who lived in Fallbrook and was tall and wore her hair in a pageboy. Mostly, I hoped nobody would remember the kid in the chair on the back of the farting truck.

We got to the school early and while Mom and Dad, with Bob tagging along, went inside to talk to the teacher, I sat outside on the school porch steps and waited, feeling pretty nervous. I wondered what kind of a school this would be, in a cabin in the woods. No real playground, no cafeteria, no auditorium. All the grades together in one room. How could that work?

When the other kids started to arrive I forgot about everything else and tried not to act as shy as I felt. A car dropped off one girl; three kids rode up in the back of a pickup. Two boys came walking up the road.

Yaak School in about 1952.

One of them came over to me and said, "You're the new girl, huh." "Yes," I answered, and then for some unknown reason I added, "My name is Doris," and from that minute on, no matter what I did, to everyone in the Yaak School I was known forever by my terrible, real name.

"Yeah, I know," the boy said. "You're in my grade."

Like everybody else, he seemed to already know about the Knowles family. "That's Billy," he pointed to a boy across the yard. "He's the other third-grader. Third's the biggest grade in school now!" then he skipped off across the yard and joined the other boy.

No other girls in my grade! I felt like a scared kindergartner. Mom and Dad came out with Bob in tow, all smiles, told me goodbye and said they'd be back at three, climbed into Jenny and went rumbling off. I hated to see them go.

Mrs. Duncan, the teacher, appeared on the porch with a brass bell in her hand. She rang it and all the kids came running.

You entered the schoolroom from the back, behind the students' desks. The south wall, to the left, was all windows, looking out toward the road. The teacher's desk was up front. She kept her own Coleman lamp there for the dark winter mornings, and the bell was kept handy too, so she could ring it to quiet the room when things got out of hand. To the right of her desk was an upright piano, and the flag was hung on a standard over in the corner. There were blackboards all across the front wall behind the teacher's desk, and rolls of pull-down maps on the right-hand wall. Below them was a long table of supplies: stacks of all different sizes of paper, lined and unlined, pencils, several cans of crayons, a box of jars of paste—the kind with brushes inside the lids, boxes of craft paints, a big stack of colored construction paper, a can full of pairs of scissors, and a stack of games and puzzles, and at the end of the table, a mimeograph machine. On the wall next to that was the pencil sharpener. In the back of the room was the potbellied stove—bigger than ours at home, with its pipe going up through the ceiling. The wood box was behind it. The rest of the rear wall was taken up with shelves and cupboards full of books.

There were about twenty desks in the room, five rows lined up one behind the other. But there were only eleven students in the school, including me. It seemed strange, having so many empty desks. The front desks on the left-hand side were the smallest; the biggest desks were in back on the right. Where you sat was determined by what grade you were in.

The teacher thought it would be a good idea to separate the two third-grade boys, so one of them had to empty out his desk and move back a desk to make room for me. These were not streamlined table-top desks with separate chairs like we had in California, able to be pushed around and re-arranged in circles or whatever the teacher wanted. These were ink-stained, scratched and carved-up wood, with black curly-cue metal sides and legs. The desk tops had a groove in the upper edge for a pencil and a round hole in the upper right-hand corner which I later found out was for a bottle of ink. Each desk had the bench for the desk in front attached to it, and the benches folded up so you could stand for the Pledge of Allegiance.

Our drinking and hand-washing water was hauled to the school in milk cans by volunteer school board members twice a week and stored in the "anteroom," a sort of enclosed porch on the front of the building. Mrs. Duncan showed me how to use the dipper to pour water into the wash basin or into a paper cup to drink, and told me not to drink directly out of the dipper and to always leave it hanging on the handle of the milk can. The anteroom was also where we stored our lunch pails. There were cubbyholes, one for each pupil. We hung our coats on a row of hooks across the end of the room.

We had two fifteen-minute recesses, one in the morning and one in the afternoon, and an hour for lunch. That was the same as in California. But in California I walked home for lunch every day. Here, everybody including the teacher, brought their lunch in lunch boxes with thermoses, and on warm days, sat outside to eat.

The teacher, Mrs. Duncan, lived in a rented cabin a few miles from the school. She had a daughter in first grade, a little girl named Ruth Ann. There were three girls younger than I, two first graders and a second grader, and two girls older, one in fourth grade and one in fifth. The second grader, Jean, was sweet-looking but seemed sad or angry, I wasn't sure which. I wondered if I might get to like her after a while. Her sister Carolyn, a first grader, was rosy and round and had the silkiest long dark hair I had ever seen. The older girls, Carol and Gail Chandler seemed high and mighty and not very interested in a new, littler girl in their school. There were three older boys, one in sixth grade, and two eighth graders. They ignored me completely and I was glad. At recess, when I listened to all the kids talking, they sounded tough and careless and I felt out of place and too citified compared to them. They said "b'fore," and "b'tween," cut their "ing's" to "in'" and their grammar was not as correct as I was used to. If you said, "Thank you," they answered "Yep," and some of the boys swore. Nobody thought anything was special about my being from California.

Billy, one of the boys in my grade, turned out to be nasty and bullyish and not smart at all. The other boy, the one who had spoken to me earlier, lived on a farm across the road and down the mountainside from the school. He had brown eyes and beautiful, pale skin and a formal-sounding name: Laurence. He told me he was "Scotch-Irish" and said he knew we lived on "the Miller place." I said we had our very own lake there. He said they had two lakes on their place. He said he thought we were lucky to have our big rig. He was talking about Jenny. They had a truck too, he said, and added, "but it doesn't run very good."

On that first day after we ate lunch, which barely took five minutes, all the bigger kids, including us three third graders, went for a hike up School Creek, "the crick," they called it, the dry creek bed that wandered up through the woods behind the school. Logs and rocks and roots were all tumbled and tangled in the bed of the creek and we had to climb over them. Before long it seemed to me we were getting an awfully long way from school and I was getting tired. I climbed over logs and rocks and pushed branches around like everybody else, but it was hard to keep up with those country kids. Finally we stopped and I was glad to sit down on a rock and rest. Nobody else seemed tired.

We were at a place where a log had become jammed in the creek bank with one end sticking way up in the air. One of the big boys climbed out to the very tip and stood up. He balanced up there on one foot, easy as pie. After a few minutes of balancing and wobbling around he sat down on the log and made it bounce. After that, he announced from his perch that the water poured down through here like *hell* in the spring.

"Yeah, like *hell*!" agreed one of the other boys.

"Like *holy hell*!" said somebody else.

"*Hell*," said the boy up on the log, "water could come right through here anytime, and wipe out the whole *goddamn school*!" Everybody laughed, so I did too. But I wasn't sure if they were kidding or not. The logs and roots were head-high, and something powerful had definitely tossed them around. But it seemed like no one was really very worried about a flood or drowning. Or even about getting back to school before the lunch hour was over.

We started walking again, up the rocky creek bottom. I was too tired and started to be scared I wouldn't be able to keep up with these kids. Finally, the oldest girl, Carol, said we better go back. Right then, I wanted her for my best friend. Boy, those Yaak kids could sure outwalk me!

When we finally got back, a half-hour late, we were in a lot of trouble. Mrs. Duncan said she'd been sick with worry. It was her responsibility, she said, if a child got lost or hurt. Did we want her to restrict us to the school ground? Did she have to treat us like first graders? Showing off, that's what it was, showing off for the new girl.

Behind her back, Laurence and Billy and the other boys made faces and mimicked her expressions. I was fascinated and amazed that they had such nerve. You would never have seen such a thing back in my California school, where everybody was scared to death of the teacher and stayed quiet as mice during class. But I thought it was funny, all the same. They told me later that a teacher before Mrs. Duncan, Mr. West, actually spanked kids, with a stick, up in front of everybody. I couldn't imagine anything worse.

The girls' and boys' bathrooms were identical privies set back in the woods on opposite sides of the schoolhouse. The girls always went in twos. One would stand and hold the door closed for the other and make sure no boys came around. The bathrooms had flies and no hole-covers and the smell was pretty bad.

The wood for the potbelly stove had been piled out by the wood shed behind the school. The two older boys got out early so they could start stacking it in the shed. At the end of the day, the flag monitors, forth and fifth-graders who raised the flag on the pole outside every morning, lowered it, properly folded it and put it away.

My favorite part of school that year turned out to be first thing each morning, when we had music, all together. In my California school we only had music class once a week and the teacher would pass out little instruments like triangles and tambourines and lead us in "play-ing" a song, which never sounded very good. In the Yaak School the teacher passed out little gray song books and we got to raise our hands and choose songs to sing. She played the piano along with us. We sang "Tenting on the Old Camp Ground," "Darling Nelly Gray," "The Woodpecker Song," "Scotland's Burning" as a three-part round, and, the ones I liked best, "A Spanish Cavalier" and "Solomon Levi," sung together, half the room singing one, the other half singing the other; the melodies fit together in harmony.

The rest of the day the teacher taught one grade at a time, having each grade come up and sit in a circle of chairs by her desk and read aloud, or answer the questions at the end of a chapter, or take turns explaining story problems in arithmetic. The eighth-graders had arithmetic races on the blackboard once a week and all the rest of us watched. I hated arithmetic. I was already worried about how I would ever learn to do the problems they did so fast, up in front of the whole room.

After a few weeks at the Yaak School, I forgot all about monkey bars and swings. The Yaak kids played schoolyard games like "Beckon" and "Dare Base." These were new to me. "Beckon" was a sort of hide and seek where "found" people had to go stand in the Beckon Box, a circle drawn on the ground by the flagpole. They had to stay there and call out, "Beckon, beckon, I want a beckon!" and as soon as they saw someone wave from a hiding place, the prisoner was free to run and hide again, while "It" was out trying to find someone else. There were dozens of places to hide in the woods and around the out-buildings and the school house.

"Dare Base" involved choosing sides and then tagging players from the opposing side when they came out from behind their safety zone—lines drawn along opposite ends of the playground. I wouldn't have believed kids could have so much fun playing games with nothing at all except a few lines on the ground.

In those days girls wore dresses to school, boys wore pants and that was that. But I was soon intrigued by something new, something you would never see in California: long stockings and garter belts. The girls started wearing them later that fall when the nights cooled down and our bare legs got cold on the way to school.

The garter belts were made of white elastic and since nobody of our straight-up-and-down age could hold up a waist band, they had straps that went up over your shoulders and garters that dangled down in front and behind. The stockings were light brown and came all the way up your thighs. They were for warmth of course, but I thought they seemed a lot like nylons and very lady-like. I could hardly wait to get mine.

Mom ordered me some from the catalog. We put the whole works on carefully, adjusting the lengths of the shoulder straps so the garters wouldn't show, and pulling the stockings up enough to fit smoothly but not pull. But by the end of the first week, I was sick of them. Once you sat down, they drooped at the knees. They were hard to fasten in back, and if a garter popped loose it snapped you on the bottom and everybody heard it and laughed. After a while the toes stretched out so you had to double them under inside your shoes, which was not comfortable. But once the weather was cold, I had to wear them, like it or not.

Mom and Dad wrote funny letters to friends and family back in California about all the experiences we were having. They laughed like a couple of kids as they wrote about the terrible roads and the monstrous wood stove and the privy. One day a letter came for Dad from his older sister, Aunt Melba.

Aunt Melba didn't see anything funny about our living in Montana. She wanted to know what on earth was the matter with Dad, to move his wife and daughters off to a God-forsaken wilderness. Mom read the letter too. She called it "scathing."

Dad was speechless. Finally he said, "God-forsaken?! Look at this place!" He gestured out the window at our lake full of sunshine. "This is the way the world *ought* to be! How can anybody call it God-forsaken?!"

Mom sent Bob and me outside to play. When we came in about an hour later, Dad had cooled down and there were a dozen or so sheets of stationery, full of lines and lines of his handwriting, wadded up on the floor. I saw the finished letter just before it was put into the envelope. It said:

> *Dear Melba,*
> *Mind your own business.*
> *Dar*

Storage turned out to be a big problem in our new house. A whole bunch of stuff had to be re-packed into boxes and stored up in the attic: Pictures that wouldn't hang straight on log walls, lots of Dad's books, record albums he decided he'd better not play on the old Victrola, all our dressy clothes and shoes, tablecloths and napkins, extra dishes and glasses and pretty knickknacks that used to be

Dad decided we needed better access to our attic. He cut a hole in the ceiling of his and Mom's bedroom and installed a drop-down stairway with sandbags as counterweights to raise and lower it. At night in the wintertime, we could hear the pack rats moving around up there.

on our furniture in the house in California. And since Jenny was too high to fit into the garage, we stored boxes out there, too. Dad built shelves in their bedroom for everyday linens, and Mom's treadle sewing machine did double-duty as her dressing table. More shelves were built in our bedroom. These were going to be for all our winter groceries. Bob and I were amazed; we couldn't imagine needing a whole wall of shelves, floor-to-ceiling, just for food!

It took some time to get the kitchen settled the way Mom wanted. The table was big and round and took up a lot of floor space, but there it was, and there it had to be, under the cooler-window with the stove on one side and all the kitchen cabinets on the other. Dad fastened a long wire hook into the ceiling above the table for the Coleman lantern. For cupboards, we had a baking cabinet with a spice cupboard on the top half and two bins for flour and sugar on the bottom. Next to that a linoleum-covered counter extended to the corner where the sink was. Above it was a cupboard for dishes; beneath the counter were two rows of open shelves. Mom finally gave up trying to find a place for the good dishes and packed them off to the attic too. She ended up driving nails into the log wall next to the wood box and hanging all her pots and pans there where they would be handy to the stove.

Our kitchen stove, for all its size, had one serious shortcoming; it had no reservoir for hot water. Mom decided the first thing she needed from town was an extra-large tea kettle to keep a supply of hot water on the back of the stove. From there, the shopping list grew every day. The old potbelly stove in the living room had seen better days, Dad decided, so we would be hauling back an entire new heating stove and new stovepipe when we went to town. He needed nails, lumber, a new axe. Mom wanted fabric to "dress up the place," make ruffled curtains for the windows, drape the fronts of all the open cupboards and shelves. Fly-tying equipment was a priority so the winter could be spent getting ready for non-stop fishing, come spring. In the 1940's everybody smoked; cigarettes were another critical item on the list. And flashlight batteries. And soap. We went through a lot of soap. Everybody needed Levis. Also—this was hard to think about that September, when summer temperatures lingered on—none of us owned a single piece of winter clothing.

All month long the mornings were bright and sunny. If you were up early you could look out at the lake and see white wisps of vapor rising from the water to the sky. Mom talked about how sweet the air was. Dad couldn't get over the quiet. On weekend mornings I would sleep late and when I got up, the house smelled like coffee. My parents would be sitting out on the front porch with their cups, watching the lake while they paged through catalogs or cookbooks or talked about some project like building a boat or fly-tying. There would already be a couple of nice fish in the sink, cleaned and ready to fry for breakfast. Later on, we would take a walk in the woods behind our house, with Mom sizing up possible candidates for Christmas trees, or sometimes we went up the path beside the creek to the river. Then we'd plan dinner down by the lake with a campfire and Dad's Golden Browns, his special Dutch Oven Potatoes.

We couldn't get over feeling like our new life was really an endless summer holiday.

CHAPTER 3

The Binders

The Binders, our nearest neighbors, lived about a mile away. They were a German-Swiss family and had immigrated and homesteaded in the Yaak in the Twenties. It seemed unbelievable to me, a one-month resident of the Yaak Valley, that the Binders had been living there for almost thirty years.

August and Julius Binder were father and son. August was in his early seventies when we first knew him, Julius was about forty-five. August's wife, whose name was Anna, although everybody called her "Mrs. Binder," spoke very little English and rarely went out, so we didn't meet her until later. But August and Julius got around the valley regularly. They had a pickup but they seldom used it. As in the Old Country, everywhere they went, they walked. The first time they came by to visit us was on a day in late September.

They looked alike: bony faces, lean, ropey limbs, sharp blue eyes. August's hair was pure white, Julius's flecked with gray. Both wore blue jeans and logging boots, summer and winter. Julius moved like a man with well-oiled bones and strong muscles. August had a rickety gait and walked with his head and shoulders out ahead and his legs following after. You never saw August without his blue-and-white bandana either twisted around his neck or fluttering from a rear pocket.

Both men were small, and August's bony hands were arthritic, but after Dad had spent time working alongside them, he claimed they were both as strong as bulls and could work circles around him. He once saw Julius shinny up a tree like a twelve-year-old.

Except for one or two trips to town per year, Julius had hardly been out of the valley his whole life and had remained a bachelor. We learned one day from our gossipy friend, Rosy Shultz, that Julius had had the mumps as a young man and that they had affected him "down below" and made him sterile.

You never knew when the Binders might suddenly be standing on the back porch, knocking at the door. It startled Mom every time. They weren't sneaking up on us, she explained, glancing out the windows to see if they might be about to appear. They were just used to walking quietly through the woods, hunting deer. Stealth was their habit, she said.

August would say, "Ah-low dere, Missus, nice vedder today," whether it was warm and sunny or twenty below. He'd be smoking his pipe and would reach down and tap it out against his pant leg in preparation to come inside. They would visit for a couple of hours and drink cup after cup of Mom's coffee.

What we didn't know, when they came the first time on that day in September, was that to the Binders, we were a little band of lost sheep. We had no idea how worried they were about the strange young family from California that had moved into their valley.

That afternoon Mom welcomed them in, and made coffee for everybody. We all sat around in the living room. Mom and Dad were glowing and fascinated, doing their California-style host-and-hostessing, loving the accented speech of our colorful neighbors. Mom offered cookies around and fussed with napkins and sugar and cream.

For a while August did his best, with a few shy assists from Julius, to answer all my curious parents' questions. The Binders first came into the valley on foot, he said, and everyone's shoes had worn out along the way, so they tied feed sacks on their feet to walk on. Their land was mostly meadow along the river. They had a small lake on their property, too. They raised cattle. August told about how his brother, Henry, had originally homesteaded our property years ago and built our house in 1927. Henry wanted to increase the size of the lake, and so, with his own two hands and a pick and shovel, widened and deepened the full length of the channel of our creek, all the way from the river to the lake. But even after all that, Henry changed his mind about living back in the trees all by himself and moved to another house a few miles away, out on the main road.

But as Mom refilled coffee and replenished cookies, it became plain the Binders had something other than Yaak history on their minds. They grew restless answering Dad's many questions about fishing flies, where to hunt, sizes of rifles, types of ammunition. And then Mom mentioned that she was looking for a used typewriter to buy, since she was thinking about starting a journal.

At that, August set his coffee cup down, slowly and deliberately. He said, "Now ve must to hef a liddle talk."

Winter would be here soon, he told us. In this country it could be summer one day, winter the next. And did we have any idea, any at all, of what the next nine months would bring?

Well, that was just what I was waiting for. "I know!" I burst out. "Snow!"

The Binders and their dog, at their home. From left: Rosy Shultz, unknown, Mrs. Binder, Julius Binder, August Binder.

I was such a shy kid that speaking up in company was unusual for me. But Bob and I had been dying for snow. We'd never seen it falling. We didn't know if it was like feathers or soap suds or what. But we could hardly wait to go sledding and have snowball fights. I was way too excited to be shy. I asked August how deep it was going to get.

He stared at me like I was the strangest kid on the planet.

"Don' voddy. Snow gonna get plendy deep," he said. His blue eyes were pointed straight at me, a serious gaze. "Plendy shuffeling, for you."

Shuffeling?...Shoveling!...*Shoveling* snow? Me? I looked at Dad. He shrugged. I'd never thought of snow as something that had to be shoveled.

Then August and Julius rattled off a series of wild, unbelievable stories about typical winter scenarios, buildings caving in, neighbors stranded, cars buried. Mom and Dad sat quietly listening.

Then August said to Dad, "You got a ex, sure."

"I'm sorry?"

August made a chopping motion. "Ex. For chop vood."

"Oh. An axe," said Dad, smiling. He and Mom were loving August's accent. "Not a good one," Dad admitted, "Just an old, single-bitted one. But we're going in town this weekend and I have one on the list."

"Double-bit ex make a big problem," said August. "Show 'em, Yulie."

Julius turned up one sleeve to display a ghastly purple scar. Bob and I gaped.

"I sharpen the axe like a razor and stick it in the block," Julius explained with a bashful grin, "then I trip and fall on it."

"I sew up dat," said August. "He youngster den. Yell a lot."

My mother winced. Julius rolled his sleeve back down.

"You buy single-bit," August said. "But maybe you buy two ex. Und vun more spare handle for ven you gonna need it....You got a saw?" He made a back-and-forth motion. "For saw vood?"

It seemed like we were a whole roomful of restless people all of a sudden. Finally, rubbing his chin, Dad asked August how much wood he thought we ought to cut for the time being.

"All you can," was August's immediate answer. "You must get vood in, in summer. Vinter too coldt, too much snow, for cutting vood."

"How much will we need for the winter?" Dad asked.

August nodded in the direction of our garage and said "Dat shed oudt dere. You pile 'im full."

Julius spoke up. "That shed holds sixteen cord. That's sixteen foot by sixteen by hate foot high, vit a little walking room."

Mom and Dad looked at each other. Fill up our whole garage? With wood?

"You don't got no garage oudt dere," said August. "You got vood shed oudt dere."

Julius nodded. "Hempty vood shed."

৪৯

Before the Binders left that afternoon, as if to mark our brains forever with an image of how tough we were going to have to be to survive in this place, August told us a story about a winter in the Yaak a long time ago.

It went like this:

In the old days most years the road to town was closed by snow for weeks at a time in the winter. Even the mail, which was carried to the Yaak Post Office by mule, couldn't always get through.

On the afternoon of December 2, 1921, August got a piece of mail that was almost a month late. It was a letter informing him that the final deadline to apply for the title to his homestead property was twelve o'clock noon on December fifth, less than three days away. He needed to appear in person at the courthouse in Libby to file the application.

He hadn't understood the importance of the deadline before; his reading English wasn't the best back then. He studied the letter carefully. He could hardly believe what it said. If he failed to appear, he lost his claim. His property could become available to anyone. He would have to re-file, and then wait another three years before he could apply for ownership to the land.

He hated to leave his family alone in such weather. That year there had been one snowstorm after another and below-zero temperatures for over a month.

"So, gutt-demmit, I got helifa problem dere," he said.

But there was only one thing to do. The family spent an entire precious day preparing for his absence. They butchered a calf, just to be on the safe side. Then he and Mrs. Binder hurried around and gathered the things he would need for the trip.

He had to have the papers for the land and his identification and proof of citizenship. And money. He would have to wear every piece of clothing he had, and two of Mrs. Binder's home-made caps (which he always wore in the winter), made from the cut-off tops of silk stockings, the cut ends tied shut with thread, the open ends pulled, one on top of the other, over his head. Mrs. Binder packed him a big lunch, all he could carry.

At four o'clock in the morning on December 4, the temperature was twenty-seven degrees below zero and the moon was out and bright on the snow. The shortest route to Libby was fifty-five miles over the South Fork Summit. August started walking.

He made the first eleven miles by eight o'clock that morning, crossed the Yaak River on the ice and started up along the South Fork trail toward the summit. Higher now, there was a hard crust on the snow. He figured if he could keep going at a good pace he would make it to Libby, another forty-some miles, by a little past midnight, find a place to spend the night, and be at the courthouse first thing in the morning. He came to a spot along the trail where he could sit down and eat some of his lunch. He knew he needed to eat to stay warm.

And then, suddenly, even before he could reach into his coat to check, it dawned on him that he had not picked up the bundle of papers from the table at home. His identification and proof of citizenship, all the vital information on his property he would need to apply for the title to the land, was still on the kitchen table, eleven miles back up the valley.

He searched madly all through his pockets just to be sure, but he knew it wasn't there; he had been in too much of a hurry to get started. There had been too many things on his mind.

At this point, telling the story, August stopped for a while. It was a hard memory, even after so many years.

"So. Iss only vun t'ing I can do," he said, "Go back und get 'em."

Before he could make it half way back, he was met by his wife, hastily wrapped in layers of clothes, carrying the papers. She was so cold he was afraid she couldn't make it back, so he went with her, all the way to the house. Then he turned around and started back to town.

By five o'clock that afternoon he had crossed the river once again and was ready to start toward the summit. The sun had set and it was nearly dark but the sky was clear. He didn't stop to eat; he ate while he walked.

Sometime in the night near the summit he sat down for a minute. He tried to figure out how long he had been walking. About seventeen hours, he figured.

All of a sudden, he woke up.

He jumped to his feet. The moon had risen. How long had he slept? Only ten minutes or so. But he was cold and his food was gone. It scared him, that he had fallen asleep. He started walking again and made good time for the next few miles in the bright moonlight.

But then he slowed down again. He was too cold and too tired. He kept sitting down, in spite of himself. Only for a minute, he would say, and then he would realize what he was doing and push himself to his feet and start walking again.

He was high on the treeless mountainside and the snowy bank rising alongside him, nearly touching his right shoulder, looked like a great, soft pillow. Two times he awoke, standing in the middle of the trail. The snow looked soft and warm. He would give anything to lie down on it, just for a minute.

He turned his gaze straight into the bright moon, willing his eyes wide open. He turned back, rubbing his face hard and digging at his eyes with his numb hands. And then he noticed the wavering shape on the snowbank beside him, rising right out of his own shoes. It moved, just as he moved. It was troubling, a frightening thing. He reached out to push it away.

Then he saw what it was.

An ostrich.

An ostrich was right there on the snowbank beside him.

He fell back a step and the creature moved with him. He sidled forward. It came along.

He thought how unusual it was to see an ostrich in Montana.

Then, for a while, cautiously, side by side and stride for stride, the two of them walked along the trail together, each keeping an eye on the other.

Then August had an idea.

Tired as he was, he lunged and made a desperate grab for the bird.

"C'mere you somanabitch, I gonna ride you!" he cried out, and snatched at what he thought was a leg. It jumped ahead of him just out of reach. He lunged again and the chase continued along the moonlit mountainside, August, bone-tired and aching to ride, the wily ostrich eluding him by inches, time after time.

The ostrich managed to stay just beyond reach all the way across the South Fork Summit. The next thing August knew, there was the smell of smoke in the air—the wood stoves of Libby. It stirred his blood and made him remember he was hungry. His legs took over, working on their own. He covered the last few miles as the sky grew light in the east.

"Und so," said August, "I make it to town. Und dat ostrich go avay vit the moon."

He watched my parents for a while, letting the tale sink in. "You know I'm vun lucky somanabitch," he said.

Dad's face was unsmiling.

"So," said August, "you don't play around vit dat coldt, dere. You, you childer, you t'ink first, ven you go oudt in dat coldt." He looked from Dad to Mom to be sure they understood. He looked at me and Bob. We all understood.

August was satisfied. He and Julius got up to leave and he clapped a hand on Dad's shoulder. "Ah ha!" he said, "you can't depend no crazy gutt-dem ostrich gonna come along, you know?" He laughed again, and there was air in the room to breathe.

"Und ven you got all the vood in, you come over." August nodded in the direction of the Binder home. "Und ve hev a liddle lunch, dere," he said, lightly trilling the 'r' with his tongue. We watched them walk across the back yard, Julius with his erect and graceful stride, August ambling, ostrich-like, beside him.

And just like that, our honeymoon in the Yaak was over.

After the visit from the Binders, Mom and Dad got down to the serious business of living in the wilderness. We came home from town a week later with our winter's groceries, two hundred dollars' worth—about two thousand dollars' worth nowadays—and crowded them onto the shelves in Bob's and my bedroom and under Mom and Dad's bed. Flour and sugar in hundred-pound sacks, fifty pounds each of potatoes and onions, cases of canned milk, soup, peaches, applesauce, tomato sauce and vegetables. Peanut butter, Cinch cake mixes. Wesson oil. Baking powder, cornstarch and baking soda. Cases of brown and powdered sugar. Jello, coconut and raisins. Catsup, mustard and mayonnaise. Pickles, sweet and dill. Something new to Mom: dried yeast. Salt and pepper. Tea, coffee, cocoa and spices. Shortening, cornmeal, breakfast cereal. Huge cans of strawberry jam and orange marmalade. A case of corned beef and a case of Spam. Canned tuna and canned salmon. Dried beans and split peas. Popcorn. Macaroni and spaghetti. Soda crackers, graham crackers, toilet paper, waxed paper, Purex, Prell, Pepsodent, Dial and Tide. Bandaids, iodine, Unguentine and Absorbine Jr., Sloan's liniment, Milk of Magnesia, Vicks, aspirin and Alka-Seltzer. A whole case of Kool-Aid for Bob and me; canned lemonade and three bottles of rum, a big foil bag of Bull Durham tobacco and a tablet of triple-length cigarette papers for Mom and Dad with a fancy, three-at-a-time cigarette roller. Wood matches—"horse matches," as they were called, several boxes. Lime for the privy, flashlight batteries, and, outside in the big cooler we hung a side of bacon, twenty pounds of cheese and two hams.

We also came home with our new heater stove, two (single bitted) axes and a crosscut saw tied across the bed of the truck. Mom changed her mind about making curtains and instead, got out the catalogs and ordered winter clothes for everybody: sweaters, boots, wool socks and mittens, heavy jackets and for Bob and me, snow pants of thick wool that unbuttoned down both sides so you could tuck in your dress when you wanted to. When the boxes arrived and we tried everything on—Bob and I each got caps with ear flaps that folded down and tied under our chins—I saw that I no longer resembled Heidi or Dorothy, and I might have been a different species altogether from my cousin Anne.

Dad and I went to Earl Stratton's to get log slabs left behind at an old sawmill. We drove up a muddy road on Earl's place and had to walk the last, steep half mile. We carried all the slabs, two at a time, back down to the truck. I got pretty hungry. We stopped at Strattons' afterward, and Earl's father fixed lunch for us. He peeled open three cans of corned beef using the little metal keys that came on the can tops, and cut the beef into inch-thick slices. He put them on pieces of home-made bread spread with butter and mustard. Dad had coffee and I had canned lemonade.

CHAPTER 4

Settling In

A few other happenings marked our first months in the Yaak. Among them, Mom took on the task of learning to drive the truck, something Dad had been after her to do. Off they went, down our road and Bob and I sat on the porch watching and listening as they lumbered along, poor Jenny's gears scraping and grinding as Mom struggled with the tough old gear-shift. Pretty soon, back they came, weaving a little, jerking along over the rocks, Mom staring straight ahead with her eyebrows stuck together and Dad sitting low in the seat with his eyes closed.

Our long-finger-nailed, skinny-ankled mom just didn't fit somehow, with Jenny the Monster Truck. But to our amazement, she learned. She mastered the double-clutching technique to shift the gears in Jenny's heavy-duty transmission: clutch in, shift to neutral; clutch out, spin the transmission; clutch in, shift into gear, clutch out, away you go. She learned how to slow the truck down using gears instead of brakes, and how to steer. You didn't actually steer Jenny, according to Mom, you hiked yourself up in the seat, hugged the wheel and "horsed" her around the curves. After a while, Bob and I actually rode along with Mom while she was driving. Dad said he'd known from the moment he'd laid eyes on her, she was a natural-born truck driver.

Another thing that happened that fall, was relatives. Dad's brother, Uncle Larry, Aunt Pearl and gorgeous Cousin Anne from Fallbrook came to visit, to see what this Yaak adventure was all about.

Talk about surprise visits.

They pulled into the yard without warning, in a cloud of dust that nearly hid their Cadillac, on an unseasonably warm Saturday in October. Mom glanced out the kitchen window and then stared.

That morning Mom had fired up another gizmo we had gotten in town, a Coleman iron that ran on white gas. The usually unruly iron was behaving nicely that day, not flaming up or overheating. So, with her hair up in pin curls and wearing jeans and one of Dad's shirts, she spent the day ironing in the kitchen. She had the record player going full blast and was singing along with the old time records, playing all her favorites, "Dardanella" and "I Married an Angel" and "When I Take My Sugar to Tea" while she worked her way through the pile of dampened and rolled clothes. My school dresses and shirts for everybody were on hangers, hung over the tops of the open cupboard doors. Next to a pot of leftover spaghetti that was to be our dinner, there was a dishpan full of the day's dirty dishes soaking on the stove.

Mom peered out the window.

"Who in the world...?" She gasped. "Oh! I don't believe it!"

Aunt Pearl got out of the car. She was wearing a yellow linen sun dress and sandals. She reached in and pulled a red alligator make-up case and a white cardigan sweater out of the car. You could see the neat, straight seams of her nylons up the backs of her legs.

"I don't believe it!" Mom said again, cranking down the iron and then grabbing at the bobby pins in her hair. "Dar! It's Larry and Pearl! I don't believe it! Girls, go pick up your room!"

It was no use. We were caught in the middle of a typical day and it wasn't a pretty sight. Dad and I had been in the woods since early morning, trying out the new crosscut saw. We had just come in, sweaty and covered with sawdust and were eating cookies, leaving crumbs all over the living room. Bob had been wading after frogs at the edge of the lake and had dried mud up to her ankles. She had put her own hair up in pin curls, four-year-old style, and was still wearing her swim suit with dried mud on the seat. She looked like some kind of a swamp creature.

As Dad raked cookie crumbs and sawdust off the front of his shirt and struggled into his shoes, I stood there like a dope, staring out the window at the approaching grandeur of our relatives. Mom, the bravest soldier in the war, threw a helpless, panicked look at us all, opened the kitchen door and did just as she always did: threw her arms wide and sang out, "Well, hi! What a wonderful surprise! For heaven's sake, come on in everybody! How was the trip?"

The best part of the visit happened that very day.

In Mom's mind the first order of business was dinner for everyone and she wasn't about to serve leftover spaghetti. We all knew what everybody wanted for dinner—fresh trout—wasn't that what this place was all about? But you had to catch it first. Well, Bob and I offered, how about if we went out and caught some?

Nobody believed we could, of course. But Dad was busy showing his brother all around the place, and Mom, with a million things on her mind, was more than happy to shoo us off somewhere, anywhere. "Fine, Girls. Go fishing," she said. "I'm sure Anne would like to go too. Be careful."

Bob and I had found a secret fishing place. Our special spot was up where our creek flowed out of the river. The inlet had a headgate to control the flow of water into the creek. Just downstream from the headgate the creek was contained in a covered flume for several feet. You could sit by the gate and let your line drift underneath the covered channel and in minutes, you had a nice rainbow or a cutthroat or sometimes a brookie. I was excited to show off our creek and our fishing hole and all my fishing techniques to my special cousin. But Anne said she would rather not. Her head was aching, she said, after such a dusty, bumpy ride.

It was disappointing. My cousin seemed very freshly-scrubbed and even more gorgeous than I had remembered her. But looking at her now, I wasn't sure I could imagine her hiking up the creek and going fishing. Bob and I got our rods and left everybody sitting out on the front porch admiring the lake.

In less than an hour we caught seven good-sized rainbows and one eastern brook. We cleaned them, nicely, with the heads off, the way Mom preferred, and packed them in grass in the creel and hauled them home. Mom was pretty surprised when we laid them out, one at a time, in the kitchen sink. Uncle Larry was flabbergasted.

Dad acted like it was no big deal. "Maybe a couple more would be nice, kids," he said, and winked at us, "we're all pretty hungry." So back we went, up the creek, and returned with four more lunkers in half an hour.

Ever after, Dad talked about the night Bob and I, still just a couple of kids, brought home all the fish for dinner.

Uncle Larry and Aunt Pearl were charmed at first with our place, in spite of the initial chaos. Mom worked her usual miracles and soon everybody was comfortable and everything was tidy. Dad got out the sleeping bags for us three girls, so everybody had a place to sleep. Then we all sat out on the front porch again, drinking in the view of the lake and the sunset.

The trouble started later that evening, as Anne and Aunt Pearl began to discover what it was really like not to have a bathroom. They came in from the privy fanning their noses.

Aunt Pearl said, "Whooh! It's a bit smelly out there, all right."

"I'm sorry, said Mom. "I'm afraid there's not much we can do about it in this warm weather. I'm told they don't smell in the winter," she added with a grin. "I guess we'll look forward to that."

Anne looked worried. "What on earth do you do in the middle of the night?" she asked.

"Well, if we have to, we just get up and go out there," said Mom, giving my cousin a look that, as far as I was concerned, was a little too sympathetic.

Anne said, "Oh *brother!*" and rolled her eyes as if to say, "why did we have to come here?"

"We have plenty of flashlights for everybody," Mom added hopefully.

"Are there always so many bugs out there?"

I couldn't stand it any longer. "Oh, for Pete's sake," I said, "they go away the minute you turn off the flashlight."

Anne gasped, "Oh! I couldn't be out there in the dark! I mean, Mother, it's *completely* dark! It's as if you've gone blind! I'd rather have the bugs!"

"Right," said Mom. "Me too. So here's a flashlight."

Later that evening, Dad and Uncle Larry appeared at the kitchen door with the contraption we had identified weeks ago as an army cot and had stored away in the attic. They brought it down thinking somebody might sleep on it. They dragged the thing into the living room and opened it up. *Voila!*

It was a bathtub.

None of us had ever seen such a thing—a floppy, rubber-sided bathtub on a folding wooden frame—and everybody got a good laugh. Mom mentioned that she just might have to give the contraption a try one of these days. Anne, looking worried again, said, "Where *do* you bathe?"

"Well, if you want warm water, there's the wash basin in the kitchen," Mom explained. "If you can wait until morning and you don't mind cold water, the lake's handy. The water's lovely and soft. It's wonderful for your hair."

"Anne won't mind that," Aunt Pearl said. "She loves to swim. First thing tomorrow, Darling, you can take some shampoo out and bathe, and wash your hair in the lake water. Won't that be fun?"

"Mother, the bottom's all gooey. It's mud."

"Well. Well, Sweetheart, it is a lake, after all."

"Oh *brother!*" said Anne again.

"Marilyn, would you mind if we heated just a little water, just enough to do Anne's hair?" asked Aunt Pearl.

"Of course not. Just let me get a fire going. It'll only take a minute."

Anne spent her time writing letters to her boyfriend and painting her toenails. She said she couldn't believe we didn't have a piano. Aunt Pearl, whose toenails were already perfectly painted, fretted when she got a run in her nylons. She seemed awfully worried about Mom and she kept asking, "But Marilyn, what on earth do you *do* all day long?"

That was how things went, for four days.

Uncle Larry and Dad had a wonderful time fishing of course, and just being brothers together. And even though I still thought Anne was beautiful and my favorite cousin, I could not think of a single thing to talk to her about.

By the time their visit was over, they weren't as enchanted as I wanted them to be with our Montana home. And I think Mom wished she could have pleased them more. It just wasn't the place for everybody, she said.

The day they left, Tuesday, was mail day. We finally got the card they had sent, telling us they were coming for a visit.

.

My parents had big plans for our place. I would lie in bed at night and listen to their late-night talks.

"First thing next spring," said Mom, "let's get a few chickens."

"With a hen house that size, we ought to be able to raise thirty or forty chickens."

"What would we do with so many?"

"Eat some of them. Maybe sell eggs."

"Nothing beats fresh eggs," agreed Mom.

"I heard of a fellow up the valley," said Dad one night, "Elmer Phillips. He has a lake, bigger than ours, and he raises trout. He sells them to the railroad for the dining cars and some to restaurants over on Flathead Lake."

"Wouldn't that be fun?!"

"Imagine, raising fish!"

One night Dad suggested, "Maybe we ought to consider getting rabbits. Remember all the rabbit we sold in the store in Fallbrook? All I could get my hands on. It's delicious fried." And another night: "Someday maybe we ought to build a lodge like the one at Puntzi Lake."

"Only nicer. I'd do the cooking," said Mom.

"Would it be fun, having guests all the time? Or not?"

"Not *all* the time."

But all the plans they talked about and everything else in the world came to a halt once we got the crosscut saw figured out and the Firewood Fiend reared his head.

You don't know what tired is, until you have been on the other end of a crosscut saw opposite my Dad. Now that I think of it, being on the end opposite an eight-year-old kid was probably no picnic for Dad either. But there was a job to do, and we were all he had. He would wear us out, first Mom and then me, then Mom again. When we started getting tired, he'd count, "One, two, three, switch," and we'd change hands. "One, two, three, switch," change again. Back and forth between hands, forward and back with the saw, slicing through thirty inches of tamarack log, one stroke, a half-inch at a time, cutting up twenty-foot, thirty-foot logs, piece by piece, cutting and splitting, splitting and loading, hauling and splitting again, and stacking, finally, in the endless, enormous space of the woodshed.

Julius Binder got us started. He showed us a hillside of old windfall, some of it downed tamarack, which, he told us, made the best firewood. We drove Jenny right into the trees, as close as we could get. Dad would pick out a log, and we'd haul in the saw and start. We would saw all day some days, then, with his new axe, Dad would start splitting the pieces into sizes the rest of us could carry over to the truck. Mom stood up on the truck bed and stacked while Bob and I carried the pieces.

Jenny the Wonder Truck and Ray Mueller, a friend visiting from Chicago.

That year, next to the Binders, the weather was our finest friend. Most years you would have had snow in the Yaak by Halloween. That year, winter came late. It saved us. We spent every possible minute in the woods. The Firewood Fiend went a little crazy. Once the wood shed was full, it was decided that for good measure we ought to fill the front porch, too. So we started piling it there, like we'd seen on other Yaak porches, with openings left for the door and the windows.

We felled only one tree, a tall dead "snag" near the edge of the lake.

Julius came over and helped Dad do it; showed him how to cut the "V" with an axe and then the two of them sawed in from the other side until the tree fell. Bob and I were made to sit in the truck but we heard the first cracking of the trunk and then saw the whole thing topple and crash to the ground, breaking in a dozen pieces when it landed. Then of course the fun was over and it was time to begin all over again with the hard part.

It was cold, the day we felled that snag. Julius left, once the tree was safely down, and Mom sent Bob and me home to get some sandwiches. We walked through the trees toward the house and noticed something drifting on the air, like ash from a distant campfire. By the time we got back with the lunch, there was more of the stuff in the air and we realized it was snow. We all sat around on pieces of the fallen snag and ate, watching the snow drifting down like tiny flecks of white sky. Bob and I were disappointed; it seemed so puny. After all the Binders' talk we expected at the very least something like cotton balls. We couldn't see how there would ever be enough for even a snowball, much less a snowman.

By that evening we had Jenny loaded full and the Fiend himself uttered the magic words, "I think we can call it good for the winter with this load, Butch, what do you think?"

Mom agreed. We all piled into the truck and drove home.

We left the truck parked in the yard with its load. The tiny snow-flakes were hardly noticeable in the evening air. We walked into the kitchen and there, draped completely across our kitchen table in gory glory, was a dressed-out deer, ready to hang in the cooler.

As if calling the thing by name, Mom and Dad both cried out together, "Julius!"

CHAPTER 5

Out of the Blue

The tiny, sugary snowflakes were still falling that night when we went to bed. In the dark you could hear them brushing against the bedroom windows. The next morning the Yaak Valley as we knew it, was gone. In its place was a snow world.

The sky and all the air was falling, sifting, drifting snow. The house, the outbuildings, the truck with its load of wood, everything was completely muffled and buried in white. In the woods, the trees crowded together, shouldering loads that weighed down their branches. Even the lake was disguised beneath the waves of snow melting into it.

Mom and Dad, still in pajamas, went chattering from window to window.

"How beautiful!"

"Like a Christmas card!"

"Can you believe how much piled up in a single night?"

"It's as if we're inside a snow globe," said Mom.

It was decided that I should stay home from school. Bob and I could hardly wait to get out there.

We hauled out all our winter gear: jackets and snow pants, hats and scarves, wool socks and "arctics"—rubber galoshes—and mittens. We buttoned, zipped and latched everything on, and out we went.

We had in mind a Hollywood version of playing in snow: rolling up a perfect snowman in the yard—we were all ready with our hat and our carrot—then pelting each other with snowballs, then we planned to build a snow fort. A big one. Big enough to eat lunch in. The thing we hadn't counted on, was that it was just so miserably, awfully *cold*.

We stuck it out for a while. We toppled backwards into the eight-or-so inches of fluff and made snow angels, which disappeared before our eyes in the showering flakes. Then we tried to make snowballs but the stuff wouldn't stay together. We tried packing it to make a snowman but it fell away in our hands like dry sand. Dad explained that this was because the snow was *too* cold, which made no sense to us at all. Pretty soon our fingers and toes started to ache. This was not fun. We went back in the house. Mom showed us how to make snow ice cream with sugar and vanilla like she used to do back in Chicago when she was a kid. We stayed inside and watched the snow falling for the rest of the day.

By afternoon, we had each gone trudging out to the privy. Each trip required putting on boots, jacket and hat. Mom got out the catalog and filled out an order-blank for a single item. It was a white porcelain bucket with a lid. It had a flared rim and a black metal handle. It would be mainly for night use, she said. Its polite name was *combinet*. Most people in the Yaak called them slop jars.

When the snow finally stopped towards evening, it was over a foot deep. Dad brought out another of our new tools, the snow shovel. He said of course it *never* would have occurred to *him*, but if August Binder thought I ought to become a shoveler of snow, he would be glad to get me started, first thing in the morning.

The next afternoon we had a very unusual visitor.

Reverend McCoy was a Seventh-day Adventist minister who had come to Montana a few years before, and had brought three or four families along with him. They all settled in the Yaak Valley and together made up Reverend McCoy's little congregation. As far as Reverend McCoy was concerned, everyone in the Yaak was part of his flock, they just didn't know it yet.

He came in a light green pickup, churning through snow well above the hubcaps. He was a tall man, distinguished-looking, Mom said. On the back porch, he kicked the snow off his overshoes as he introduced himself, Bible in hand. Under his heavy winter jacket he wore a suit and tie—an unusual thing to see on a man in that part of Montana, winter or summer. He looked so elegant, Bob and I couldn't help staring.

Soon he was sitting with us at the kitchen table, eating a piece of cake and drinking a cup of hot chocolate. Hot chocolate was not an easy thing to come up with on the spur of the moment, but he'd said no thanks to coffee, he didn't use it, so Mom got out the canned milk and the powdered cocoa and put together hot chocolate for him.

They visited a while and then he smiled at Bob and me. "What sweet girls," he said. "Maybe we'll see you at Sabbath school on Saturday?"

Saturday? Wait a minute. Bob and I were confused. Wasn't church supposed to be on Sunday?

Mom shushed our questions and Reverend McCoy moved along to another item. He asked Mom and Dad about their church backgrounds. Mom's was pure Methodist. Dad's was shady.

Reverend McCoy looked serious. He pulled a tablet out of his pocket and made a note. "Let's see now, Mrs. Knowles," he said, peering at Mom, "your Christian name again?"

"Marilyn."

"Ah. Marilyn." He wrote it down. He peered at Dad.

"Darwin," said Dad.

Reverend McCoy put down his pencil. He leaned back in his chair and looked long and hard at Dad, a gaze that slid down his nose, ski-jumped up over the table and landed on Dad in a heap.

"Now...ahh...Darwin," he said, "you wouldn't be one of those fellows who thinks we all came from monkeys, would you?"

Dad's fingers laced together slowly on the table in front of him. He leaned forward on his elbows and lobbed a stare straight back at Reverend McCoy. "You're not one of those fellows who's going to try to tell me the world was created in a week, are you?"

"Six days," said Reverend McCoy, lifting a halting finger. "Six. God rested on the seventh."

"Surely," Dad said, "you don't actually believe that. Six days? Twenty-four-hour days?"

"Says so right here." Reverend McCoy tapped the Bible. "And I do most certainly believe it."

Dad said, "Then, sir, I may as well tell you right now, you and I are not going to see things eye-to-eye."

"Well, sir," said Reverend McCoy, "if you don't mind my saying so, it's my job to change your mind."

And so it began. World War Three. Wrangling arguments that lasted two, three, four hours at a time, sometimes far into the night and drove everybody else out of the kitchen and kept some of us awake way past our bedtime. Fueled by coffee and hot chocolate, cookies, cake and pie, the battles between Dad and his arch-enemy, Reverend McCoy, over theology, the Bible, creation and the impending end of the world, spanned the years of my childhood.

Both men were drawn to the feud like magnets. Dad would spot the green pickup pulling into the yard and a gleam would come into his eyes and he'd begin clearing space at our chronically cluttered table. As time went on, things became less formal. Reverend McCoy came by in his overalls. They called each other "Dar" and "Mac." Conversations started out friendly, the latest fish story or the weather. Then one or the other of them would make the first move and all at once they were like flint and steel and sparks were flying. Reverend McCoy would switch to Dad's full first name, Darwin, as if to remind himself and God who this enemy was, and what misguided ideas filled his head and endangered his immortal soul and the souls of his wife and daughters.

Moses and Kierkegaard, Isaiah and Einstein, Matthew, Mark, Luke and John, Dad's main hero, Alfred North Whitehead, and even Charles Darwin himself, drew swords and dueled at our kitchen table. No argument was ever resolved. Reverend McCoy would finally leave, hoarse and frustrated. Dad would pace around the house afterwards, claiming he couldn't sleep, the man got him so upset. "Well, why don't the two of you just agree to disagree and let it go at that?" Mom suggested late one night, sitting up in bed, waiting for him.

Dad said, "He's an intelligent man! How in hell can he think the way he does? How in hell can an intelligent man be that silly and that stubborn?!"

Wide awake in my bed, I could actually hear the look on Mom's face. Finally, she blew out the lamp and shuffled down under the covers. Dad continued to pace in the dark, planning his strategy for the next round.

After the first storm of the season, the cold front blew through, the snow became rain and the yard turned into a slushy mess. The weather stayed wet and nasty, but relatively mild, into November.

One rainy Saturday, Dad saw something odd out in the lake. On the far side, there was a lone tree stump that stuck a few inches out of the water, about thirty feet from shore. There was something on top of that stump, Dad said, something sort of rust-colored. We got out the binoculars and looked.

Nobody could make out what, but we all agreed it was some kind of small animal. It was about thirty-five degrees outside. The heavy sky dragged gray curtains of rain over the lake. Bob and I started in:

"Oh, the poor little thing!" we whined. "Dad! Oh, Daddy, please, we have to go get it!"

Dad wasn't about to take us along, but he decided he would walk around to the other side of the lake to see if he could at least identify the animal. No telling what kind of wild creature it might be, he said. He set out, bundled up against the wind and rain. We stood with Mom and watched him walking miserably along the edge of the lake. Bob and I wished he would hurry. We were worried about that poor little creature.

Dad was a little over half-way around to the far shore of the lake when he stopped and took another look through the binoculars. He turned right around and headed back.

As he came up to the porch he said, "It's a cat. A house cat. Can't imagine how it got out there, that far from shore. You can almost hear it meowing from here." Bob and I went into hysterics.

Shortly, the rickety rowboat, which we had inherited from the lake's former owner, had been hauled out of dry dock—a clump of willows by the creek—righted and launched, and Dad was rowing across the lake in the driving rain. Bob and I were out on the front porch with the binoculars, watching his progress.

After what seemed like an hour, Dad began jockeying the boat around in the wind so he could get as close to the stump as possible. I happened to be the one looking through the binoculars when suddenly, with a sizeable stretch of water still between stump and boat, the animal leaped crazily from its perch and landed square in Dad's lap. I called out the action to Mom and Bob:

"Omigosh! It jumped into the boat! It's climbing into Dad's arms! Ooh, the poor little—Oh! It's climbing up onto his head! He's trying to grab…Uh-oh! There goes his hat in the water! Now the cat's stuck to his back! Dad's trying to get a hold… *Whoa! Dad!*"

The boat was pitching wildly. Dad nearly went over the side, trying to catch hold of the animal clinging onto his back.

Mom grabbed the binoculars. "Let me see! What on earth?! The crazy thing! It's up on his head again! Oh, Dar! Oh, shoot! Wait. There, he's got it. He's trying to hold it. It's frantic! It's stuck to his arm. He's taking off his coat. He wrapped the coat over it. Oh, good idea! The cat's inside. He's got it down in the bottom of the boat. Thank heaven! He's coming in. Oh, poor Dad!"

Poor Dad, phooey. Bob and I were worried sick about the cat. We went running down to the lakeshore in the rain.

As the boat approached, Dad called out a warning, "Get back away from here, you kids. This animal is scared out of its wits."

The bow of the boat slid onto the bank. I could see blood beading along several scratches on Dad's face and ear. He was holding the bundled-up coat down in the bottom of the boat with both feet. "Get back out of the way," he said again. "I don't have any idea what it's apt to do."

He raised his feet and got carefully out of the boat. The bundle didn't move.

Bob wailed, "It's been killed!"

"It's far from dead," Dad said, and with one of the oars he lifted a fold of the coat, gently nudging the package. Still, nothing happened. Dad bent cautiously and caught hold of a sleeve and pulled off the coat. A big, orange-and-white striped cat huddled, unmoving, in the bottom of the boat.

"Oh!" Bob and I cried out together.

"Stay away!" Dad said. He pointed out his scratches. "Look here, at this."

Just then the cat looked up and blinked its eyes. Black and orange eyes. It opened its mouth and out came a hoarse, "Meow-yow?"

We bypassed Dad and were in the boat before anybody could stop us. Bob squatted down and started petting and cooing, "Oh, poor itty kitty!" The cat sat and looked at us without moving. The next thing we knew Bob had it in her arms. It lay there, dirty, soaked, but calm as could be, shivering with cold. "Pooor baby," Bob cooed.

"Well, hell," said Dad.

We named her "Ching," Dad's idea, since, as he pointed out, she was wearing spurs. And the mystery of how she ended up out on the stump was never solved. Probably, we decided, she had been lost by someone passing through, and then been chased by some sort of predator, maybe even a pack of coyotes—lately at night we had been hearing their eerie howls—and she had been frightened enough to take to the water.

Still, after the mauling she gave Dad, she was hardly a favorite of his. He wasn't a cat person anyway; he was a dog man. But Mom said we needed a mouser, so we put the word out on the Grapevine and when no one claimed her, Ching became ours.

And wouldn't you know it, she turned out to be your basic rotten cat.

Dad, Mom, and Bob holding Ching.

She stole food off the table, clawed the furniture and roamed the house at night meowing and jumping up on people's beds, usually Dad's. She carried off wool socks and mittens and they were never seen again. Worst of all, as far as Dad was concerned, she could steal a fish right out of a man's creel. After her busy nights she spent most of the day asleep on a favorite windowsill in the living room. Meanwhile, mice ran rampant.

One day Mom came into the kitchen and there was Ching, way up on top of the high cupboard, eating coconut frosting off a newly frosted cake. Coconut didn't agree with Ching and a while later the frosting reappeared as a nasty mess on the living room rug.

"That's it," said Mom. "I'm sorry girls, but that's the last straw. Maybe there's someone else who might be able to appreciate Ching more than we do."

Bob and I pleaded. Ching was an *orphan*. Dad saved her. She had a *double meow!*

Mom gave in, but only on the condition that Ching would become an outdoor cat. Ching had other ideas. Once outside, she climbed up the screen door and hung there, howling, until we gave up and let her back in.

A favorite stuffed animal of Bob's, another cat named "Patches," was Ching's final victim. During the night, Patches was horribly disemboweled, his innards scattered all over the living room. Bob, in shock, declared that, "Daddy should have left Ching out on the stump!" The decision was made to find Ching another home. If possible.

The dilemma only lasted a few days. Then, according to Dad, a miracle occurred. Reverend McCoy dropped by and happened to mention that he was having trouble with mice at his house.

"Dar, shame on you," said Mom, as Reverend McCoy drove away with his new cat. Dad was glowing. "I agree with Mac about one thing," he said. "The Lord truly does work in strange and wonderful ways!"

CHAPTER 6

Moiling

By the time I was nine years old, I had picked up smatterings of insight into our family philosophy. Dad had his convictions and Mom had her standards. Dad got all riled up and hifalutin whenever he talked about things like justice, responsibility, honesty, and good grammar. Mom said he was a throwback to another time. He was noble and rare and we were lucky to have him, she said, but sometimes he didn't fit into the real world.

Mom's standards, as I understood them, had mostly to do with cleanliness, good manners and the importance of three square meals a day. Also, if you had a sense of humor, she liked you, if not, she found somebody else to talk to.

Dad was smarter but Mom was always right. He adored her. My sister and I understood these things from birth.

Also, until I was nine, I thought we were rich. There were lots of reasons why I had this idea. There was the time back in California when Dad came home with a brown paper bag, grease-stained like the ones he often brought from the bakery, and handed it to Mom as if it were a dozen doughnuts. Her arm dropped all the way to the floor with the weight of the bag and it burst open. It was chuck-full of silver dollars, a bonus from a car deal Dad had just concluded. I was completely dazzled by such a pile of wealth.

Then there were three of Dad's brothers, my Glass-Factory Uncle, my Shoe-Store-Chain Uncle and my Liquor-Store Uncle. They were all rich, so it seemed only natural that we were, too.

And there were the stories Mom told, about when she was a child and her family lived in the big house in Chicago with the electric garage door-opener that sent the door sliding sideways at the flip of a switch. Their car had silver bud vases by the back seat windows and

Mom sometimes rode to school with the little girl next door, who had a chauffeur. In my mind I could easily transfer that lifestyle to our family, never mind the log cabin we lived in and the truck we drove.

But lying in my bed that winter, listening to my parents' late-night kitchen conversations about our family economics, I began to discover to my surprise that the family fortune was not so huge as I thought. The "Savings Account," that endless source of the means to buy everything, was shrinking faster than Mom and Dad had expected. That had to stop. All the plans for our Montana home were still just plans, and now it was winter and not much could be done to start up a fish hatchery or a rabbit farm.

"Where's it all going?" Dad wanted to know, sounding worried. Mom, keeper of the budget, answered, "Honestly, I don't know. Here and there. We've needed so many things." They settled back into the nighttime, sitting at the cluttered table, sipping coffee, having their smokes.

Oh, there was no doubt about it, they agreed, it cost next to nothing to live in the Yaak Valley. Our home was paid for. Our expenses were minor. Gas for the truck at around twenty cents a gallon. Lamp fuel. Clothes were worn until they wore out in this neck of the woods. "Style" was not a word in anybody's vocabulary here. Our meals were built around either venison, fish, or the local livestock. For that, if you didn't raise your own, you traded with something more valuable than money: a few hours' work. Dad's skill as a carpenter was becoming known and he had already helped a man down the valley, Earl Stratton, design and build a bridge across a creek. At the end of a week's work he had come home with a hind quarter of beef. After introducing Toni Home Permanents to the local ladies, Mom had come into demand herself and often had jars of jam or home-canned venison pressed upon her for her services.

We paid a few cents a gallon for milk from the Binders. Rosy Shultz gave us all the butter we could use and sold us eggs for next to nothing. Oh, sure, there were still a few groceries that had to be ordered up from town, but when it came down to it, except for the infrequent trips we made to Bonners Ferry, there was no place to spend money. So, they wondered, where did it all go?

Except for the hissing of the Coleman lantern, silence filled the kitchen.

Nevertheless, it was a surprise to find out that Dad had plans to stop further erosion of the nest egg. With our belated winter waiting in the wings and Christmas right around the corner, he went over to the sawmill on the West Fork of the Yaak River to see if Carl Cummings, the mill owner, might give him a job.

Carl Cummings drove a new powder-blue Cadillac with his name, "Carl D. Cummings," written in fancy gold letters across the hood.

It was a small sawmill situated in a clearing on a hillside above the rushing, tree-shaded West Fork of the Yaak River. There was a teepee burner in the mill yard and a log-pond ringed by scrubby willows at the rear of the mill. The mill itself was built on a series of wood platforms and the main works—the head-rig saw, edger and trimmer— were covered by a tin roof. About a dozen workers lived with their families in the "mill shacks," tar-papered cabins on skids, situated around the mill's perimeter and down along the banks of the West Fork.

It was after hours when Dad came by, so Carl Cummings took him out and showed him through the mill. They walked from the winch, which pulled the logs up out of the pond, over to the head-rig, where the sawyer sawed the logs into long slabs. Then to the edger, where the bark was pared off the edges, then to the trimmer, which cut the pieces into different lengths. Finally they got to the green chain, twin conveyer belts made of linked metal, which ran along a long platform and carried the newly sawn lumber out of the mill. From the chain, the lumber was sorted and stacked as it moved along, according to size. Dad and Carl walked the length of the platform and Carl pointed out the different sizes of lumber, stacked in several piles on either side, waiting to be trucked to town. He needed all the help he could get, Carl said, and sure, he would be happy to have Dad join the crew. He could start out right there on the green chain. It was where all the new guys worked. It paid ten dollars a day.

The Knowles family business, all those years ago in Salt Lake City, had been lumber. "Two-by-six, eight foot, two-by six, ten foot, two-by-eight, fir and larch, spruce boards..." Dad said it all started coming back to him as they walked along, talking lumber talk. He loved the smell of it. He loved the look of it, so clean and new. It would be good, healthy work, out in the fresh air. He told Carl he could start Monday morning.

There were two ways to get to the mill from our house. Either you drove the long way around, a distance of about seven miles, or you could ford the Yaak River where an old bridge had washed out on the West Fork road, take a short cut through the woods and get there in a mile and a half. It was decided that since Mom needed the truck to drive me to school, Dad would go on foot by way of the shortcut.

Mom packed him a lunch, two big sandwiches made with extra-thick slices of bread, a piece of cake and a thermos of coffee. He set out walking, with his waders over his shoulder. After he crossed the river he stashed the waders in the bushes on the far side.

When Dad got to the mill they were firing up the generator and the place was coming to life. One of the workers was a woman, Mary Ward. Dad saw her burly figure across the mill yard and couldn't believe his eyes when he spied the long blond hair hanging down her back. She tucked her hair up under her cap and climbed up behind the winch that pulled the logs out of the pond and started to work right along with the rest of the crew. She looked to be as big and strong, and as tough, as any man in the mill.

Once things were up and running, Dad climbed out onto the green chain platform to await the first pieces of lumber. A few of the men nodded to him. Soon lumber began dropping onto the chain and moving toward him. It occurred to him as he looked around at the men up in the mill, that it was a good thing he had spent the past several weeks sawing firewood himself; at least he was in decent shape for this kind of work. It also occurred to him that the rest of the green-chain crew was late for work.

First to come along was a big piece of larch, a three-by-twelve, sixteen feet long. Dad put on his gloves, looking for the right stack for that size, and, seeing that the stack was down near the end of the chain, stood back and waited, letting the chain carry the wood along. As it neared the stack, he grabbed the piece of wood and pulled. To his complete surprise, it didn't budge.

"It's called a green chain," he explained to us later, recounting the day, "because the lumber is green, wet. But I still couldn't believe how heavy it was. It might as well have been made of granite. And when I looked up, here were half a dozen more pieces coming right at me."

Finally he managed to hoist one end of the piece of wood across to the edge of the stack and rest it there. Then with a mighty heave, just before the chain carried it away, he slid the monster into place. Just in time to catch hold of the second piece nearly on top of him and haul that one over. Then here came another one. No, this one was eight feet long, it went on the other side. He jumped across to get at it. Here came a third ten-footer. He got the eight-footer off, but the ten-footer got by him. It dropped with a *clunk* off the end of the chain and landed on the ground.

Carl came striding down the platform just as another eight-footer got past Dad and fell off the end.

"Sonsabitches're heavy, ain't they?" Carl called.

Dad answered, "Yes sir, they are. Where are the other fellas?"

Dad said Carl just looked at him kind of funny. And that's when it dawned on him: there were no other fellas.

Carl said, "You'll get the hang of it."

And of course, Dad did.

But Bob and I watched Mom rub Sloan's liniment into his back and arms, night after night those first few weeks. And he asked her to fix him bigger lunches—three sandwiches, he said, and two pieces of cake. One day we got a package from Sears with a dozen pairs of leather work gloves inside. Dad would go to bed right after dinner and be sound asleep in minutes. But eventually, our dad turned into a regular Charles Atlas.

The December days got shorter and it started snowing every day. The river began to freeze but the ice was patchy and wading across it in the dim early mornings was dangerous. So for a few weeks, all four of us had to pile into the truck every morning and leave with time enough to drive over to the mill to drop Dad off. Then Mom, Bob and I would head on down the dark, snowy Yaak Road to the school. After school Mom would be there to pick me up and we would go home, then back to the mill to get Dad. The short days were long for all of us.

As soon as the river was frozen hard, Dad started walking again. He was walking in the dark both ways now. He ordered a miner's carbide lamp from the catalog, to wear on his hat to light the way. It was amazing that those little gray rocks could put out such a brilliant light. He was able to see a good twenty feet out ahead as he walked. But Mom didn't like it when he started out on those dark mornings, especially if it was snowing hard. And she would start watching for him every evening as soon as it grew dark again. She would sit on the arm of her wingback chair, watching out the living room window until she finally spotted the tiny point of light, way across the lake. "I see Dad!" she'd cry out, and I could hear the relief in her voice. She'd stand and watch as the white spark bobbed nearer, and finally we could make out Dad's shape against the snow. And then he'd be home.

There came a night when Dad wasn't too tired to read to us. It had been a long time since he'd done that, and we missed it.

"*There are strange things done in the midnight sun, by the men who moil for gold*," he read.

"The Cremation of Sam McGee." We loved that wild, grisly tale. Dad always said, "taint being dead, it's my *aawful drrread…*" and, "to hear him *sssizzzle so!*" and then he'd laugh with us at the silly, ghastly story. When he finished, we wanted more. He read "The Shooting of Dan McGrew."

More, we said.

Something nicer, Mom put in. So he read "The Village Blacksmith."

We loved listening to Dad read and laugh and tell stories about when he was a kid. But I started to think he was like these poem-men now, with all their working and worrying and trudging through the snow. With "muscles in his brawny arms, as strong as iron bands."

CHAPTER 7

Dashing Through the Snow

Every morning, the first sound I heard was the scraping of the damper in the living room chimney as Dad turned it open. Then he opened the creaking door of the heater-stove and stoked up the fire, added a few pieces of wood, *ka-thump, thump,* and closed the door again. The fire popped and crackled and started to roar. I heard him go into the kitchen and light the Coleman and lay a fire in the kitchen stove. It would be a little after six o'clock, and except for the splash of light on the snow from the Coleman, as dark as could be outside.

Heat flowed into our bedroom and I would snuggle down and go back to sleep for few more precious minutes.

Mom's soft whisper came close by my head, "Dee. Come on, honey. Time to get up." I would roll out of the warm covers. She had my bathrobe ready and we would tiptoe out of the dark bedroom and close the door so Bob, the lucky dog, could sleep a little longer. Dad would be hauling in an armload of wood and would say something like, "Snowing to beat the band out there!" or "Stars all over the place!" as if the spectacle outside was a show just for us. I would sit at the kitchen table and wake up with a glass of chocolate milk. Bob and I still hated the stuff fresh from the cow, even thoroughly cold. In order to get us to drink it, Mom had started stirring a couple spoonfuls of Nestle's Quik into our milk every morning.

Of course, keeping anything thoroughly cold was no problem that time of year. Our kitchen window cooler had its winter coat on, a heavy layer of burlap that rolled down on the outside and fastened at the bottom. It kept most things from freezing except in the coldest weather.

The teakettle of hot water was there, on the back of the stove, and I would pour a basin full and wash and brush my teeth at the kitchen sink. I got dressed for school in the dark living room, standing in front of the heater, while Mom fixed breakfast and packed lunches and Dad brought in two buckets of water from the creek and set them, bottoms ringed with snow, beside the sink.

The pump had been drained in November so it wouldn't freeze. Now breaking through the ice on the creek and filling the buckets and packing them up to the house was a regular chore, twice a day at least. Dad hauled it all, but I had a feeling he had his eye on me for the job. I was ready to take it on. I was beginning to realize a change in myself. I was feeling better. I got cold, sure, like everybody else, but I didn't *have* a cold all the time. I was more energetic, more like Mom. I overheard my parents say I was beginning to fill out, and that I had roses in my cheeks. I was anxious to prove I could do a hard, important, slippery job like hauling water.

As I got dressed, I could watch out the front windows. With the warm, dark living room around me, I could see the silvery shoulders of the mountains across the lake. I could touch my bum against the stove and feel the sting of heat while I looked out at the pure, white cold. Everything, everywhere, was covered, buried, smothered, in winter.

Our breakfasts had gotten bigger as we went about the demanding business of getting around in deep snow. We would have bacon, sliced thick from the slab, or ham, or venison steaks or corned-beef hash, and always eggs. Then there would be cereal or pancakes or sometimes Mom made a batch of "French Puffs"—they were Dad's and August Binder's favorite—a sweet, spicy muffin with the tops dipped in melted butter and cinnamon-sugar. And if it was really cold, Mom would make corn meal mush the night before and then fry it in butter the next morning. Corn was the best thing, Dad said, for heating up your inner furnace.

Getting me to school became a never-ending problem. It was eleven miles, and that was a long way on the Yaak Road, especially in the winter. Week after week, morning and afternoon, Mom drove me in the truck, fifteen miles per hour, hauling poor Bob along. We'd sing to pass the time, "When You Wore a Tulip" or "When It's Springtime in the Rockies," Mom harmonizing, Bob and I singing the melody.

Sometimes Mom would drive Dad and me to the mill and I would ride to school with the two oldest of the three Cummings girls. The third daughter, Gracie, was Bob's age. Mom would stay and visit Mrs. Cummings and the two little girls, who were crazy about each other, would play together. We three older kids would pile into the massive cab of one of the lumber trucks, lunch pails clattering, and ride to school, shouting all the way over the roar of the motor, watching to see if the poor, harried driver might break down once in a while and smile about the situation.

At school in the winter, recess depended upon the weather. Mrs. Duncan made us go outside any time the temperature was above twenty degrees. And I finally discovered that snow could be fun. One week when the daytime temperatures rose to thirty-five degrees and the snow was nice and sticky, we chose sides and built snow forts out of huge snowballs lined up side-by-side. That took two days. Then we had an all-out snowball fight and the winners—us—stormed the losers' fort, and destroyed it. It was the most fun I'd ever had. I told Mom and Dad and Bob all about it and they talked about how lonesome Bob was, and that it would be better when she and Gracie Cummings were both in school.

If the temperature was below twenty degrees, you could stay inside during recess if you wanted to, if it was down below zero, you had to stay in. We had board games to play, Monopoly, Sorry, Parcheesi, Chinese checkers. Sometimes we would sit in circles on the floor and play jacks or marbles. There were tons of jigsaw puzzles—there was always one of those to work on. Or sometimes Mrs. Duncan would read to us. Once she got going, she didn't like to stop. She would sometimes keep reading all afternoon and pretty soon it would be three o'clock and time to go home and we'd all be sitting there, completely wrapped up in a story. We heard *The Wonder Stick*, about a cave man named Ru the Sparrow-Hearted, who invented the first bow-and-arrow, and *Quest in the Desert*, a story about Genghis Kahn, and *The Yearling*, which we loved, and which made even the boys cry.

When I got home from school, it would be nearly dark and I had chores to do. I shoveled more snow than I knew existed in the world. Every few days, as Dad had time to split up the bigger chunks, Bob and I had piles of kindling and holding wood to stack. This was the job both of us hated more than any other, and it was never-ending. We felt terribly sorry for ourselves. It was a shame, we thought, that two little children should have to work so hard all the time.

And it was my job to keep the lanterns filled. The kerosene, and the white gas for the Coleman were kept in five-gallon cans out on the back porch. That job required bare hands and it was cold work. Every once in a while I'd forget, well, maybe not forget, just shake the Coleman and judge it to be full enough to get by for another night. And then we'd be half way through dinner and all of a sudden the Coleman would start getting dimmer and dimmer. Everybody would roll their eyes and give me the *look* and I'd get a lecture from Dad about responsibility.

In the wintertime, when Earl Stratton hauled hay to his cattle, he had to push the deer out of the way so the cows could eat too.

Hauling water, I was sure, would be a much better way to teach responsibility.

On one cold December weekend, Mom and Dad brought down the folding bathtub and decided to give it a try. They set it up in the kitchen and checked it over for any obvious holes. Dad hauled buckets of water and filled the wash boiler on the stove. Mom hung a blanket in the archway between the kitchen and the living room so there would be a "bathroom" to bathe in. When the water was hot, she poured bubble-bath onto the soft, grey rubber that made up the tub. "You don't think it will leak, do you?" she asked, and they looked it over again. It seemed perfectly fine. Using kettles, they bailed in hot water. Midway through the job, Mom, perspiration dripping, said, "I hope this is going to be worth it!" About then, they realized they were standing in water. It was spewing out of the tub from a wide crack that had just opened up along an old fold in the rubber. They bailed water back into the boiler as fast as they could. Mom ended up taking down the blanket and spreading it on the floor to sop up the water while Dad folded up the tub and stuffed it back into the attic where it belonged.

Before we knew it, it was Christmas time. Mom had picked out our tree weeks earlier, a blue spruce about a quarter of a mile into the woods behind the house. Getting our own Christmas tree was fun, and it was a perfect tree. But we decided that getting to it, digging it out, cutting it and dragging it all the way home, all in thigh-deep snow, was more work than hauling a whole truckload of firewood. Next year, we decided, we would find our Christmas tree close to the house.

All the Christmas shopping had to be done through the Sears Roebuck and Montgomery Ward catalogues. Every week, boxes came in the mail and were stowed away in Mom's closet. I hoped there were some Bobbsey Twins books in there. I was crazy about the Bobbsey Twins.

We baked cookies and tried out candy recipes. We had our successes and our failures. Mom said it was asking a lot to try to make divinity on a wood cook stove. She figured out how to make Danish pastry, though, with all the butter Rosy Shultz was always giving us. She would layer the dough and the butter and then set it outside on the snow to chill, then roll it out and layer it with more butter. Then she coiled strips of dough into "snails" and baked them and spread them with frosting and nuts. They were absolutely luscious and we ate them about as fast as they came out of the oven.

August and Julius showed up the Sunday before Christmas, driving their big old plow horses and pulling their hay wagon, which had been turned into a sleigh; the wheels had been removed and replaced by runners. They had the sleigh piled full of hay. We all climbed aboard and headed up to Rosy and Gus Shultz's house to see Rosy's famous Christmas tree with real candles on it.

It was about four miles to the Shultzes'. We picked up two more people along the way. They were newcomers, an older couple, the Taylors: "Shorty" and her husband, Taylor. They were renting Mrs. Wheeler's little cabin, the one that had replaced her burned house. Taylor was a millwright and worked at the sawmill. They were glad to see us come driving up in the sleigh and invited everybody to come inside for a visit. We could barely all manage to crowd into their cramped little space. They had a skinny Christmas tree sitting on top of their kitchen table. Shorty wanted everybody to have a "toddy." Taylor poured a little whisky into some coffee mugs and Shorty added sugar and cinnamon and filled them with hot water from her teakettle. Bob and I were given cups of warm cinnamon-sugar water and it tasted pretty good.

They were lonesome, Shorty said. They missed their kids and their grandchildren, especially now, at Christmas time. But they had to go where the work was, and so they were here.

Shorty Taylor was a musician, and played, of all things, the bass fiddle. She kept the instrument in its case right there, in the middle of everything, in that tiny little cabin. It wouldn't fit anywhere else, she explained. It was the first thing you saw when you walked in. It reminded me of our kitchen stove—a too-large, black heap that took up a lot more than its share of space.

But then she played it for us. And for a few minutes we weren't standing in a crowded wooden shack. We were in another place, bright and airy and soft with snow and as sweet and peaceful as stars, where your heart ached inside of you but you wanted to stay there all the same. When the music was over we were all very quiet. Shorty looked out the tiny kitchen window and there were tears in her eyes. It was a Christmas piece, she said. It was her present to us. Dad said, "That was just beautiful," and I looked up and saw a tear on *his* cheek! He told Shorty her fiddle was worth whatever space it required to be in her house.

Shorty loved singing, too. When we started out in the sleigh again, she wouldn't give up until she got everybody singing, even Julius. When we came to Schultzes' hill, Dad and Taylor got out of the sleigh and walked alongside while the horses puffed steam out their noses like a pair of steam engines as they pulled us all the way to the top.

There were several pickups parked in Shultzes' yard when we got there. Lots of people had come to see the tree and we knew a few of them: Jack and Dorothy Cross, old time Yaakers from down the valley—Dorothy was Rosy's niece; Gib Hall, another friend of Dad's from the sawmill and his wife, Dede, with their little boy, a holy terror of a kid named Jerry; bachelor Earl Stratton, another old-time Yaaker, had come and brought his quiet, frail father along.

We entered, as always, through Rosy's "milk room"—the enclosed porch where the separator was—and in the middle of the floor there were three wash tubs full of crushed ice, each with a hand-crank ice cream freezer buried in the middle of it. The ice cream was ripening, we were told. Bob and I had never tasted homemade ice cream. And Christmas seemed like an odd time to be having ice cream, but our mouths watered at the thought.

As soon as it was dark, we gathered in the living room to light the candles on the tree. Rosy's tree was a Douglas-fir, a different shape from ours, wide and open, and the candles were out on the very tips of the branches in tiny wire holders that pinched onto the branches and held each little white candle straight up. Everyone gathered around as Rosy and Dorothy lit the candles; there were twenty-four. Then the lamps in the room were carried out to the kitchen and we all stood in the darkened room and admired the tree. Shorty started to sing again, "Silent Night," so everybody joined in.

I noticed a movement behind a half-open door. Rosy's husband, Gus, was standing back in the dark hallway all by himself. I wondered why he wasn't in the room with the rest of us.

When the singing ended, we looked at the tree for a few more minutes and then Rosy and a few of the others started blowing out the candles. Bob and I each blew one out and that was it; the Christmas tree lighting was over. And everyone headed into the kitchen for ice cream.

But I looked back and noticed Gus again. He moved heavily from behind the door, his wide back swaying from side to side as he moved down the dark hall into the living room and stood for a few minutes by the tree. He was carrying two buckets full of water.

Bob whispered, "What's he doing?" and I thought about the scary warnings we got from Dad all the time, and about Mrs. Wheeler's house. "Fire," I whispered back. And the Christmas tree took on a spooky look, standing there in the dark with smoke rising from its limbs. Gus waited a few minutes more and then carried the buckets out the front door and dumped them in the snow. I realized that our dad wasn't the only person who worried a lot about fire.

Along with the ice cream, there was Rosy's famous fruitcake. The slices were thick and heavy, full of candied fruit and had a strong, sweet smell that Mom told us was brandy. The adults were crazy over all of it. Bob and I tried our best, but to us, the ice cream, just like Binder's milk, tasted like the cow. And the fruitcake was much too terrible to eat. Neither one of us could swallow a second bite.

The trip home was in the dark, but Julius said the horses could see the way. Going down the hill, which seemed a lot steeper at night, August and Julius pulled together on the reins to keep us slowed down.

Once we were on the flat, the horses took off. They knew they were headed home and they were anxious to get there. Nobody sang. We were too busy hanging on.

And guess what. Sleighs really can fly at night!

CHAPTER 8

The Dead
of Winter

By the time January was upon us we had lived in the Yaak five months. Winter was no longer a stranger.

We kept three paths shoveled from the back porch out through the snow: one to the woodshed, one to the privy and one down to the creek. The sides of the paths were chin-high on me. Bob, if she could be spotted at all, was a red tassel bouncing along on the top of a stocking cap.

It seemed to me we were burning wood faster than we had cut it. Half the wood stacked on the front porch was already gone and there was a roomy, open space in the woodshed that got bigger every day.

Washing clothes was a major chore in the cold weather. It became a family project, done on weekends. Water had to be hauled from the creek, ten buckets, six for the wash boiler, which was set on the stove to heat, and four for the rinsing tub, set across two chairs in the middle of the kitchen. Mom would pour in the Tide and do the whites first, plunging for about a half hour with the wash plunger. Then we would all wring them by hand and drop them into the ice-cold water in the tub, where Bob and I would stir them around with pieces of broom sticks. Then wring again, then out to dry. Dad kept the water coming and the fire going and took over the wringing when it was time to do jeans. Mom hung most things outside on the clothesline to "freeze dry." You had to be careful not to break the brittle clothes when you brought them inside. I didn't believe this tall tale at first, so I tried it out on a pillowcase. Sure enough, if you bent the frozen-stiff fabric, the threads broke and the pillowcase was in two pieces. Amazing. "Don't try it again, please," Mom said.

The lake was covered with ice except for the narrow stretch of moving water where the creek flowed in. One day we noticed a Canada goose, swimming there all alone. We watched her every day—we had somehow decided that it was a "she'"—expecting her to take off and fly south, as all her flocks of relatives had done much earlier. Some days she would waddle up onto the ice and sit for a while. But then she always got back into the water and just swam around near the edge of the ice. She might have been injured, Dad said, or maybe she was a young one and had gotten separated from her flock. Whatever the reason, she seemed to be set on staying where she was for the time being. We named her "Lucy." We wondered what on earth she might be finding to eat. Mom went out and scattered cornbread on the snow near the creek but Lucy ignored it. The opening in the ice got smaller and smaller. Still she stayed on, swimming round and round in her little circle. One morning we looked out, and the open water had frozen over. Lucy was nowhere to be seen. We watched for her all that day and the next, but she was gone.

"Where?" Bob and I wanted to know. But we were afraid we already knew. It was probably not a happy ending for Lucy. Dad said that was Nature's way. Weaker creatures didn't always survive. It was a lesson you learned first hand when you lived in the wilderness.

One night I woke up in the middle of the night and heard the truck running. I got up to see what was going on and Mom said go back to bed, that it was below zero outside and Dad had started up the truck to keep the engine from freezing. This went on for several nights. Some nights Dad got up as many as three times to start the engine and let it run long enough to warm up, so we would be able to get it started the next morning.

The cold was a solid thing, pressing down on the valley, freezing even sound. Car horns, shouts, Dad's axe chopping a hole through the ice on the creek, the frigid air silenced it all.

The temperature got down to twenty below zero and the sawmill shut down and we thought that was cold. Then it got down to thirty below, school closed, and we thought that was really cold. Then one morning we got up and it was forty-four degrees below zero. That, said Dad, was *damn* cold.

Out in the woods, frozen trees cracked, sounding like gunshots. In the early morning hours, the ice on the lake moaned and hooted like a herd of goblins. Our window panes were completely iced over, inside and out. Bob and I scratched holes so we could try to see out, but they froze over immediately, as if to seal us inside.

Dad alone went outdoors on those days, just long enough to empty the slop jar and get wood and water. Standing at the kitchen door wiping his overshoes while Mom took the ice-encrusted water buckets from him one at a time and set them by the sink, Dad told us he had to be quick when he was dipping up water from the creek. "The hole in the ice tries to freeze over before I can get the bucket back out," he said. We didn't know whether he was kidding or not. He said no, he wasn't kidding. Then one morning he went out to start the truck and Jenny's battery was as dead as a doornail. Not that we wanted to go anywhere. But it seemed odd and maybe a little scary, that we couldn't go anywhere, no matter what.

The extreme cold lasted about ten days. Mostly, we just stayed inside and watched it. The sky was absolutely clear and blue. Nothing moved except the sun and the ice crystals sparkling in the air. The dry snow squeaked underfoot. The kitchen door froze shut between uses and had to be given a sharp jerk to open it. We kept fires in both stoves all day and all night; Dad got up two or three times during the night to add wood. As long as you stayed away from the windows, where frost leaked in and grew white fur on the panes and sills, the house was comfortably warm. Mom and Dad were pleased about that.

When the weather warmed up, the truck thawed out and Dad was able to get it running again. So I went back to school for a few days. It started snowing. And kept on snowing.

One day Julius came over, walking on snowshoes. He had a second pair slung on his back; they were for Dad to borrow until spring, he said. Then, sitting at the table with a cup of coffee, he told Dad it would be a good idea to shovel the snow off our roof. Just to be on the safe side, he said.

Dad didn't even seem surprised. He just nodded thoughtfully and admitted that, yes, he had thought about that himself.

I couldn't believe it. Our wonderful, sturdy, log house? The roof might actually cave in?!

They talked about how the snow was so heavy this year because there had been rain early on and it had turned to ice. And now the snow was nearly five feet deep. Julius said that the Westovers, down the valley, had lost their barn. "She collapse right on top uff the cows," he said grimly, slapping his hand on the tabletop with a thud.

Dad managed to get the ladder situated in the snow, up against the roof of our outdoor cooler. From there he was able to climb onto the

roof. He went up two or three times and looked around, surveying the job. Then he got the shovel and started. Mom took a picture of him standing up there on a bare patch of roof, shoulder high in snow.

He got it done. It took four days.

With snow still falling heavily, Dad works to clear the cabin roof.

Elmer Phillips lived about eight miles farther up the valley from us, and had a lake much larger than ours. He raised fish in his lake and he and his wife, Alma, and Mom and Dad became friends. We went up there for dinner once in a while and they came to our house. Elmer had a bulldozer, the kind everybody calls a "Cat," that was big enough to do the job of plowing the roads. Lucky for us and everybody else, Elmer wasn't busy in the winter. So he took care of the upper end of the main road and managed to get to most people's houses in our end of the valley every couple of weeks.

One day after plowing his way up our road and clearing our turn-around, he left the Cat idling out in the yard and came in for a quick cup of coffee. He told us that he had run into a bull moose that morning not far from his house. It stood square in the middle of the road and charged the Cat again and again and refused to let him go by. They played "Cat and moose" for quite a while, Elmer said, but the animal was in a rage and would not give up. Finally Elmer had to take the bulldozer and plow a swath through a stand of jack pines so he could drive around the moose to get by.

We heard later that the Cat and the moose tangled again on the way home. This time the moose took its stand in front of the narrow bridge across Windy Creek. After a while Elmer saw he was running low on diesel. He tried to discourage the charging animal by raising and lowering the blade. After several collisions the impact of the blade finally killed the moose. Elmer had no choice but to push it off the narrow bridge into the creek so he could get home.

Carl Cummings had a Cat at the sawmill. A man named Casey Zimmerman drove it, and plowed most of the middle part of the valley. Still, we had three and four days at a time when we couldn't get Jenny out to the main road and I missed an awful lot of school. We kept busy at home. We were getting more relaxed about being winterbound. Dad and Mom played Honeymoon Bridge and both became pretty good at tying fishing flies. I finished all four of the Bobbsey Twins books I had gotten for Christmas, and even read one of them to Bob.

With the short days and long, dark evenings, we depended more and more on an old radio Dad had bought from his friend, Earl Stratton. It was the size of a bread-box and made of wood, with tuning and volume knobs on the front. It had a large battery that fit into the back—an "A-B battery," Dad called it. We could sometimes get radio shows all the way from Seattle: Phil Harris, *The Great Gildersleeve*, *Lucky Lager Dance Time*, *Amos 'n' Andy*. Bob and I looked forward to the kids' shows, *Straight Arrow* and *Bobby Benson* and *Challenge of the Yukon* with Sergeant Preston of the Mounties. Mom followed a couple of soap operas. She and Dad both listened to the news and weather. But wouldn't you know it, in the middle of the coldest, darkest part of January, batteries being batteries, the radio reception started to fade. And once it started, it was gone in a week. A new battery could be bought only in town. So we said goodbye to the radio and put it up in the attic until spring.

Deep as we were in winter, Dad decided to reach for a piece of good old summertime. He got out the axe and a digging bar and set out to punch some holes in the ice to go ice fishing. The ice was as hard as concrete and two feet thick. Dad cut four holes in different parts of the lake and we all went out to set out the lines. We made up four sets of rigging, each with three hooks per line. We baited the hooks with tiny slices of bacon and fixed them so the bait would be at different depths. Dad tied each of the lines to a stick of wood and laid the sticks across the holes and that was all there was to it. We went in the house to wait.

Two hours later we had a dozen fish; one on every single hook. They were all eastern brook trout, no rainbows or cutthroats. All we ever caught ice fishing were brookies, don't ask me why. But they were pale and quiet as we hauled them up, not at all like the colorful fighters we caught in the summer. It was as if they were hibernating. They were good to eat but almost no fun to catch. After a couple more effortless hauls, we gave up ice-fishing altogether.

The first Saturday night of every month was Community Hall night in the Yaak Valley. The Community Hall was located on the main road about midway between our place and the Yaak Post Office. The hall had been built in about 1925 by all the Yaakers living in the area then, so they would have a place to get together for dances and parties. It was a log building about thirty feet wide by fifty feet long with a wood cook stove and long tables in one end and a potbelly heater stove in the other.

For a Community Hall Halloween party, Mom copied the Aunt Jemima Pancakes label. She blacked her face with burnt cork, put her hair in a turban, and wore a red-and-white checked skirt. Another year she went as a pirate with a mustache made of witches' beard moss.

Long benches were built along the walls on both sides of the room. The rest of the space was for dancing, and there was a wind-up record player like the one we had, that provided the music.

Jack and Dorothy Cross lived near the Hall. Jack was a gentle, soft spoken man in his fifties who had worked for the Forest Service for many years. His wife was a wide-smiling, friendly lady with a big laugh and a loud voice and who everybody said liked to run everything. They would go down early on Saturday and get the fires going and the coffee pots on, so the hall was warm and ready when everybody else got there.

Even so, when you first walked in, the building smelled damp and musty; it sat empty so much of the time. But as people kept coming, the room got warmer and the smell of coffee took over. On a good night, the crowd swelled close to fifty.

Some of the kids I knew at school didn't come to Community Hall night because their families were Seventh-day Adventist like Reverend McCoy and didn't believe in drinking coffee or dancing or, especially, drinking alcohol. And alcohol was part of the doings, although it stayed outside. Men, mostly, would stand in huddles around the backs of parked pickup trucks, all bundled up against the cold, passing a bottle around. Once in a while, usually later in the evening and with a lot of commotion and laughter, a few of the ladies ducked outside too.

The Cummings girls were usually there. Gracie and Bob played all over the hall together. I hung around with the two older girls, Carolyn and Jean. We ran and slid on the big, bare floor, played tag and showed off in our best dresses, which we always wore to the meetings.

Everyone brought food. Platters of sandwiches, fried chicken, potato salad, cookies, cakes and pies.

Being cake connoisseurs, Bob and I took inventory as the selections arrived. My favorite was Mrs. Whitcomb's chocolate fudge cake. It had frosting that was smooth and dark and looked like it had been poured over the cake and then cooled to a glossy, fudgy coating. Mrs. Whitcomb said she baked it for Jess, her husband, and it had no butter in it at all. It was, in my opinion, the most completely luscious cake of all cakes in the world. Bob, and lots of other people, liked a lemon layer cake Alma Phillips usually brought. Mrs. Phillips was the queen of cooking in the Yaak Valley. Mrs. Obermeyer sometimes brought a white cake with jam in the middle that a lot of people made a fuss over. Bob and I never even tried that one because we knew we wouldn't like jam in a cake. Rosy Shultz's cakes were always decorated with really bright-colored frosting—sometimes orange and green, or purple and pink. Bob and I noticed the adults didn't seem to care for such colorful cakes. We felt sorry for Rosy so we always took a couple pieces each of her cake.

The community meeting would begin with just that, a meeting. There would be a secretary's report and a treasurer's report and maybe an argument over the dues—one dollar per family per month was the rate then—some people thought it was way too much but some said it barely paid for coffee and toilet paper. Then people made announcements, like Dorothy Cross announcing that poor Ben Deyerle was sick and Amy could use help doing chores, or Ernie Starr asking if anybody needed a ride into town next week, because he was driving in. Rosie Shultz quietly told Mom that nobody spoke up because nobody in their right mind would want to ride into town if Ernie was doing the driving. Then the dancing began. The record player got a work-out and everybody took turns winding the player and changing records.

Many of the people living in the Yaak Valley in those days were like the Binders, immigrants who had homesteaded in the valley in the 1920s. We heard all different kinds of accents around us at the Community Hall—German, Norwegian, Swedish. There were different kinds of dancing, too. People waltzed and jitterbugged of course—from the minute they set foot on the floor, Mom and Dad were the hands-down champion jitterbuggers—but Bob and I loved to watch the polka and the schottische. When they played "Varsouvianna," Mom and Dad watched for a while and then got out and tried it. In this dance, the lady stands in front of the man, with her back to him, and slightly off to his right. They hold hands. Both people start out with their right heels out in front. The music goes, "Put your little foot, put your little foot, put your little foot right out," and with each "put your little foot," both dancers tap their right toe across their left foot, then take a step forward. With "right out," they change sides, the lady passing in front of the man so she is then on his left. Couples follow each other around the hall, all heeling and toeing and changing sides together. I thought it was wonderful and like a minuet in a movie. It was popular and got played a lot and even most of the kids could do it. After the first few times, Dad came and got me, and Mom got Bob and they taught us how. We joined the parade. It was the most fun I'd ever had.

The January meeting that year was our third time to go to the Community Hall. Mom and Dad were still getting acquainted and hadn't met some of the people who lived fifteen or twenty miles away from us, at the lower end of the valley. During part of the evening, Bob and I sat on the long bench at one end of the hall, watching the goings-on and being introduced to somebody new every now and then by Mom, who thought it was important that we meet everybody, whether we wanted to or not. The dancing had just gotten started when somebody hollered, "Pack rat!" and everybody stopped dancing and looked up into the big expanse of open rafters overhead.

There was a gray, long-tailed animal creeping across on one of the logs. It was about the size of a squirrel. I had no idea rats got that big. Mom said neither did she.

Somebody turned off the music. Jack Cross went over to the corner of the room near the door and worked his way through the twenty or so pairs of galoshes that were scattered there on the floor. From somewhere in the corner, behind bunches of coats and purses hanging from hooks on the wall, he pulled out a .22 rifle. By that time the rat was about half-way across, overhead. Jack raised the rifle and shot. The rat fell to the floor with a soft flop, sounding very dead. Somebody brought a paper bag and carried the critter outside. It was the first time Bob and I had ever seen an animal shot.

"Happens all the time," Rosy said. "This place is full of 'em."

Bob and I spent the rest of that night watching for rats in the rafters, not sure, if we saw one, whether we would holler out, "Pack rat!" or not.

Everybody in the Yaak shot deer out of season. But, Dad said, while driving home that night, a person needed to use common sense about it. There was an "understanding" with Riedlinger, the game warden, that Yaakers only took meat when they needed it. They usually shot barren does, if they could find them, since they were always the fattest and the best to eat and didn't have fawns. So Riedlinger looked the other way. But if he caught you

Dad and Gib Hall were fishing along the shore of Hoskins Lake, catching a few small ones. They came around to the creek inlet, where dozens of huge trout had gathered. They both waded in and, in minutes, scooped armloads of trout onto the bank. At the far end of the lake someone appeared, walking toward them: the game warden. They looked at their fantastic catch flapping in the grass, then scooped them all back into the water.

red-handed with a deer out of season, Dad said, he would have no choice but to do his job.

As soon as the words were out of Dad's mouth, three deer jumped into the road and started running ahead of us, trapped between the high drifts of snow left on both sides by the plow. We knew they would run on and on if we kept going; they didn't have time to climb out. So Dad stopped and waited. Finally all three animals got tired of staring at our headlights and found places to climb the drifts and get off the road.

After the pack rat incident at the Community Hall, I felt hunter instincts coursing through my blood. We had become venison eaters. We needed meat. As we watched the last of the three deer clamor over the lumpy drift, I said to Dad, "That one looks pretty good. Why don't we shoot it? I knew that Dad kept a rifle stashed behind the truck seat, like everybody else in the Yaak.

Dad said this was exactly the situation Riedlinger wouldn't want to see, big blood stain right in the middle of the main road and everything. No, he said, we'd get our deer closer to home and off the road, if possible. And anyway, he added, didn't I think it would be better if the deer had at least a sporting chance?

I knew what was coming then. I recognized the signs. Before Bob and I knew what hit us, Dad launched into a car lecture.

He loved to do this when he had us trapped, captives with a lesson he thought we ought to learn and a long drive home ahead. We squirmed. We hated car lectures. But Dad was in the mood, so we were in for a long one. He started with the principles of sportsmanship: every person's responsibility to the animals and other hunters and why the laws ought to be obeyed. Then he segued to the subject of the morality behind the laws and whether or not it was right for a game warden like Riedlinger to go along with people who broke the law in certain circumstances like here in the valley, where deer were starving and the local people needed meat. From there he moved on to the animals themselves and how in winter the deer were in danger of starving and needed to conserve every calorie of energy they possibly could. We were invaders in their territory and somehow they had to get across the roads we made in this valley and they didn't need to be running extra miles in front of cars. On and on the lecture went, explaining to us how animals' bodies stored fat and how they withstood the terrible cold and adapted to different foods and ate some things in the winter that had no nutritional value but just filled their stomachs, and so on, and so on. Bob and I were exhausted, but Dad was just getting warmed up.

We rounded a curve and suddenly a deer jumped into the road directly in front of us. "Oh!" Bob and I burst out together, as Mom cried, "Oh no!" Dad tromped on the brake. "Damn!" he said, and the truck skidded sideways and stopped. But not soon enough. We heard a sickening *bump-bump* and felt the impact of the deer against the left front wheel.

Dad shut off the motor.

"Everybody okay?"

We were. We all sat still a minute. We were shaken.

In a small voice, Mom said, "I hope it's dead."

Dad opened his door and got out. "Don't look," he said.

We didn't want to.

He pulled his rifle from behind the seat and closed the door. Mom put her arms around us and pulled us tight against her. A second later, as Bob and I reached up too late to block the sound, Dad's rifle exploded in our ears.

Dad came around to Mom's side of the truck and opened the door. He was shaking his head.

"Damn," he said again, and looked at Mom.

He touched her hand. "Okay?" he asked.

She nodded.

Dad said, "Well, we may as well take it home, Tweet. The meat's in good shape."

After a minute, Mom said, "You're right. I guess we should."

The two of them looked at me and Bob. We were wide awake now. Twice in the same night we'd seen animals killed. This time it was terrible. We just sat there.

"I don't think it suffered," Dad said.

Mom said, "And it's true, we can use the meat." And after a minute more of waiting there and watching us, Mom loosened her hold on the two of us and got out to help Dad.

In a few minutes they had the deer loaded onto the truck and we were on our way home. Dad backed the truck up to the wood shed and threw a rope over a rafter in the front corner of the shed and hoisted up the deer. Mom brought out the Coleman lantern and Dad began the job of dressing out the animal.

Bob and I had seen a deer dressed out once before and it was a long, disgusting, messy process. But even though it was past two in the morning, we didn't feel like sleep. We were all warmed up and excited now that the catastrophe was behind us. We stayed outside, playing around in the plowed clearing in front of the woodshed, doing the Varsouvianna and shining our flashlights out into the dark. "Wasting batteries," Mom said, but she was busy helping Dad so we kept it up.

After a while I heard her say, "Dar, are those *eyes* out there?"

"Hold the light a little higher, Tweet," he said.

Mom kept peering out into the woods. "They *are* eyes! Girls, get in here. Now!"

We knew serious when we heard it. In we came.

"Shine the flashlights over there into those trees," she said, pointing. We did.

Less than thirty feet from where we were standing, pairs of eyes flashed back at us from the dark woods. We counted five, six, maybe eight pairs. They were staring straight at us, or at the deer carcass and the tub of innards that was steaming in our midst.

"Don't you girls move an inch!" Mom said.

"Coyotes," said Dad. After watching the eyes for a minute, he told Mom to take the Coleman and get us girls into the house.

"Oh, Dar, I don't—"

"Do it quick, Tweet. Leave me the flashlights. And get back out here."

Without a word, Mom herded us up the icy path to the house. She closed the door behind us and scrambled back out to the woodshed as fast as she could go. Bob and I had our noses glued to the window. We wanted to get another look at all those eyes! Talk about creepy! Dad, we saw, had gotten the rifle out of the truck and was leaning it against the side of the shed just as Mom nearly slid into him with the lantern. After a few minutes I hollered out there, to see if they'd let us come back out.

"No!" they yelled in unison.

Pretty quick, the two of them came slipping and sliding, lugging the deer carcass as fast as they could, up the path to the cooler. Dad had one flashlight propped in his jacket pocket, trying to keep it shining ahead so they could see their way.

They made it to the cooler and slammed the wooden door shut behind them. We could hear them struggling as they hung up the meat. Then they hurried back out together, rounded up the lamp and the gun and the tools from the woodshed and came slipping and sliding back again into the kitchen, red-faced and panting and smelling like raw venison.

Now the woodshed was dark. We turned the lantern out and all stood at the kitchen window, watching the clearing. After only a few minutes, a shadowy shape, black against the snow, came creeping out of the edge of the trees. It stole across the clearing and stopped for a minute beside the truck. Then another shape, much smaller, came up behind it. The two then moved across and disappeared into the woodshed. Almost immediately, three more animals ran from the woods across the clearing and directly into the shed. We stood watching, breathless, excited, nobody saying a word. All together, we counted nine animals.

Dad said we might hear some fighting. We did. Wild snarling and growling. Chilling, desperate-sounding cries.

Mom said "Dar!" and shook her head, looking down at Bob. Bob was glued to the window. Dad bent over and picked her up. She was round-eyed.

Dad said, "They're wild dogs, honey. They have to fight over who gets the most, that's all."

The next morning Dad came in from the wood shed and told us that the wash tub was empty and that every speck of the deer leavings, even the head and the hide, were gone. They licked the platter clean, he said.

CHAPTER 9

The Princess
and the Pea

During that winter of 1949-50, four-year-old Bob had too much time on her hands. Usually it was too cold to be outside and Tinker Toys and coloring books were only fun for so long.

We had a set of *The Book of Knowledge* and each book had a section called, "Things To Make and Things To Do." Mom worked her way through the set, helping Bob grow salt castles in bluing, mix vinegar and soda to watch it fizz, make weird clay out of cornstarch and water, cut paper snowflakes, cut chains of paper dolls and stand them up on the record player to watch them go around. But it was Mom who ended up doing most of the "making" and the "doing," and at the end of the day her own work was still there, waiting to be done.

In desperation, she brought my roller skates down from the attic. My skates had done their miles on California sidewalks before; now they bumped along over the wood floors in our cabin in the woods. Bob shoved off from Mom and Dad's bedroom door, worked up speed across the living room and coasted through our bedroom to the dresser—a distance of maybe twenty-two feet. It kept her busy for a couple of weeks.

Jumping rope was Mom's next idea. She cleared the middle of the floor in our bedroom, tied a rope to the doorknob and became a rope-turner. After school, I joined in. We got Bob started with the basic jingle: *Bluebells, cockle shells, eevie, ivie, over.* I showed her how to run in, and run out, and we went through all the other rhymes:

Motor boat, motor boat.
Mabel, Mabel, set the table.
Ish-kabibbely, oggazoggle, bungalary, out.

Eventually Mom rigged up a second rope on the doorknob and Bob graduated to jumping double-Dutch. But there was still the same problem: Mom had too much work to do to be much of a playmate.

Bob spent hours listening to records—we had "Little Orley" and "Let's Pretend" fairy tales and *The Wizard of Oz*. She played them until she knew them by heart and they got scratchy from the dull needles on the wind-up Victrola. One day she decided a sharper needle was needed and she knew just where to get one. She ended up with the needle of the sewing machine stuck through the tip of her finger.

One particularly icy morning Dad decided he should drive himself and me to the sawmill so Mom wouldn't have to be driving the slippery roads. I then rode to school with the Cummings girls and after school Mrs. Cummings brought me home. As soon as I walked through our kitchen door, I knew something was wrong. The house was too quiet. The kitchen stove was cold.

Where was everybody?

I called out, "Mom?"

Sounding distant and unavailable, Mom answered from her bedroom, "In here."

I went in. She was down on the floor, on her knees beside the bed. Bob was sitting on the bed in front of her. It appeared to me that they were both staring straight up at the ceiling. I couldn't resist the latest smart-aleck phrase going around at school:

"What's up, Doc?"

Mom gave me a quick, irritated glance. Then I saw the crochet hook. She had a crochet hook stuck up Bob's nose. Way up.

"Mmmmmmuuuuhhh!" came from Bob. Mom said, "Keep still!" and Bob closed her mouth. I saw a tear come dribbling down her cheek.

For at least a full minute, Mom worked away with the hook. Bob's face was beet red. Except for my toes, which were curling, I was paralyzed, watching the operation. I started to ask, "What—?" but I stopped myself. This was not the time.

After several tense minutes, Bob started to whimper and more tears came and Mom finally pulled the crochet hook out and sat back on her heels. She let out a long, "Whooh!" as she stood up and rubbed her back. Then she pulled Bob against her and said, "Shoot!"

That was as close as Mom ever came to swearing. But it packed the punch of the real thing. Bob started crying, out loud.

Mom looked weary. To me, she said, "She has a pea up her nose."

So that was all! Was I relieved! I said, "Bob, you dope! There's even a song about not doing that."

"Don't," said Mom, "it's not funny. We have to get it out before it swells any more. Oh, I wish we could get to a doctor."

"Can't she just blow it out?"

Mom shook her head and Bob kept on crying. "Come on, sweetie," Mom said, "you mustn't cry. That'll make it swell up faster. We have to just keep trying."

Mom sat Bob on the bed again and got back down on her knees. Up went the hook. I could hardly stand to watch.

"Now hold very, very still," Mom said, and went at it again. Bob's eyes were wide but she didn't move a muscle. Mom started talking quietly, like she was having a nice time, just frosting a cake or something.

"We'll get it pretty soon now. We'll get it. I know you didn't know it would go up so far. You were helping Mommy make split pea soup. There were lots of peas, lots of peas. We can get it out if we hold very, very, very still…".

But after another siege of torture Bob gave a little shudder and Mom had to quit again.

Mom said to me, "Would you see if you can start a fire? It's cold in here." She sat down on the bed and took Bob on her lap and they rocked back and forth. In her softest voice, Mom said, "Poor little one. We've been at this for hours. Poor little one…"

With the truck gone, by the time Bob had confessed about the pea, there was nothing Mom could to do but try, all day long, to get it out. It dawned on me that it had been a couple of days since we had split pea soup. "When did she put it up there?" I asked.

Bob glared at me and croaked, "Day before yesterday!"

"She's tired of explaining," Mom said. "We've been all through it. Go build a fire. It's cold in here."

But I wasn't as tired as they were and I wasn't ready to let up either. I said, "I just can't believe *anybody* would be *dumb* enough to—"

"Build a fire," said Mom. "Now."

At me, Bob hollered, "I did it lots of times! In my ears too! And I always get 'em back out!"

Mom's eyes went wide. "You what?!" She stood Bob up in front of her and stared at her. Bob started crying again.

On the end of the bed was a collection of discarded tools that they had already tried: The bulb syringe Dad used to wash wax out of his ears, tweezers, tooth picks, even a nut pick. The pea itself was way up as far as you could see in Bob's nose. It was big and hard, and everything Mom used just seemed to push it up farther.

But minutes later they were back at it again. I couldn't watch any longer. I went in and started a fire in the kitchen.

This was my new skill. Dad had showed me how to place the hatchet across a narrow slab of wood, then lift wood and hatchet together and bring them down, not too hard but hard enough, on the edge of the wood box, splitting off a thin stick. Six or seven sticks were all it took. Wad up three or four magazine pages, tightly, so they would burn hotter, put them in the fire box. Then crisscross the sticks of kindling over the paper. Open the damper three-fourths, open the drafts on the front of the stove, touch a match to it. In a few minutes, when you heard the wood crackle, close down the drafts and there you had it: heat.

When I went back to the bedroom they were taking another break. Mom looked like she was at the end of her rope. She rubbed her neck and pushed her hair back—she had let it grow long and was wearing it pulled up in the latest style, called a pony-tail—it was all falling down now, around her face. She pulled out a loose hair pin and started to push it back in, then laid it in the palm of her hand.

A new tool.

She straightened it out and bent a little pea-sized hook in one end. Up went the hook, into poor Bob's nose.

Just as Bob started another, "Mmmnuuh...." Mom gave a little cry, and there, in her hand, was the pea. She sat back on her heels. "Thank heavens!" she said.

I wanted to get a good look at the thing. It was yellowish white, and puffed up to the size of a small marble. Mom put it in an ashtray and pressed her fingers over her eyes. I saw how exhausted she was. I decided I better not do any more harassing. Mom picked Bob up in her arms and squeezed her and said, "I hope you've learned your lesson, young lady!"

That night Mom and Dad had an argument. It was five degrees below zero outside so there was no place they could go where we couldn't hear every word. That's one of the problems with a cabin-sized house. Bob and I sat in our bedroom with the door closed while it went on.

"It could have been serious!" Mom said. "Those things can get infected!"

"I shouldn't have taken the truck," said Dad.

Mom said, "What if that pea had somehow worked its way down into her windpipe?! I hate to think—! I just don't know how safe it is, Dar, being home alone with a child and no way to get help!"

Dad said, "From now on, the truck stays here, no matter what."

"You certainly can't walk to and from work in this weather. It isn't safe!"

"Then we'd better have you drive me so you can keep the truck."

"It's a nuisance, driving that road so many times every day. I don't have time!"

"Then, Tweet, what would you have me do, honey?"

"I don't know. I'm too tired to think about it."

After a while Dad said, "Maybe we should get another vehicle." Mom didn't say anything. We all finally went to bed.

But after the pea-up-the-nose episode, I was ordered to spend more time playing with my sister. It was one of my regular chores. And just when we needed it most, we ran across the motherlode of wintertime entertainment: an endless source of comic books. Casey Zimmerman, the cat-skinner at the sawmill, had a bunch of grandchildren in town who had been going through comic books by the dozens for years. Casey hauled boxes full of them up to the mill and when the Cummings girls were finished with them they gave them to us. We got a foot-high stack, every week. It didn't take long to discover that I could get my poor, bored sister to do anything I wanted, if only I would read her a comic book. She would put away my clothes and make my bed, fix me a sandwich, any old thing. Pretty soon I had the arrangement working beautifully. I had a slave! If we ran short of comics we switched back to the Bobbsey Twins books. I had five of them by then; enough to last for the rest of the winter, I figured. Every so often Bob would ask if we could read my new *Nancy Drew, The Clue of the Black Keys*, I said no. Nancy Drew was my private territory and not to be shared with a little sister who puts peas up her nose.

Mom had always loved to cook. Week by week, as she got better at managing the stove, cooking became her wintertime entertainment. Whenever she had a little free time she would get out a cookbook and be off in her own favorite, private world. Before long she got up the nerve to start having company over for dinner.

When the snow was several feet deep, Bob and I climbed into the attic and dared each other to jump out the window into the snow. We couldn't get up the nerve. We decided the cat would love it. We carried her up and dropped her, legs flailing, and she sank about two feet into the snow. We were waiting for her as soon as she climbed out, so she could go again.

Mom had come from California with her mother's dinner party recipes and her bridge party repertoire of delicacies most Yaakers had never even heard of. She introduced them to the whole valley. Chips and dip, which everybody thought was pretty strange at first, was a huge hit. Mom served the first baked potatoes with sour cream and the first Roquefort cheese dressing anyone had ever tasted and people raved. Mom's spaghetti and meatballs with garlic bread became a legend. At the Community Hall it was her chocolate cake with the secret ingredient—coffee and mayonnaise—and her coconut cream pie that made her famous.

But what everybody really loved were her chocolate eclairs. Icie Betzer ordered them by the dozen. Mrs. Fix, who supplied the cream for the filling, said they were heaven on a plate. In fact, there was so much fuss made over Mom's chocolate eclairs, that it began to seriously irritate Alma Phillips.

"I don't think she likes me very much," Mom said one night as they stood at the kitchen window, watching Phillips' taillights disappear in the trees. Alma and Elmer had just been down for dinner.

"Sure she does," Dad said, but he grinned and squeezed her shoulders. "Maybe she'd like you a little better if your cream puffs were soggy or your coffee wasn't quite so good."

"She hardly ate a thing," Mom complained. "Whoever heard of eating rice without the chop suey?"

"She said she just doesn't care for foreign food."

"Oh, phooey. Chop suey's as common as anything."

"Maybe to an exotic Chicagoan."

So without realizing it, Mom started a feud that winter, between herself and a nice lady whom she would have liked to have for a friend, especially since Elmer and Dad enjoyed each other a lot. Dad said Elmer was one of the smartest men he'd ever met. Among other things, Elmer was an expert at raising fish. He had run hatcheries for the state and raised and sold trout to restaurants and to the Great Northern Railroad for their dining cars. He had built his own fish hatchery on his lake. And Elmer was interested in Dad's idea of raising fish in our lake. He could supply us with all the fry—the baby fish—we would need, from his hatchery, he said. He and Dad talked about it by the hour.

But as far as Mrs. Phillips was concerned, she was still the Yaak's reigning queen of cooking, and the newcomer from California had stepped on her toes. A war was on, whether Mom knew it or not.

And Mom went on introducing one goodie after another. She made a Lord Baltimore cake—with just a *touch* more rum than the recipe called for—that disappeared at the Community Hall as fast as she could slice it. An enchilada casserole with tortillas out of a can, turned out to be Jack Cross's new favorite dish. And when she got out one of *her* mother's cookbooks and tried a strange Italian recipe called "pizza-pie," it created a sensation.

One night in late January we had Rosy and Gus Shultz over for dinner. Bob and I loved it when Gus Shultz was around. He was a storyteller. His grammar was the worst we'd ever heard. He said wonderful things that made Dad laugh and cringe at the same time, things like, "clumb up a tree," or, "ketched aholt of," or "th'owed a rock," and he knew a million tales about all the old timers in the Yaak. Gus was one of the earliest settlers in the valley and had owned his homestead since 1914. He had helped build the Community Hall and in 1920 he organized the few neighbors around, and they built the "Federal Building"—a tiny log cabin at the end of the mail run in the upper end of the valley. It had a wood stove and benches and was a meeting place for valley people to visit while they waited for the mail truck on Tuesdays and Fridays.

Gus wasn't much to look at. A couple of his upper teeth were missing, the rest were stained from cigarettes and strong coffee. His hair was thin and gray. His nose was like the Yaak Road: bumpy and crooked. His hands were big and gnarled and all that was left of his right index finger was an inch-long stub. Like so many Yaakers, he dressed logger-style: plaid shirt over long underwear, red suspenders, heavy pants cut off at the ankles and logging boots.

Rosy was Gus's second wife. They had been married a little over ten years. Mom had heard all about Gus's earlier life from Rosy. When he first came to the Yaak Valley in 1910, Gus married a girl named Ester Robards, the daughter of another homesteader. They had one son named Scott and another little boy, Robert. Robert drowned in the river when he was only two years old. Eleven years later Gus's wife died. Poor Gus and his son were left alone and then as soon as he was old enough, Scott left the Yaak Valley and moved to town. Once I knew about all this, I tried to see if Gus showed signs of how sad it must have been to lose his wife and have his little boy drown. It didn't show. Gus looked as tough as rocks.

Gus was known all over the valley for his woodpile. He had the tallest one in the Yaak. You could see it from a long ways away as you came up their road. He spent all his extra time splitting wood and throwing the pieces high up on the pile. He'd hold his axe in one hand, a piece of wood in the other, and split the pieces off as fast as you could deal a deck of cards. Dad said he wished he could handle an axe like that. Dad said that wood pile was Gus's monument to himself.

Gus knew lots of stories about bears and old timers. He told one story about a miner who was being chased by a bear that was so close behind him he didn't have time to open his cabin door to get inside. So he ran past the cabin and straight into his privy and slammed the door just in time. The bear ran around the privy a few times and then started clawing at the sides, rocking the building back and forth until it fell over. The bear looked up through the bottom of the privy and saw the miner. He charged, and got his head up through the hole. Then he couldn't get it back out. He started dragging the whole works backwards. The door was on top, so the miner opened it, climbed out and ran to his cabin. The last he saw of the bear it was headed off into the woods with the outhouse stuck on its head.

Dad told us that maybe once in a while Gus's stories were taller than they were true, but we didn't care. We could have listened to Gus for hours.

He told another one about a trapper who ran a line of traps way up on the East Fork. He built himself a log cabin so he could stay through the winter and trap. There were a few other miners and trappers in the area and they all thought he was crazy because he wasn't getting his wood cut for the winter. Then, when he started building a second cabin, an even bigger one, around the outside of the little cabin, they thought he was even crazier. They knew he would freeze to death and they told him so. Still, he spent all his spare time on his big, new cabin and finished it just before winter. After the first bad snowstorm someone went to check on him and got a surprise. The trapper was snug as a bug, inside the second cabin, sawing up the first one, which he used for firewood all winter long.

We'd had a wonderful time that night. Outside, the winter darkness was deep and cold and both our stoves roared to keep up with it. The house smelled like good food. The kitchen was bright with the hissing Coleman overhead, and full with the six of us, gathered to the shoulders around the table, wool-stockinged feet crowded underneath. Rosy was full of gossip—yes, she now knew for sure, Icie Betzer and George Lang were living together. He was around there all the time, in plain sight; they weren't fooling a soul—and Gus was full of stories. We were all full of Mom's venison spaghetti, coleslaw with sour cream dressing, and graham cracker cake.

It was nearly eleven when Rosy and Gus finally got up to leave, a process that took some time, all the putting-on of boots, jackets, scarves, mittens, hats. Gus went out and started the pickup to let it warm up a few minutes and then the four of them stood on the back porch finishing off their visit and saying goodnight. Bob and I went in to get ready for bed.

The next thing we knew, the kitchen door banged open. Somebody was moaning.

We heard Rosy's voice saying, "Careful!" and the movement of heavy feet on the kitchen floor. I made it into the kitchen just in time to see Mom being carried in by the other three, Dad, Gus and Rosy.

The moaning was coming from Mom. It was the worst, the scariest sound I'd ever heard. In between moans her voice was a little whimper. She said, "Oh, my leg. Oh, my leg." over and over.

They carried her into the living room and laid her on the couch. Rosie pulled the afghan from the back of the couch and spread it over Mom's shoulders. Bob and I were frozen in our footsteps.

Gus and Dad tried to pull the right leg of Mom's jeans up, but she cried out, "Oh! Ow! Ow! No! No!"

Without taking her eyes off Mom's face, Rosy said to me, "Go get your mother's scissors."

As fast as I could move, I went in and grabbed them from the sewing machine drawer. Dad took them and carefully cut the leg of Mom's jeans from the cuff to the knee. We all looked at Mom's leg. In the middle of her smooth, skinny, right shin, there was a weird, pointed bump sticking up about an inch.

Dad put down the scissors and reached for Mom's hand. "Oh, hell! Oh, honey," he said, and kissed the inside of her hand. He held her hand there, across his mouth. She had her eyes closed and wasn't looking at anybody, just moaning. Bob started to cry. In my whole life, I was never so horrified.

Gus said, "We'll have to splint this real good in order to get her to town, Dar. Get some towels and a couple magazines and some sticks of wood from the kitchen. And we need some socks. Several pair of socks."

Dad gathered everything up in no time.

"You got some whiskey, don't you?" said Gus.

"Rum," said Dad.

"Give her four, five gulps," said Gus. "Marilyn, this has got to be done. And I'm sorry."

This was not the fun, jokey, storytelling Gus Shultz with the terrible grammar. In a heartbeat everything and everybody had changed. This was a man with a deadly serious voice and a grim face. The room was filled with fear. It was as if we'd all died and gone stiff with it.

Rosy was sitting on the couch by Mom's head. She reached out and stroked Mom's hair back from her forehead. She smoothed the afghan again and then got up and took Bob and me by the shoulders and herded us into Mom and Dad's bedroom.

"Stay in here until we come and get you," she said. "Your mother's broken her leg. We have to get her ready so we can take her to town to the doctor."

"How did she—?" I began, but Rosy turned around without another word and went out of the room and closed the door behind her.

We weren't brave. We were as scared as it was possible to be. We didn't even know if we could move. We didn't want to move. We didn't want to hear or even feel. But we couldn't escape this awful thing. We couldn't go anywhere. We had to be there where we were, and *stand* it.

Something flew into my head. Almost without thinking I said, "I'll be Nan," and felt a tiny relief.

"And you're Flossie," I went on, feeling a little better. "This is *The Bobbsey Twins in Terrible Trouble*. It's Chapter One: 'Mother's Broken Leg.' Mother just broke her leg and we're getting ready to take her to the doctor. Okay?"

Bob was instantly into the game. We assumed our fake, Bobbsey voices:

"Oh, Nan! What should we do?!"

"I don't know, Flossie! Get her some rum! That'll help!"

"Yeah! Rum!"

"Hurry. Bring magazines and socks!"

"Yes! Here!" (Bob holds out pretend magazines, socks and rum.)

"Here, Mother dear, have some rum." (I raise pretend Mother's head on the bed, tip pretend glassful of rum.)

"Here, Mother dear, here's a magazine to read." (Bob offers pretend magazine.)

This went on, I don't know how long. We put lots of socks on Mother's poor broken leg and brushed her hair back and brought more glasses of rum. But I felt like I was watching somebody else do all these things. In my stomach was a terrible, crying ache. I was afraid it would be even worse if I let it out.

The door opened. It was Dad. Nan and Flossie vanished and we were us again and it was now, and real. Dad closed the door. His face was set, chin forward, biting hard like he always did when he was worried. I searched his eyes. I didn't want to see him scared. If your father was scared, all must be lost.

His voice was calm. "Your mother is going to be all right," he said. "but we have to get her to the doctor in Bonners Ferry. Gus and I are going over to the mill to borrow Carl Cummings' car so she can lie down in the back seat on the trip into town. Rosy will be here with Mom. I want you both to be very quiet so Mom can rest until we get back. Get some things together so you can go home with Rosy tonight. I'll have to stay in town with Mom. She will have to be in the hospital for a while."

At this, I had to let loose some panic.

"In the hospital?! How long?!"

"Sshh! I don't know right now. She's broken both bones and Gus says—"

"Both? Both legs?!"

"No. Not both legs. There are two bones here." He touched his lower leg. "Gus says it's a bad break but it will heal. He's done a fine job of splinting it. Now," he sat down on the bed and held us, each one by an arm, in front of him. "you kids are going to have to be soldiers. Dee, you're in charge. Bob, be the biggest girl you can be. Rosy is glad to have you both. I'm counting on you."

Dad was always telling us to be soldiers. When you had a splinter that needed taking out, you had to be a soldier. When your feet were freezing but you weren't finished stacking kindling, you had to be a soldier. Now, being a soldier was not possible. I needed to ask a hundred questions. How much was it hurting her?! Was she still moaning that sad, awful moan?! What happened? Did she fall? How? Where? How could this have happened to *our mother*?!

But then he was out of the room and gone. In minutes we heard Gus's pickup rumbling out of the yard.

The Coleman lantern had either run out of gas or someone had turned it out. There was a kerosene lantern burning low, on the kitchen table. Bob and I tiptoed quietly across the dim living room. Mom was a still, silent mound on the couch with her head in Rosy's lap. Rosy held her finger to her lips. I was afraid to see Mom. It wasn't bearable, to have your mother badly hurt. It was the worst thing possible. I didn't want to be me, going through this. For Nan Bobbsey, it would be easier:

Quietly, in our room in Lake Port, Flossie and I gathered up our stuff, just a few things, pajamas and underwear. We were going to stay with Aunt Pry for a while.

"It might be fun to stay with Aunt Pry. Don't you think so, Flossie?"

"No."

The game had worn out. We sat on my bed in the dark bedroom for what seemed like hours. There wasn't a sound from the living room. Bob fell asleep. I think I must have. Then I heard a car. I woke Bob and we saw headlights come across the yard. It was the Cummings' sedan, covered in snow, looking like an igloo with portholes. Shultzes' pickup followed. The car turned around and backed up to the house, as close as the snow banks would allow. Dad got out and opened a rear door. Both vehicles sat out there, engines running, exhaust pluming, headlights beaming through falling snow.

More sounds: The kitchen door opened. Gus's and Dad's voices, speaking low. Kitchen chairs being moved aside. Scuffling footsteps in the living room, more voices.

"Careful."

"I've got her."

"That's it."

More feet moving.

She was going! We couldn't stand it. We ran into the kitchen just as Mom was carried out the door, head first, by Dad. Gus supported her right leg with both hands. It stuck out straight and was wrapped in a towel and nested in a magazine. Two pieces of kitchen stove wood were tied tightly, one on each side, bound in place with Dad's socks, all knotted together. Gus guided the leg carefully through the door. Rosy was holding blankets around Mom's shoulders. They got onto the porch and Gus said, "Careful now. Chrissake, don't nobody else slip."

I watched them move out the path to the waiting car. It seemed like they spent endless time settling Mom into the back seat, Dad at one door, Gus at the other, Rosy on her knees in the front seat. Finally they closed the doors. The igloo puffed and rumbled and began to move slowly out of the yard. Rosy came walking up the path to the house.

She said, "You still awake? I thought you kids'd both be asleep by now. Get on inside and close the door, child! Where's the little one?"

Bob was there behind me in the dark, stuck like glue. We got back inside and closed the door.

"Got your things all ready to go?" said Rosy. "Look there, it's two-thirty. We've got to get on home."

We went back into the living room to get our stuff. Rosy looked us over and sat down on the couch. "C'mere and sit down for a minute," she said, so we did.

"Now, your mom is going to be all right," she said. "She's in pain, but she'll be all right. Gus, he knows how to take care of things like this. And your dad, well, your dad is the gentlest man I ever saw. My god, he does love that woman. You two are lucky little girls and don't you forget it."

I wasn't sure why Rosy was telling us this. I didn't feel one bit lucky. I saw the car lights flash from the road across the lake and watched them disappear in the dark. They were on their way. How I wished I could have gone with them!

I guess Rosy was just trying to make us feel better. She thought it would help if she told us our Dad would take good care of our Mom. She wanted us to feel lucky we had such parents. We already knew we were. But a lonely thought entered my head: parents don't always belong to their kids. Especially at times like this. At times like this, parents belong to each other. Kids are extra. And even with Rosy looking after us, we were on our own, like soldiers.

CHAPTER 10

Nosy Rosy, Galloping Gus

That night as we drove up Shultzes' icy, rutted road, past the barn and outbuildings to the house, Bob and I were both lost in the gloom in our heads. I heard Rosy mutter complaints at the pickup as she wrestled it over the road with her one good, and one not-so-good, arms. "Ever since that stroke," she grumbled, "I'm not much good at this driving business."

But we finally pulled into the yard and she ushered us through the back door of the house, through the milk room and then into the kitchen. She lit a lamp and carried it along as we went into the living room at the far end of the house. A stairway divided the living room from the main bedroom and went up to another small room in the attic. We would be staying up there once we were settled, she said. But for tonight, the couch would do.

The living room was dark and close with lots of furniture and small windows. Schultzes' furniture was covered with layers of crocheted afghans, all the same bright and deep colors as Rosy's cakes. Crocheted doilies were on all the tables, starched and ironed to stand up in stiff ruffles around Rosy's dozens of knickknacks.

Bob and I unloaded our stuff onto a chair while Rosy put wood in the stove. Neither one of us had to go, but she made us go out to the privy anyway, where we managed as best we could in the freezing dark. Finally we were settled on the living room couch, heads at opposite ends, feet overlapping in the middle, afghans piled on top of us. We were both asleep by the time Rosy took the lamp and went into the bedroom.

The Shultzes were one of the few Yaak Valley households that had a telephone. The original line had been strung by the Forest Service after the forest fire of 1910, to connect the lookouts on Mount Henry and

Mount Baldy with the ranger stations and the town of Troy. There were some fifteen people on the line and, since Gus had worked for the Forest Service, he got a telephone put in to his house. Shultzes' telephone didn't look anything like the streamlined, black, table model we had in California. It was a wooden box mounted on the wall in the kitchen. It had a black mouthpiece, a black earphone that rested on a cradle, and a hand crank on the side that you turned to make it ring. Shultzes had their own special ring—one long, two shorts and another long—and all the telephones along the line would ring no matter who was calling whom.

The next morning all Bob and I wanted to do was be miserable together and sit in Rosy's big kitchen and look out her windows. She had one facing east that looked out at their road, where I imagined Dad might somehow come driving up to get us, and one above the sink facing west that looked out over the North Fork, not far from the place where we had camped last summer, in what seemed now to be a much happier time. So when the telephone rang, it startled us. Sure enough, it was Rosy's one-long–two-shorts–one-long, ring, and it was Dad. Rosy talked to him for just a minute and then we got Bob up on a chair so she could reach, but she wouldn't talk. She only listened and nodded her head and then she started to cry. So Rosy took her and sat down in the rocking chair. Then it was my turn. Dad sounded far away but I could hear him okay. He said he had to talk fast because he was calling long distance and didn't have much change. He sounded fine. He said Mom was fine. Gus had done such a good job of splinting Mom's leg, he said, that the doctor hardly had to do a thing before he put it into a cast. Dad would be staying in town for a week and Mom would have to be in the hospital quite a while, maybe three more weeks. He told me not to worry and they loved us and he was counting on me to take good care of my sister. We said goodbye and I put the earphone back into the cradle and the call was over. I turned around. Bob had stopped crying. I told her the news. Three weeks! It was forever!

Rosy said, don't be silly, the time will fly. The first thing we were going to do was get settled in the upstairs bedroom. "Then," she said, "I can sure use some help around here."

Gus got home that afternoon. He had hitched a ride with someone else coming back from town. We all drove over to our house so Bob and I could get a bunch more of our clothes. Rosy started a fire and washed up all the dirty dishes in our kitchen. She and Gus talked about coming over every day or two to start a fire and warm things up in the house. When we got back to their house, we carried all our clothes upstairs and Rosy helped us hang our clothes on a row of hooks along one wall of the little bedroom. Besides the bed, there was a dresser with a mirror and bench that had belonged to Rosy's mother. We each got a drawer. We would be sleeping together in the bed and Rosy gave us our own slop jar. The chimney from the stove below went right up through the middle of the room so it was nice and warm, but at night Bob thought the chimney was scary. We had forgotten to bring any flashlights from home and Rosy said she was sorry, she didn't even own one. We would just have to get used to the dark and try not to bump into the chimney if we had to get up. Bob slept on the side of the bed away from the chimney with me in between, so she couldn't see it. We put the slop jar on her side of the room, close to the wall, so we wouldn't knock it over.

Months later, after all this was over, people were still hearing from Rosy Shultz about how she sure wished she could have kept those Knowles girls a few weeks longer. It would have done them a world of good, she told everyone. We were the laziest pair she'd ever run across. "Your mom is a lovely woman," she told us, "but Lord in heaven, she's got the two of you spoiled!" She was amazed that we didn't wash all the dishes at our house and said, "Well if that isn't the height of something or other!"

After dinner our second night, she set a dishpan full of dirty dishes in front of me, put Bob on a stool at a second dishpan full of rinse water, showed me how to scrub everything from plates to pots, and Bob how to dry.

By the next afternoon, Bob was sweeping the floor and I was peeling potatoes. Hauling water from the river became my regular chore; never mind the steep path to the house from the river, or that the ice on the river was dangerous and I could be pulled into the hole by the current, or any of the dozens of other hazards Dad would have found to worry about. I thought about Gus's little boy every time I went down there, but as far as Rosy was concerned, I was a big enough kid to be doing the job and that was that.

Bob and I both carried in wood from Gus's famous pile and Rosy showed me how to empty the ashes from the cookstove and scatter them on the paths so they wouldn't be slippery. Which, she said, is what we should have been doing at home. Then our Mom wouldn't have fallen.

Rosy told us she had had a stroke a few years back and ever since, her right arm had been bad. One thing she needed help with was washing butter, she said. I thought "washing butter" sounded completely loony but pretty soon I was doing it. Rosy could run the separator and churn the cream but then she would dump the clump of butter and whey out into a wooden bowl where it had to be washed with water, and that was the part that was hard for her to do. She showed me how to use the wooden paddle to work the whey out, tipping the bowl and spilling whey over the edge into a bucket, then adding more water and working it until the butter was nothing but pure butter. I thought my arms would break for sure.

Rosy said our parents were fine people but she was surprised they hadn't taught us better. Kids these days weren't learning how to work, and now, boy, did she have *her* work cut out for her! There was no reason, she said, why Bob wasn't perfectly capable of standing on a chair and plunging the laundry in the wash boiler. And I was certainly capable of hanging out the wash and bringing it in and folding it. She showed me how to use the sadirons that were always on the back of her stove and I ironed simple things like

Mom didn't like boiled coffee. She preferred brewing it in a Cory vacuum brewer, set on a trivet to protect the glass bottom. She put eggshells in, to help settle out the coffee grounds. Eventually two pots got broken atop the wood stove. She and Dad finally learned to like instant coffee.

her aprons and our blouses. I told her about Mom's Coleman iron and she said she wouldn't give house room to one of those crazy, flaming things.

We also helped with the outside chores. Bob was given the job of feeding Rosy's cats, which was right up Bob's alley. The Shultzes had mules and cows and chickens, and Gus took care of the mules and cows, but Rosy showed me how to feed and water the chickens and rake the manure out of the chicken house, which I didn't much like. Bob got to gather the eggs. Rosy showed her how to slip her hand underneath a hen, ever so carefully, so she wouldn't get pecked, and feel around for an egg in the nest. Bob was good at it, too. I decided Rosy liked Bob a little better than me. Probably because Bob was the little one, and blond.

"I wasn't raised to sit around and twiddle my thumbs," Rosy said, "and no kids in my house are going to, either." So when everything inside and outside was done, she sat us down and taught us how to crochet. She had dozens of spools of crochet cotton, all in Rosy-type colors: bright orange, dark blue, mustard yellow, blazing pink, grass green. We started little doilies and she let us mix colors any way we pleased. We decided to make doilies to give to Mom when she came home.

Most of the other people on the Yaak telephone system were like Gus and Rosy and had lived in the Yaak for many years. There were the McIntires, John and his wife, Jeanette Nolan, who were movie stars and who had owned their summer home up near the East Fork summit since 1937. Next down the line were Phillipses; then the Shultzes. There was a telephone at the Upper Ford Ranger Station; it was about five miles down the valley from our place and built in the 1920's. Then there were Jack and Dorothy Cross; Jack's uncle homesteaded their place in the early '20's, and Icie Betzer at the Yaak Post Office had a telephone. There was one farther south at the Ranger Station at Sylvanite, and a few more, mostly in the homes of Forest Service employees.

But whenever Rosy's phone rang, no matter whose ring it was, Rosy dropped what she was doing and hurried over to it. She would put a hand over the mouth piece, then, very quietly, lift the ear phone off the cradle and put it to her ear. She'd listen a minute, frowning, her eyes wandering around the room. Sometimes she would stare right at the two of us, but it was as if we weren't really there. After a few minutes more she'd reach out one foot and hook the leg of the kitchen stool. Slowly and carefully, like slipping a hand underneath a hen, she would slide the stool underneath her bottom so she could settle down for a good listen.

And so Bob and I discovered how it was that Rosy was always up on all the latest gossip in the valley. Gus got a kick out of the whole thing. "Nosy Rosy," he called her. He told Bob and me that once when she was listening in on somebody, right out of the blue, one of the people on the line said, "Isn't that right, Rose?" and she got all flustered and hung up.

One day Bob and I went with Gus to skid some logs in from the woods. Gus told us it was a good day to be outdoors because we were having a chinook—a warm wind from the south. It was about forty-five degrees outside and the snow was soft. Bob and I were warm enough in sweaters. Gus put harnesses on his two mules and fastened coils of heavy chain to each harness. Then he helped each one of us climb aboard a mule, and off we went, Gus on snowshoes, leading the team. We were about as scared as we were thrilled, to be way up on top of those animals, with the chains clanking on the harnesses like sleigh bells.

We headed north up toward the "line," as Gus called the Canadian border. He said it was only a few miles from his house. It was a forty-foot-wide clearing in the trees that went as far east and west as the eye could see, clear across the country actually, and divided the United States from Canada. I wanted very much to see this real, live map-line on the earth but Gus said we couldn't get that far in the snow. It would wear out both him and the mules, he said.

After a ways, we turned off the road and Gus led the team into the trees. The snow was deeper here, and the walking was hard for the mules. Up on top of them, the ride got rough and we had to hang onto the harnesses to keep our seats. We finally came to a clearing where a mound of snow turned out to be a head-high pile of ten-foot logs. Gus told us to slide off the mules, which we did, and sank into snow way up past our knees. He helped us climb out and then made us stand back while he attached chains to four of the logs and used the mules to pull them off the pile and into position to be towed home.

"Now I ride and you walk," he said, taking off the snowshoes and fastening them up on one of the mules. "You kids'll have a good trail to walk home on." Then he stepped up on the logs and whistled to the team and they took off at a trot, pulling the four heavy logs as if they were nothing at all. And there was Gus, jumping and balancing back and forth from one rolling, slippery log to another as they twisted and bounced along through the snow. From back where we were, he looked like the scarecrow in the *Wizard of Oz*. We ran along behind and kept up as long as we could. Then Gus and the mules pulled ahead. They beat us back to the wood pile by about fifteen minutes. Riding the logs looked like loads of fun, I told Gus. But he said nobody shouldn't be doing nothing like that without they had a lot of practice. In fact, he said, "nobody probably shouldn't be doing it at all."

At the end of the first week Dad came home from town. Rosy fixed him dinner and said he looked tired. He said all he needed was a good night's sleep.

The sawmill was up and running again and Dad had to go back to work until Mom came home. Then he would have to take time off and stay home to take care of her. So he went back to our house, and we stayed there with Rosy and that was the way it was for two more weeks. And even though Rosy kept us busy and sometimes we even had fun, time didn't fly. We were dying to see Mom. Sometimes Bob would cry after we were in bed at night. I was missing a lot of school. But there was nothing to be done about any of it.

Dad came every few days to see us. Rosy told him, give her a little more time and she'd really have us whipped into shape. Our mother wasn't going to know us. We were twice the kids we'd been when she first got her hands on us, she said.

The day Mom came home, February 17th, Gus and Rosy let us ride in the back of their pickup, sitting down behind the cab, on the way back to our house. The air coming around the pickup cab was so cold it made your cheeks numb when you peeked around to look ahead. But we didn't care; we kept looking ahead anyway, we were so anxious to get home. In the yard there was a car we didn't recognize, parked next to Jenny. We were so excited to see Mom, we hardly noticed it.

There she was, lying on her bed in the middle of the living room. Dad had made a place for her, right in front of the windows. Her broken leg was sticking out in front of her, propped up on pillows. It was covered by a fat plaster cast that went all the way from her toes to the middle of her thigh. She had on a plaid shirt and a pink scarf tied on her pony tail and she looked wonderful. She told us she would have to stay in that cast for six more weeks. Then she would get another one, a cast she could walk in. We were afraid to hug her in case we would hurt her leg but she said it didn't hurt at all anymore, it just itched like mad. Bob crawled right into the bed beside her and I sat on the other side. It was so good, it was like Christmas, to have her home.

The car parked outside was ours. A black, '46 Ford. Dad said he still couldn't believe he'd bought a Ford. But he'd gotten a good deal. The main thing was, as soon as Mom could drive again, she would have her own transportation.

CHAPTER 11

Survival
Techniques

Dad knew how to cook one thing: egg salad sandwiches. We would manage just fine, he said. He had his grocery list made out for the next six weeks: eleven jars of mayonnaise, fifty-six dozen eggs, and a hundred and twelve loaves of bread. We would fill in the blanks with cocoa. Bob and I thought it sounded fine. Mom said we could try it for a couple of days.

For the rest of February and the month of March, Dad stayed home from work to take care of Mom, and I stayed home from school to help. Mom, pretty much confined to her bed, finally had plenty of time to spend with Bob. They sat in Mom's bed together and read by the hour, comic book after comic book. Bob soaked it up and was as happy as a clam.

We didn't get through the six weeks alone. Mrs. Binder, whom Mom had finally gotten to know, sent over two loaves of bread every single week. We got casseroles and even a baked ham from neighbors up and down the valley. A few days after Mom got home, Rosy and Dorothy Cross showed up with a big box full of little presents. They were all for Mom, from all the ladies in the Yaak, many of whom she barely knew. There was a gift to open every day while she was home in bed. Just small things, like pot holders and hankies and embroidered tea towels and a tiny hourglass that was a three-minute egg timer. It was a wonderful thing, Mom said, the way people in this valley took care of each other. You certainly didn't see that every day.

Dad learned how to cook, more or less. With Mom coaching, he made her famous "Sick Soup," a beef and vegetable soup with big chunks of potato, and it was almost good. He made coleslaw once but skinned his knuckles on the grater. One night he decided to doctor up

Mom's spaghetti sauce and we got stomach aches from all the spices. The house got cleaned, after a fashion. I had to admit, three weeks in Rosy's Reform School helped. I took over the job of hauling water. It was a job I liked, for some reason, even on laundry days.

Dad served Mom all her meals on a tray brought to her bed and he always tried to fancy it up a bit by putting a rolled-up napkin in her cup handle or a bow on her fork or, one time on a Sunday morning, an "ice sculpture"—a rabbit, made out of snow.

We had to wait on Mom hand and foot. Dad brought her the wash basin every morning, on a tray with her toothbrush and towel. I got pretty good at brushing her hair into a pony tail. The hardest thing was getting her up to go, on the slop jar. We were afraid she was going to fall and her crazy, heavy, big leg was always in the way. With practice she

learned to pivot while Dad or I supported her leg, then she would slip off the side of the bed onto the jar. This was the worst part, she said, going potty in the middle of the living room.

She couldn't get over her fingernails. Sitting around, doing nothing, they grew beautiful and long, so she filed and polished them like she'd done back in California. "Too bad they won't reach down in this cast, though," she said, poking one finger down as far as she could and scratching. Dad straightened out a coat hanger and made her a scratcher so she could reach down in there.

One blustery day in late March. Mrs. Binder came for a visit. Julius drove her over in the pickup and dropped her off. Dad was washing dishes at the stove when she knocked on the door. She was carrying a load.

Anna, Mrs. Binder, dressed in her best for their wedding anniversary.

She started chattering away the minute he let her in. She spoke her own Germanflavored lingo, fast, and without stopping. She was a tiny, wrinkled little thing, less that five feet tall and probably eighty pounds. She always wore a house dress and, depending on the weather, topped it with a layer of shirts or a long-sleeved sweater or two, never a coat, and always socks and black canvas high-top tennis shoes on her feet. She had no teeth and it was generally known that she lived on bread, cheese and coffee, period.

Dad took the things she had brought for us: two loaves of bread and a cold roast of venison, and then ushered her into the living room. She pulled her chair close to Mom's bed and there she sat, talking for most of the rest of the day.

Mom had spent enough time with Mrs. Binder by then that she actually understood her most of the time. Mrs. Binder was a kick, according to Mom. She complained and cussed about August a lot—the cussing was in English and plain as day—and talked a lot about the "old country," which made Mom wonder if she really liked living in this one.

At the end of the afternoon, when Mrs. Binder finally got up to leave, it was obvious she was planning to walk home. Oh, no, Dad said, he'd be happy to drive her. She objected and chattered at him, several long sentences, but Dad insisted. He guided her as she chattered, into the truck and off they went. When he got back, he said he had learned his lesson and he wouldn't do that again; Mrs. Binder had scolded him all the way home.

One good thing happened though, he said, a sign that spring was around the corner. On the way back from the Binders', a grouse had flown right into the cab of the truck through the open window and nearly scared the life out of him. It put up as much fuss as Mrs. Binder, before he was able to shoo it out of the truck.

Finally it was the first of April, the day Mom was to get her cast changed. Dad was the happiest one of all. He said he would be glad to go back to the sawmill where the work was easier. He took Mom into town, and Bob and I spent the day over at the mill with the Cummings girls. The mill road was still buried in hard-packed snow and there was a wonderful hill that went from the mill down to the bridge across the West Fork and then up again on the other side. The Cummings girls had three sleds and a couple of dish pans and we spent the whole day on their perfect sledding hill. Once, we tied all the sleds together and tied one dishpan on a long rope at the end. Gracie rode down in it and laughed so hard the dishpan was full of pee when she got to the bottom. I decided *that* was the most fun I'd ever had.

Mom came home that night and it was like a miracle—she could walk. Her new cast was shorter; it came to just below her knee and had a steel peg sticking out of the bottom, underneath her foot. She could stump right through the snow on it. Dad started calling her Long John Silver. She said, thank heavens she could move around again! She could hardly wait to get at that house of ours!

April 7th was August Binder's birthday. Mom baked a batch of the French puffs that were such a favorite of his; he called them "cookies." Dad, Bob and I decided to walk over to Binders' to take a platter of the puffs to August. The three of us were hiking up Binders' road, when we began to notice a cow or two, here and there in the trees. Before we knew it, we were standing in the middle of Binders' herd.

Binders' cattle wandered all over that end of the valley. The Open Range Law, Dad explained, meant that cattle were free to roam and had to be fenced out, not in. If you didn't want them on your property, you fenced it.

Usually, no one minded cattle. They roamed loose all over the Yaak and had so much room you hardly knew they were around. Binders, however, never dehorned their animals and several of the cows had horns that looked like they could skewer a rain barrel if they wanted to. And Binders' bull was the meanest looking beast imaginable. August had weighted his horns so that they grew downward alongside his face, and were therefore harmless. The effect, though, was horrible. The down-turned horns gave him an evil expression and to Bob and me, he looked ready to attack the first thing that moved.

When we realized we were surrounded by the animals, Dad said, "Don't act scared. Just look straight ahead and walk right along with me. Stay close. They'll leave us alone." Pretty soon a cow came trotting into a clearing just off the road ahead of us. She stood there with her horns in the air and stared at us. We could hear the breath shooting in and out of her nose.

"Uh-oh," Dad said, and stopped. "She must have a calf here somewhere." As he said that, the cow ran around in a nervous little circle and stood facing us again, breathing even faster.

"We better get back in the trees," said Dad. But there wasn't a tree nearby that didn't have another cow or two standing under it. We looked over on the far side of the road and there stood the horrible bull, horns cocked and ready to charge.

The cow trotted towards us a few steps, shaking her head from side to side. The bull stood stock-still, a monster of pure, staring hate. Dad set the tray of French puffs on the ground and pointed back down the road. "Those trees back there!" he said, "Go now!" We ran for it.

We made it to a clump of trees. Dad was looking around on the ground for something to throw but the surface of the road was nothing but slush. The cow broke into a trot and was coming straight toward him. Dad picked up one of the French puffs and raised his arm. The cow stopped short and snorted.

Dad threw the puff with all his might. It floated a few feet, like a wad of cotton, and landed on the ground in a soft little pile. The cow stood stock still, nostrils flared. Dad picked up another puff. He wadded it in his hand and threw it. It carried farther and plopped on the cow's shoulder. She shied as if she'd been shot. She blinked at Dad a few times and then turned and ambled off into the woods on the far side of the road, bawling for her calf. Meanwhile, the bull had come forward. He eyed Dad and kept coming, his huge tongue taking a swipe over his nose. He owned the road and he knew it. Dad picked up a third puff from the platter and raised his arm menacingly. But this beast was not going to be startled by a cupcake. He came straight on, lowering his head to the ground.

In the middle of the road, he stopped at the smashed French puff. He pushed it around with his lips and then picked it up, munching, his beady eyes fixed on Dad with a deadly stare.

Dad grabbed another puff and tossed that one off to the side of the road and the bull moseyed over and ate that one, too. Dad picked up the platter of puffs and waved to us to come on, and we got through the rest of the herd.

We hated those cows, we told him. He said he didn't like them either but he felt safer as long as he was carrying a tray full of his trusty French puffs.

At about that time I was able to get back to school regularly. A few kids asked me if I was going to be able to catch up since I'd been gone so long. "Of course!" I said, certain it would be easy; schoolwork always was. I wasn't about to let my two boy classmates think I was worried about catching up with *them*.

We were doing geography in my class and the three of us had to take turns reading aloud out of our geography books. Doing anything alone, in front of the roomful of other kids was not something I enjoyed. But I was a confident reader because I was good at it, better than students in higher grades. Glancing down at my paragraph though, I saw a word I had never seen before: "Europe."

Who or what was "Europe?" I had no idea how to pronounce it. Part of my brain scrambled madly through all the phonics I could think of, while the rest of me, on automatic pilot, began reading aloud. By the time I reached the odd combination of letters, the best pronunciation I could come up with was "*oh-rope*," accent on "*rope*." Kids giggled all over the room, especially Laurence Harding and Billy Sims. My face caught fire.

"It's 'Europe,' Doris," Mrs. Duncan corrected.

Yurup?! How could it be Yurup? Yurup was spelled with a "Y"!— wasn't it?

Mrs. Duncan made me repeat the sentence, pronouncing the word that rhymed with "syrup," correctly. My two classmates, I saw, were happily satisfied to find out I was not as smart as I thought I was.

CHAPTER 12

The Science
of Farming

Bea Harding was a tall, hard working, no-nonsense kind of gal who loved to laugh and drink a beer now and then. She didn't like to waste time doing her hair and wore it pinned up in pincurls and tied in a scarf most of the time. She wore men's clothes, jeans and shirts and "engineer boots," which were calf-high, black leather with a sturdy heel, square toe and a snazzy strap riveted at the heel. Mom thought she was wonderful. She said Bea Harding was an honest-to-goodness Montana rancher if there ever was one. Mom planned to get her own pair of boots like Bea's as soon as she got her walking cast off.

Mom got to know Bea when she started taking me down to school again that spring. Now that the roads were better, she was driving our new car all over the place. If she wasn't waiting to pick me up after school, chances were she would be across the road and down the hill at Hardings' ranch, visiting with Bea.

One day Mom and Bea decided to drive our new car into town. They did some shopping and then Bea talked Mom into going to a cattle auction. Bea bought two feeder calves. They brought them home in the back seat of the car. On the way home they stopped at a café for a hamburger. When they came out of the café there was a gathering of onlookers around the car. One of the calves was in the front seat, sitting behind the wheel. Mom said it made such a good story it was worth the near-ruination of the upholstery.

Bea and her husband, Herschel, an easy-going, pleasant man who always seemed a little amazed at his wife, made a decent living off their farm. Most people agreed that the Harding place was the best piece of property in the valley. There were acres of meadow, two lakes and the Yaak River running alongside it all. The house itself was another matter. Part of it seemed like a collection of small sheds lined up and connected together by an outside porch. I never knew how many rooms it had, but the porch was long. The two main rooms were built over a slope and it was downhill from the kitchen to the living room.

But the living room was cozy and the kitchen was comfortable and messy and I loved being there because I loved the Harding boys. There were three of them. Bill, the oldest, was tall and handsome and had a big, bright smile. I didn't get to know him until after he had graduated from the eighth grade at the Yaak School and was going to high school in town. When he was home he would come up to the school and visit and all the kids would be glad to see him and crowd around him to hear what he had to say. Gary, the middle brother, was two grades ahead of me. He was not a handsome boy; he was tall and gawky with flaring teeth and a big Adam's apple. But he was the smartest kid they'd ever had in the Yaak School, and the funniest. He could do voices and make noises that were better than any cartoon. He and I invented a language only we could understand. It was a combination of Pig-Latin and Arp—the fake 'languages' adults use when they don't want kids to know what they're saying. We called it "Piganized-Arpalat." If I said, *"Arp-ey-harp-ay, Arpary-garp-ay, arp-an-carp-ay arp-ou-yarp-ay arp-un-der-arp-ay-arp-and-starp-ay arp-e-marp-ay?"* he would answer, *"Arp-ure-sharp-ay arp-I-arp-ay arp-an-carp-ay!"*

Our other secret form of communication was the sign-alphabet from the school encyclopedia. We could spell things back and forth during class:

i-h-a-t-e-m-a-t-h
i-t-s-e-a-s-y
n-o-s-i-r

My favorite of the Hardings though, was Laurence, the beautiful boy in my grade. He had no idea how beautiful he was. He just wanted to some day be a mountain man and trap and hunt for a living. We were pals and went around together a lot and I would walk home with him after school when my mom was visiting his mom. He showed me all their ranch. They had chickens and cows and a pen full of the world's meanest pigs. Laurence fed them buckets of garbage and scraps and they gobbled it up in seconds with snapping teeth and jaws like crocodiles.

Laurence could bake a cake in nothing flat, without a recipe. He'd just dump in flour, sugar, eggs, butter and milk, stir it all up and bake it, and it came out fine. The Harding boys had another delicious con-

George Beck, Laurence Harding, and Dee at school.

coction that, awful as it looked, was completely luscious. They would pop corn and make fudge and pour the fudge over the popcorn. We'd eat it by the handful right out of the bowl. What a mess! It was heavenly.

Maybe it was getting to know the Hardings that finally nudged Mom and Dad into beginning our own little farm.

Dad started off our first venture, chickens, with careful research. One of his favorite sayings was, "If a job is worth doing, it's worth doing well." So he had books and articles sent up from the library and the County Extension Office about types of laying hens, designs for chicken houses and all the latest scientific methods for raising egg-producing hens. Dad concluded that the best type of chicken to raise for eggs was White Leghorns. We needed fifty of them. He wrote to the grocery stores in Troy to see if they could market farm fresh eggs for us if we sent them down on the mail truck. They could.

As soon as the order for fifty birds was placed at the feed store in Bonners Ferry, Dad began overhauling our log chicken house. He fixed the leaky roof. He re-did the chinking, put in a ceiling and insulated it with sawdust. He built nesting boxes. He made a compact section of roosts in one corner with a tin reflector in the middle so a lantern could be hung beneath them for warmth. Chickens would lay all winter, he said, if you kept the place light and warm and fed them correctly. He built a bin for laying mash and wheat, and a feeder and holders for water and grits. He hauled a load of shavings from the sawmill and spread them several inches deep on the floor. In the doorway, in addition to the main door, he installed a screen door made of chicken wire. As soon as the weather was warm we would let the chickens run around outside, he said. They would stay home because this was where the food was. Being outside made for better-flavored yolks, he said. Just in time for the arrival of our fifty youngster-hens, our state-of -the-art chicken house was finished.

We hauled the poor birds home in two cardboard boxes in the back of the truck. Bob and I sat one on each side of them all the way, and I thought the jouncing over the road would kill them for sure. But they survived, and we put them into their new house and closed them in for the first few days.

Mom gathered information from Bea Harding and Rosy and anyone else who had advice about chickens. Dad began calculating the profits we might expect to earn from selling the eggs. He said the only way an operation such as this could work was if a man figured out how to make everything cost-effective and used the latest scientific methods to maximize production.

There were several factors to consider, he told me one night after dinner, sitting with pencil and paper at the kitchen table.

Climate. Genetics. The quality of your feed. The amount of stress in the environment. All that affected the productivity of a laying hen.

"Actually, according to the latest research," he said, "the most you can depend on is one hen laying about an egg and a half every two days.

"Now let's see…" He was getting the paper all squared up. I cringed. I knew what was coming: Arithmetic. Dad loved it; I hated it.

"Would that be the same as a hen and a half laying one egg a day?" he asked, hoping to pique my interest. He got up and took a paring knife and sharpened his pencil to a needle point. "Come on and let's see if we can figure this out. This is a good problem for you, Dee."

He was positive I shared his itch; I was his daughter, after all. I only wished I did. But I didn't want to disappoint him, so I hunched over the paper and tried to appear fascinated. Like a convict in a cell, I endured, while he took us through the scenario:

"If a hen and a half lays one egg in one day, how many eggs will fifty hens lay in a month?"

Enthralled, he set down neat rows of figures for me to examine. "Three hens would be two eggs in one day. One hen would be two-thirds of an egg in one day or twenty eggs in thirty days. Fifty hens would be a thousand eggs a month!" He drew a line under the "1000."

"On the other hand," more figures, "with one hen laying an egg and a half every two days, fifty hens would do seventy-five eggs in two days, eleven hundred twenty-five eggs in thirty days. Almost a hundred dozen a month! Imagine that!" He drew two lines under "1125."

"Actually," he went on, "the exact figures are really closer to an egg and a third. So. Now. If one hen lays one egg in one-point-two-eight days…"

And on we went. No matter how we figured it, when it was over I had to admit, the number of eggs was impressive. We were in business. We were on our way to becoming egg magnates.

But the real substance of our fortune was going to be made in meat, Dad said. Rabbit.

Every time he brought this up, Mom gave him one of her looks. But he kept reminding her of how popular a meat rabbit had been in the store back in Fallbrook. Hasenpfeffer, that was the way a lot of people prepared it in those days. Mom said that was before the war, when it was okay to be German. Well, fried then, Dad said, just plain fried rabbit was delicious. And as a business, raising rabbits had two advantages. Number one, rabbits were easy to keep, even in this northern climate. Number two, well, everybody knew number two.

Dad approached the grocery stores in Troy once again and the response, while not enthusiastic, was positive enough—he thought—to proceed with the rabbit plans.

Baby rabbits were ordered. Two bucks and four does. Another trip to town. This time Dad went to town by himself and came home loaded up with rabbit pellets and the makings for rabbit hutches along with the rabbits themselves in a large, wood-and-wire shipping crate from the feed store.

Dad drew a design for the rabbit hutches. There would eventually be eight of them, each twenty-four inches square with shed roofs and wire mesh bottoms and doors, and little drawers that pulled out in front, so you could put in feed and water without bothering the inmates. The hutches would all be lined up against the south wall of the woodshed, out of the north wind, up on legs high enough so that rabbit-eating varmints couldn't get at them. There would be a little nest-box in the back of each hutch where they could crawl inside and be warm and have all their babies.

But the rabbit hutch project had to be put aside because suddenly Dad had his hands full battling an unexpected enemy: beavers. In a single night they crammed enough willows into the channel of our creek to cut the flow down by half. It took Dad hours to untangle and pull out the mass of branches. The next day they were back again in a different place. For a couple of weeks Dad spent nearly every day after work removing beaver dams. Early mornings he was out patrolling the creek bank with a flashlight and rifle, trying to catch the sneaky beasts at their work, but he never did.

Bob and I thought the rabbits were the cutest things we had ever seen. We watched them for hours, hopping around in their shipping crate, temporarily situated on a pair of sawhorses next to the wood shed. Dad told us to remember, this was a business. These were farm animals here, being raised for meat. Rabbit stew. Fried rabbit. We said yes, we knew that. And who was going to get to take care of Brownie, Ringeye, Polkadot, Snowball, Princess and Sam?

He said it had better be his job.

That spring Mom jumped with both feet, or rather, with foot and peg-leg, into the business of mountain-style housecleaning. Living in the mountains, she said, was no excuse for a dirty house. She always said you could tell a good housekeeper by the bathroom. That rule applied, even if the bathroom was outside.

She broomed and mopped every inch of the privy, inside and out. We were supposed to keep the door closed and latched—there was a leather loop that you could fasten on a cup hook if you were inside, and a wooden latch that fastened the door shut when you came out—and we were always supposed to wipe our feet on the door mat, and use the lime, and keep things tidy in there. As careful as we all tried to be though, somehow a swarm of wasps managed to sneak in and in no time at all, build a huge nest high up on the back wall at the peak of the roof.

We were out of DDT and Dad tried everything else he could think of. The nest was up too high to douse with a bucket of hot water. He thought if he could somehow pry it loose and drop it quickly down the hole and slap the lid over it, maybe that would do the trick, but as soon as he stepped up on the bench with a shovel, the wasps got nervous and started buzzing all over the place. There were *lots* of them.

Next he put a ladder against the outside wall and climbed up and hit the roof with the side of the axe to try to knock the nest loose from the outside. Wasps appeared from out of nowhere and he got stung in two places on his neck before he could get down. Pretty soon we all got nervous about having to go in there at all. It was a situation.

Dad had one final idea. Wasps were dormant at night, he said, and much less likely to attack, so he would have to work in the dark. That night he went up the ladder with a can of kerosene while Mom stood down below, shining a flashlight on the peak of the roof. He poured kerosene into the crack at the top, hopefully soaking the nest. The next morning we saw that the only thing that got soaked was the entire roof of the privy. The wasps were fine.

So it was decided that since the privy had already been doused with kerosene anyway, we would just have to go ahead and burn it down. That's what we did. Our nice, perfectly decent privy. With the washtub full of water and a bucket close by, Dad set it on fire early the next morning while the wasps were still asleep in their hive. It went up like a torch, wasps and all.

Fortunately there was plenty of lumber on hand for the rabbit hutches, so Dad used some of it to build a new privy. He went to the trouble to make some improvements. The hole in the seat was oval-shaped and sanded, so there were no scratchy edges. The lid fit just right and there was a shelf for extra paper. We kept the leather loop from the old privy as a souvenir and used it on the new door. Dad put hinged openings—like small windows—high on each wall that you could close in the winter and open in the summer to let the smell out. To discourage wasps and moths, he covered the openings with some of the wire mesh that was intended for the bottoms of the rabbit hutches. When he was finished, we had an even nicer, perfectly decent privy.

Meanwhile, Mom marched along with her cleaning crusade. She washed curtains and bedspreads and took rugs outside and hung them on the line and beat them with a broom—like her grandmother used to do, she said. The house had been shut up all winter and everything, even the log walls, needed a good dusting. On Dorothy Cross's advice, she wiped the logs down with a kerosene rag wrapped around the broom. It cleaned the logs, but made the house smell terrible. She wasn't doing that again, she decided. Those logs needed to be varnished.

She ordered brushes and three gallons of clear varnish from Sears. Dede Hall came over and helped her and they put a coat of the stuff on every log. That week, with nighttime temperatures still down in the thirties, we slept with all the doors and windows wide open, and a fire going in the heater stove, until everything was dry and the varnish smell went away. Mom thought it made a wonderful difference. The logs were prettier and would be easier to clean. Trouble was, she said, now the nice, shiny logs made the chinking look dingy. She ordered white paint and more brushes. She spent two weeks with a narrow little brush, painting every inch of the plaster chinking a nice crisp white. Along the way, small areas of chinking fell out and we could see how Henry Binder had done the job. Between the logs there were lots of small nails driven in, close together, some going down into the lower log, some going up into the upper log. The interlaced nails held the mortar in place. Dad was able to borrow a bag of mortar from August and re-chink the broken spots. Mom painted them as soon as they were dry. More nights with wide-open doors.

As soon as the nights were warm enough, Dad got our wonderful kitchen pump re-started—hauling water was over for the summer—and Mom made good use of it. She kept the teakettle full of hot water on the stove and scrubbed shelves, counters, window sills, even the porches with Fels Naptha soap. Dad built her a fire-ring out in the back yard and she used it to heat water in the wash boiler for the laundry. From then on, we did the washing outdoors in the summer.

For a while Mom made a study out of baking bread. It was one of the hardest things, she said, to learn to do well. She had to bake twice a week, two loaves plus dough for an extra goodie like cinnamon rolls or dodgers. She ordered an extra-large mixing bowl from the catalog. It was blue and weighed about ten pounds. She would start her dry yeast, sugar, salt, warm water and Crisco in the bowl and when it was "working," would begin to add the flour, cup after cup, kneading until she was gooey with dough to the elbows, then kneading, kneading, adding flour until it wasn't sticky but sat in a big, plump pile. Back in the bowl, she set it up on top of the baking cabinet to rise. When it was ready she made sure the fire was right, and by the end of the day the house was filled with that smell everybody loves. We always ate a slice apiece, while it was hot. If she decided to make dodgers, we waited for them instead. She would pat out a circle of dough, cut it in wedges and fry them in butter. Right off the grill, you pulled open the wedge and spread the inside with butter and strawberry jam.

But it wasn't all work all the time. Even with added chores, Mom and Dad managed to get in lots of fishing. Nearly every evening after dinner they would grab a fly rod—the rods were kept handy resting on nails on the side of the house nearest the creek—and walk down to where the creek ran into the lake. That, we had discovered by then, was the best fishing spot overall. They would each throw a few casts and usually both catch at least one. Sometimes they would send them swimming back into the creek if they weren't hurt by the hook. Sometimes we would have trout for breakfast.

One Saturday morning I got up early, around six, unusual for me on a weekend. The house was quiet. Bob, the sack rat, was still sound asleep. I wandered into the living room, barefoot and in my pajamas. Breakfast remains were on the kitchen table. Dad was up the creek, no doubt checking for beaver dams. I padded over to the front door, making not a sound with my bare feet on the cool, smooth wood. Mom was sitting out on the porch steps with a cup of coffee in her hand.

She was watching the lake. I went and sat beside her and her free hand cupped my pajama-ed knees and pulled me against her. After a minute, she said, "Listen," so I did.

The lake was a bowl of blue sky, mirror-still, easy on my sleepy eyes that time of day. By afternoon it would be crackling with squint-bright sun. The witch's-beard moss hung on the pines, limp and motionless. And there wasn't a sound to be heard. Not with your ears, anyway.

But there was something. More of a sound you felt, as if it reached your hearing through your skin. It was in the sun on our arms and in the warm porch boards under our legs and seeping in through our eyes. A sort of long, flowing sigh.

"What is that?" I asked.

"I don't know." She was in one of her dreamy moods. "The mountains breathing, maybe."

Her eyes moved from the trees near the water, over the lake to the shadowy slope of Zimmerman Hill on our left.

"I didn't know mountains breathed," I said.

"Me neither. I don't think many people get to hear them."

"We're lucky, huh."

"Yep. We are."

It was a good thing we weren't sleeping with all the doors open the following week, because Binders' cattle came in the night and took over our yard. The whole herd—close to fifty cattle—came right up to the house and were helping themselves to our grass when we got up the next morning. The bull was standing in the middle of the back yard.

Probably waiting for a French puff, Dad joked.

Mom didn't think it was funny. She said we couldn't have this; this was ridiculous. There were cow pies everywhere. She stumped out on the porch in her cast and pajamas and tried to get them to move off by waving a dish towel. They just looked at her. Dad went out and started up the truck and took a few runs at some cows. They ambled off into the woods. Finally, the bull followed. Mom and I used shovels to clean up the messes in the yard as well as we could.

June brought long summer days. We were amazed at how long they were. Daylight from five in the morning until ten at night. To Bob's and my dismay, Dad couldn't seem to forget about firewood, even in warm weather. He insisted we spend an occasional evening in the woods, getting an early start on next winter's supply. We weren't such greenhorns when it came to doing that job the second time around. Dad had learned how to keep the teeth of the crosscut razor-sharp. He knew how to drive a wedge into the cut to reduce the drag on the blade and how to drip a little oil to make the saw slide easily. Mom could maneuver Jenny through the woods as easily as if she were pushing a shopping cart in a grocery store and could always get within a few feet of whatever log we were cutting. Bob and I were both bigger and a lot stronger. We could stack half a truckload of wood in a single evening.

Our young chicks were feathering out. Dad reminded us that farming was a science like everything else, and it paid off when you knew what you were doing. Feed, water, grits, laying mash, all was being properly measured and fed to our young hens. The chicken house was kept as warm and as light and clean as possible. Pretty soon the young birds were able to be outside all day. They fluttered their scrawny, half-feathered wings and scattered when we walked through the middle of them, but surprisingly enough, they all seemed to realize this was their home and nobody strayed very far. If you went into the chicken house, they all followed you in, and gathered around the wheat bin, chirping and chattering and waiting for their coffee can full of wheat. Mom liked them. She said they were her kind of creatures: they stayed around home and loved to eat.

Our rabbits were growing too, looking more like full-grown rabbits. We were on our way to becoming a real farm. It wouldn't be long, Dad said, before we started producing. He must have said it too loud. The next day the rabbits exploded.

It was seven a.m. and Dad and I had just climbed into the truck and were setting out for the mill. I was going along to visit the Cummings girls for the day. Bob was up early, out nosing around the rabbit crate as usual.

Dad turned the key in Jenny's ignition. The needles in the gauges popped to attention, just as Bob poked her head up over the crate, grinning from ear to ear. "Baby rabbits!" she announced.

Dad turned off the key and the needles flopped over. He rolled down his window. "What?"

Bob was beaming. "Babies! A whole bunch of 'em!"

Dad and I got out and went over to see what this was all about. Bob held up the lid of the crate and presented the evidence: three separate bundles of tiny, naked baby rabbits. All mixed up in rabbit fur, all tumbled over each other and being tumbled over in turn by the other rabbits in the box. "Dammit all to hell!" Dad said, sounding like a real Yaaker. "Well, we'd better get them out of there before the bucks get them."

Bob asked what did he mean by that, and he had to explain the ugly truth about male rabbits to her, that they sometimes trample their young. Bob suddenly saw Brownie and Sam with new eyes. She stood guard, watching over the crate as if it held the baby Jesus while I went with Dad to find something to put the new babies in. Dad was aggravated. He said he *knew* he should have built those hutches! "Between beavers and wasps and cattle in the yard! Dammit all to hell anyway!"

We finally came up with temporary housing for the rabbits. We used the crate from a case of canned peaches and a couple of the new nesting boxes from the chicken house with chicken wire nailed over the tops. We divided the three families—two litters of seven and one of eight with the mother rabbits Ringeye, Polkadot and Snowball—and put the two bucks and Princess together, back in the shipping crate. Our rabbit population had more than quadrupled. There were twenty-eight of them.

Dad and I left for the mill. He was running late and grumbled all the way, vowing he would get at least one hutch built that very night. After work when we got home we discovered that Princess, too, was a proud mother of eight. We were up to thirty-six.

That week, sawing and hammering went on into the wee hours, every night. By the end of the weekend, five hutches were almost finished. There was one small problem: after using the wire mesh for the vents in the new privy, there was only enough left to do the doors of the hutches, but not the floors. We would have to wait until we could get to town to get some more. Dad came up with an idea for temporary hutch bottoms. He cut one-inch wooden slats and nailed them across the bottoms of each hutch, far apart enough to let the rabbit droppings fall through but not the rabbits. It worked as well as wire. And now each rabbit family had its own home and there was a separate hutch for the bucks.

One morning a few weeks later, after Dad had left for work and Bob and I, in full-on summer vacation mode, were still asleep, Mom burst into our room. "Girls! Get shoes on and help me catch rabbits!" she ordered.

"What happened?" I asked, still in a haze.

"They chewed through and got loose!" Mom called out, as the screen door banged shut behind her.

We were up in a flash. The rest of the morning we hunted, chased, scrambled and pounced until we had caught Ringeye and her escaped family. We put them all in with Princess and her eight kids. After investigating the empty hutch, we discovered that two of the wooden slats had been chewed through in the floor of Ringeye's hutch, back inside the nesting box where you couldn't see the hole unless you crawled underneath the hutch.

The next week Ringeye and Princess both let themselves and all fifteen youngsters loose in the night. As luck would have it, Dad had gone into town that weekend to get, among other things, wire for the bottoms of the rabbit hutches.

We ran ourselves ragged again. And we could only find fourteen; three babies had slipped away and run off somewhere. By then the baby rabbits were not so tiny, so we crammed both families into the hutch with the two bucks for the night. Bob kept on searching around outside and didn't want to go to bed without finding the three lost rabbits. It got dark. When we started hearing coyotes, she fell apart. Mom had to rock her to sleep around midnight.

With all those coyotes out there, Mom said, we needed to be sure the chickens were all safe in the chicken house. So I took a flashlight and went outside. The howling stopped immediately. I shined the light all around, into the woods and underneath the rabbit hutches. I would have jumped out of my skin if I'd seen anything move. I knew they were out there and it gave me the creeps. The inky darkness of the valley at night was scary sometimes. I remembered when Bob said it was too big. That night I knew what she meant. I stamped my feet on the porch and hollered, "Get outta here, coyotes!" and then I forced myself to go marching out there blaring, "Fee, fi, fo, fum! I smell the blood of the coyote scum!" slashing the light all over the place, like some kind of a weapon. I shut the chicken house and everything else up tight, even the privy, then scuttled back into the house as fast as I could and slammed the door behind me and locked it. Safe!

When Dad got home the next afternoon and heard the whole story, he was too tired from the drive to be very sympathetic. He did say he wished we hadn't put Ringeye and Princess in with Brownie and Sam. But it was too late now, he said, it only took them a few minutes.

Sure enough, in another month our herd of rabbits exploded again. Now we had fifty-three.

CHAPTER 13

Summer
Lightning!

There was a mid-summer dance at the Community Hall. Mom and all the other ladies spent most of a Saturday decorating the hall with crepe paper. They hung long strands of white back and forth across the ceiling, weaving them in and out to make a bunting. Then they took more crepe paper, pink and yellow strips, and pinched them into twists with pale green, so they looked like flower chains, and hung them down from the bunting. It made the drab old hall look like a giant garden. That night we all went to the dance and there was a square dance caller from Troy and nearly everyone square danced—even the kids. Mom found out she could do-si-do and twirl around like an ice skater on her walking cast. Dad said he had to get her out of there before she broke the other leg.

In the midst of this busy time, Mrs. Binder started coming to visit Mom regularly. She came in the morning and stayed all day. Mom said she had far too much to do, to spend so much time visiting, but Mrs. Binder was lonely, poor thing.

Mrs. Binder decided she wanted Mom to give her a Toni home permanent. Mom ordered one from town. Mrs. Binder's hair was shoulder-length and she didn't want it any shorter, so the finished "do" was a billowing froth of white curls. She loved it.

As Mrs. Binder continued to come visiting, Mom said they were beginning to understand each other pretty well. And there were things that might surprise you, she told Dad one night, after Bob and I were in bed. Some of it was pretty spicy stuff.

"Like what?" Dad wanted to know.

"August does the laundry."

"Why?"

"So they'll have clean clothes. She says she doesn't do laundry. Never has. And you know the garden by the house? It's hers, but it's for flowers. Only flowers. The vegetable garden is down by their lake and that's August's job, too. And she doesn't cook either. Julius does most of the cooking."

Dad said that didn't sound too spicy to him.

"Well," Mom lowered her voice but I could still hear, "she told me she and Henry had a romance, years ago."

"Really? Henry? August's brother?"

"Yes. She told me when Henry built this place, our place, it was supposed to be for her. He enlarged the lake just for her. Wanted to entice her over here to be with him instead. 'Ach! He luf me so too much!' she said."

Dad was astounded.

"I'll bet she was something in those days," Mom went on. "She told me she comes from a...I didn't quite get what she said...but, from some kind of important family back in the Old Country. Social standing and considerable wealth. Anyway, after Henry built our place and she wouldn't leave August and come over here to live with him, Henry sold this place and moved out there on the main road. He wanted to be where he could see August's place and watch over Anna for the rest of her life. Kind of a lovely, bittersweet story, don't you think?"

"Certainly not one I would have dreamed up," said Dad. "That ancient little lady!"

"You never know." Mom said. "Besides, you might change your mind when you see her with her new permanent."

The conversation came about the day Mom saw a hawk swoop down and snatch up one of the chickens.

It was horrible, she said. She could hear the poor thing squawking in the hawk's clutches! And there were coyotes howling again too, all night. And yesterday she had to chase the cattle, again. It was easier now that she had her cast off and could wear her new boots. But still, she said, it was high time.

Bob's and my ears perked up. We knew what was coming. We'd been to the brink of this discussion before. We fixed our eyes on Dad.

"Its high time we got a dog," said Mom.

In previous, long, three-against-one, begging sessions, Dad had held his own. It wasn't that he didn't like dogs; he'd always said he was a dog man. But we had a regular menagerie to deal with around here already—cattle, beaver, coyotes, not to mention rabbits and chickens.

If we had a dog, we said, he would chase the cattle away and we wouldn't have to worry about them! It was the same with coyotes! And just think, no more surprise company because we would have a watch dog. Besides, we needed a pet.

Dad said after Ching, nobody on earth could blame him for being hesitant about having another pet.

We reminded him that Ching was a cat.

Dad said we all had too many chores already.

"Farm dogs aren't work! Farm dogs help!"

"You'd sure think," said Dad, "with all these animals..." He was shaking his head! It was a sign of wavering! "...we *sure* wouldn't want another one!"

"A dog would keep away those chicken-stealing hawks!" said Mom.

Dad knew when he was licked. He sighed, a beaten man.

"Okay, all right, I guess," he said. But he, he alone, was going to go about the business of finding the right animal.

Later in the evening, Mom mentioned she had heard that Reverend McCoy's dog had a litter of puppies. They were ready to wean.

"Mac's dog?" said Dad, "Ha! That'll be the day!" Then he grew thoughtful. "Mac has an Australian shepherd, doesn't he? Hmm. Probably a pretty good dog. Australian shepherds are some of the smartest dogs there are. Probably expects a fortune for the pups."

"No," said Mom. "I don't think so. "He gave one to Earl Stratton. To replace Earl's poor old dog that was blinded by the porcupine."

"Hmm," said Dad. He narrowed his eyes and looked car-dealer devious. "Well, we'll have to see."

It was as good as done. Bob and I knew it. Dad would figure out a way to bargain Reverend McCoy out of a puppy and we had already picked out a name: "Lightning!"

The puppy didn't come cheap. Reverend McCoy said he would make

Dad a deal, but only because Mrs. McCoy was so fond of that big orange cat. "You can have the pick of the litter, Darwin," he said, "if you bring your family to church for the next three months."

At first Dad wanted to forget the whole thing. It was too big a price, he said. But he was caught in the three-against-one squeeze again, so every Saturday for the rest of the summer, we got all dressed up, Mom in nylons, Dad in a tie, and went to church. The services were being held temporarily, until a regular church could be built, in the McCoy home. Bob and I and the rest of the kids were given Bible verses to learn every week because there were too few kids for an actual Sabbath School class. We would come to know The Truth, Reverend McCoy said, if we had ears to hear, and eyes to see.

We had to stand and recite our verse each week, in front of everybody. I hated it. Mom helped Bob memorize hers, since she couldn't read yet. But I usually ended up memorizing mine in the car on the way to church. It was a struggle; I didn't want to know The Truth. The Truth was scary.

I Peter 4:7. *The end of all things is near. Therefore be clear minded and self-controlled so that you can pray.*

Revelation 22:7. *And behold, I am coming quickly. Blessed is he who heeds the words of the prophecy of this book.*

Acts 2:19. *I will show wonders in the heaven above and signs on the earth below, blood and fire and billows of smoke.* The kids in church all said see, that was the atom bomb they were talking about, right there.

It was not safe to approach Dad after we had been to church. He'd drive home shaking his head, muttering to himself. Then he'd strip off his church clothes as if they'd been sprayed by a skunk and go fishing for the rest of the day. To get his head back on straight, he'd say.

Meanwhile, though, we got our dog.

Lightning!

The cutest, wildest ball of fur in all the world. He piddled and pooped all over the house, of course. Mom said this was only natural for puppies and he would have to learn. We loved him and cuddled and played with him and he slept in our beds. He chased Bob and me all around the house and out in the yard. He made a few playful runs at our feathering young hens and Dad pointed out that in a few weeks he would learn who and what to chase and who to protect.

He chewed up socks and slippers and mittens but he was so cute, no one cared.

"Look at those eyes," Dad would say. "That's intelligence."

He dug holes in the yard.

"Feel this muscle-mass across his shoulders," Dad would say. "That's fine breeding."

One day Lightning! got hold of a pretty spray of tail feathers Laurence Harding had given me. Laurence had shot the bird with a B-B gun and trimmed it out and preserved the feathers himself, following directions out of a book on taxidermy. Much as I loved Lightning! I wasn't too happy about losing my feather fan.

"What kind of a bird was it?" Dad asked.

"A hawk."

"I knew it," Dad said. "The dog's a natural."

But then, as we stood by in helpless amazement, our beloved family pet began to turn into the Dog of Disaster. Slowly at first, then faster and faster like a roll of toilet paper coming to an end, Lightning! ran amok. The bigger he grew, the worse he got.

It started with coyotes. Sometimes there were so many of them and they were so near, Dad worried about the rabbits. The chickens were safe, he said, they were completely enclosed in the chicken house. But he sure didn't want one of those critters creeping around the rabbit hutches. That was just too close.

One night when the coyotes set up a chorus in the woods behind the wood shed Dad said, "Now's the time to get this dog started. Let's put him out there and let him bark his head off."

We all stepped out on the back porch as Lightning!, ears forward, sauntered across the dark yard. We waited for him to bristle at the outrageous yowling coming from the darkness. Instead, he stood quietly. After a minute he sat down, curling his wavy tail around his feet, and listened. Finally, lifting his nose skyward, he let out a piercing howl that sounded more like a coyote than a coyote. The chorus answered him. They struck up a duet. It went on for several minutes. Lightning! was having a wonderful time.

"Well. I guess this isn't going to work," Dad observed. Mom agreed. We dragged Lightning! back in the house where he continued to howl back and forth with his friends in the woods for the rest of the night. Dad explained that the dog wasn't quite old enough yet to feel protective instincts.

But he was growing by leaps and bounds. He got bigger than the average Australian shepherd. Bob could ride him; he carried her all over the house. He ate anything and everything. All our table scraps, dog food that Mom ordered from town by the case, but we still ran out. He ate both chicken feed and rabbit pellets. From a box of groceries left unguarded in the kitchen, he gobbled a pound of margarine, part of a head of lettuce and several packages of Jello. One day when we were cleaning out the attic, he ate an entire box—swear to God—of glass Christmas balls. It didn't faze him.

But then a wonderful thing happened that made us forget all about Lightning! for a while. One of our blooming brood of chickens laid an egg.

There it was, right in the middle of a nesting box, just like it was supposed to be. Dad called us all out to see it. It was like some strange, unheard-of miracle.

Within a week, eggs were popping out right and left. Small, yes, but perfectly white and egg-shaped! And they were edible! They were good! They tasted just like real eggs!

Bob and I haunted the chicken house and stood over the poor birds, waiting for the next prize to come along. Mom and Dad were smug and business-like, carefully keeping track of the developing production and watching over their brood, like mother hens themselves.

Then, catastrophe.

Mom scolding, "*Oh no! Bad dog!*" and a yelp from Lightning! were ringing in our ears as Bob and I jumped up from breakfast and ran outside to the chicken house. There stood Mom, shaking her stinging fingers—she had just given Lightning! a swat—and there lay Lightning! at her feet, cringing in shame, even as he licked the last of a glob of egg yolk from his chops.

"Oh no," I echoed. "How many did he eat?"

"All of them. I don't know. *Bad, bad dog! No!*"

We all scolded him and he lay there in a shivering heap, taking it. It was pathetic.

Mom suggested she'd better be the one to tell Dad about this. He wasn't going to be a bit happy. The three of us agreed to keep a constant eye on Lightning! until he learned the chicken house was strictly off limits.

Mom asked several people for advice. Filling a blown-out egg shell with pepper was the only thing anybody had to offer, other than the unthinkable: get rid of the dog.

But pepper didn't work. Lightning! carefully avoided the doctored eggs and found plenty of good ones to feast on. He started hanging around the chicken house door whenever he was outside, waiting for a chance to sneak in. A week passed. Bob and I realized Mom hadn't told Dad what was going on yet. We were grateful.

As it turned out, she didn't have to tell him. Before long, Lightning! discovered something he liked even better than eggs.

Chicken.

And there was no hiding this evidence. We came home one day to a yard full of bloody feathers and three mangled, partially eaten hen-bodies. Lightning! was nowhere to be found. Finally, as we stood there, surveying the mess in shocked silence, he came skulking out of the woods, stopped at one of the bloody corpses and turned over onto on his back. He was so sorry!

Dad took the situation in hand immediately. He got a rope from the garage and tied Lightning! up. There he was to remain, lashed to a tree in the front yard where he couldn't get near the chickens. Lightning! chewed through four ropes in two days. After that, we tried everything, anything anybody suggested, to stop our cuddly, fun-loving dog from killing our chickens. We fenced them in, and Lightning! was underneath that fence and inside the chicken house in a matter of hours. We kept the chickens in the chicken house with the chicken-wire door fastened shut and one day while we were gone, Lightning! pawed a hole in the wire, got inside and had himself a heyday with the trapped hens. He killed three more that day. We spanked him within an inch of his life. Spanked him *with* a dead chicken. "Get rid of the dog," came from all sides, as the only solution. Bob and I couldn't stand to think about it. Gib Hall said if we tied a dead chicken around the dog's neck and left it there until it rotted off, that would cure him. The process took two and a half weeks and the smell was ghastly. We felt terrible, leaving him outside all the time, all night long with that *thing* around his neck like an albatross, just hanging there. It was barbaric, Mom said. And it didn't work.

The amazing thing was, we never actually caught him in the act. Only afterward would we know he was the culprit, when he'd come creeping back to confess, shame-filled and repentant. By the end of the summer he had us down to thirty-one hens.

He was hopeless, Mom said. Even Bob and I lost our faith in Lightning!

Dad took to calling him "Mac."

"Well, that's who he reminds me of," he said, looking narrow-eyed at our shaggy problem, who was lying on the back porch watching every movement of the hens. "He's wily. He waits and watches and then when he gets you to trust him, *whup!* he grabs one. Oh, you can bet on it, he's not going to give up until he gets 'em all."

Much as we didn't want to, we started keeping the solid outside door to the chicken house closed most of the time, and only letting them outside in the sunshine for short periods, like recess, when somebody had the time to stand guard.

So it was no great surprise when "Mac," as we all called him by then, didn't become a first class watch dog either. He still howled back and forth with the coyotes, but he never barked at anything. Binders' cattle were welcome guests, as far as he was concerned. Mac just rolled in cow pies to his heart's content and then waited on the porch for somebody to let him in and feed him.

Sometime later, Bob and I learned that after losing the first several chickens, Dad had decided to do away with our dog. He asked Mom to keep me and Bob in the house so we wouldn't know what was going to happen. He got his hunting rifle and he took the dog and they went deep into the woods. An hour later they both came back.

As Dad always said, he was a dog man.

CHAPTER 14

The Cuccaburras

That summer Bob and I became playmates. It wasn't so bad. Besides, what choice did we have?

We got braver and braver about wandering in the woods around our place. We built a tiny little cabin in the trees behind the house. It was a lean-to. We had seen the directions for building it on one of the Straight Arrow cards from a box of Shredded Wheat. We nailed a pole across two trees and leaned branches against it to make a wall. We put a blanket down underneath and ate our lunch out there. We rounded up rocks and made our own fire ring and Mom let us have a camp fire as long as we were careful. Then we decided we wanted to sleep out there overnight but to that, she said no.

We beat a regular path up the creek to the river. We started following the river farther and farther up- and downstream. Up the river, we found a place Julius Binder told us was called Garrigus Meadow, where there were wild flowers galore. We watched out for the moose he said we might see there. One morning we heard it splashing across the river and saw its black rump disappear in the willows on the other side. We explored the abandoned houses on two homesteads Julius told us about, the Hoskins place and the Benefield place. Downriver one day, we came across a deer's bed, all lined with fur. We visited it again and again, hoping to see the fawn, but never did. We picked tons of flowers, trillium, sego lilies, tiny blue violets and Johnny-jump-ups that were the identical flower in yellow, Oregon grape blossoms, which we called "clusters-of-gold," and our favorite, the calypso orchid, which looked to us exactly like the toe of a fairy shoe. We found a great bouncing log and spent hours riding it.

One rainy day, close to home, we explored the attic of our own chicken house. It was musty up there under the old roof, but pleasant enough with rain pattering on it. We decided it would be perfect for a club house, so we started a club. The Cuccaburra Club. I was the president, Bob was the member. We got the Cuccaburra idea out of a book of children's songs and Mom helped us read the notes so we could sing our club song:

Cuccaburra sits in the old gum tree.
Merry, merry king of the bush is he.
Laugh, Cuccaburra, laugh Cuccaburra,
Gay your life must be.

We had meetings whenever we were in the mood to climb up the ladder into our attic club house. Mom donated an empty scrapbook she said she would never use, so we decided to do a club project. We would collect all the flowers and tree needles and shrubs we could find, mount them in our scrapbook and label them with their correct names, once we figured out what they were. We found a few of our wildflowers in the *Book of Knowledge* but we needed somebody who really knew the local plants and trees. We decided that person would be Julius Binder.

By that time, Julius had gotten used to us. His English was almost perfect, so he was much easier for Bob and me to understand than August. We started bringing out our club book whenever he came around, showing him all the sprigs and twigs and leaves taped in place with adhesive tape. He would scratch his head and hem and haw around and sometimes come up with a guess, but we finally figured out that he really had no idea what anything was. We pestered him: "How come you don't know? You've lived here all your life." He started kidding around with us: "Tree," he would say, pointing out a sprig of pine needles. Or, "blue flower," or, "weed." Ah, here was one he did know. "That one there," he said, "vit the red berries. That's kinnikin-

Our cat was trying to make off with a just-landed fish and managed to hook herself. Hours later, Mom and Dad were still trying to get at the hook in the cat's mouth, one working with pliers, the other trying to hold the cat. They tried tying her up. Then they tried tying her to a chair. The idea was to use a dish towel to attach her front legs together to one arm of the chair and her back legs to the other arm. We all tried to help. We discovered that you can't tie a cat—up or down. We finally let her go. Eventually the hook worked its way out by itself.

nik." We laughed and didn't believe him. No plant had a silly name like that.

We told Julius all about the stuff we saw on our jaunts in the woods and he took it upon himself to pass on to us, the members of the Cuccaburra Club, some rules he thought children—"childer," as he said it—ought to follow. Mom said they were wise advice. We wrote them down in our Cuccaburra Book. "The Rules of Julius," we called them. And since we were always making fun of Julius's accent, I wrote the words exactly the way he said them.

THE RULES OF JULIUS
#1. Nefer go in the voods vitout telling somebody.
#2. Turn around vunce in a vile so you know how it looks
    going back.
#3. If you tink you're lost, stay put.

Late that summer, just before school started, something wonderful happened. Rosy Shultz came to visit, and she brought along a couple of friends for Bob and me.

Their names were Mike and Francine Conley, and their family lived in Spokane. Their father owned a chemical company, Conley Chemical and Supply. They had a summer place on the river just a few miles upstream from us.

Each summer when school was out, Mrs. Conley would come up with the five Conley children. Patricia, "Pat," was the oldest. Francine was just my age. Mike was Bob's age. The twins, Mona and Bobby, were a couple of years younger. The Conleys brought a nanny along to watch the younger kids so Mrs. Conley could go fishing whenever she wanted. And since Mr. Conley had to stay in Spokane and run his chemical business, they had a hired man, "Hef," who lived in his own little cabin, down on the river bank.

The Conleys liked to be real ranchers when they came up to the Yaak, so they brought everything along with them to make their place into a ranch. They trucked up a milk cow and a bunch of chickens with a huge, white-feathered rooster. They brought a black-and-white collie named "Lassie," a cat named "Calico," and best of all, they brought horses; one for each one of the kids. Pat had her own special palomino, "Babe," who had won lots of trophies and couldn't be ridden by anyone but her. Francine's was a black mare with a white blaze, named "Roxy." Mike's was a sorrel, "Jasper." The twins had Shetland ponies named "Boy" and "Carmel."

That first day, when Rosy brought Mike and Francine over, Bob and I were excited about having friends our own age close by, even though they would be leaving to go back to Spokane in a couple of weeks. Rosy told Mom that the Conley family was having a big dinner party for everyone in our end of the valley, and we were all invited.

Francine and I seemed to be made to be friends together, right from the start. We sat outside in the bed of Rosy's pickup and talked and talked until Rosy was ready to go home. I could hardly wait for the dinner the following weekend.

The Conleys' house was a big, open log cabin with two kitchens, one along the north wall of the big room and one in a separate room, off the east end of the house. They had something I loved: a big rock fireplace. And they had a pump organ that Francine was learning to play.

For the dinner, they had a long table set up in the main room with places for all of us to sit. Mr. Conley stood at one end of the table and carved up turkeys and hams, and the nanny, Lorraine, and Mrs. Conley and Pat delivered the rest of the food, in huge bowls, to the table. They served wine, in wine glasses, to all the adults. Mr. Conley said grace—the Conleys were Catholics—and after dinner he made a speech telling everybody how lucky we were to live in the Yaak Valley and saying welcome, to us, the Knowles family. Two of the people there were real movie stars: John McIntire and his wife, Jeanette Nolan. Their summer place was up on Basin Creek. They were sitting across from us and up at the other end of the table. Jeanette Nolan had long black hair and the sweetest smile you ever saw. Mom and Dad muttered quietly to each other that they recognized both of them and had seen them in lots of movies. The McIntires had two children, a boy and a girl, but they hadn't come to the dinner. Francine told me that their daughter, Holly, was the prettiest girl she had ever seen and had dark hair that hung all the way to her waist.

After the dinner, Francine showed me all around the Conleys' barns—they had two—and we climbed up into the hayloft that was above where the cow was kept, and sat in the hay and talked.

We only saw each other a few more times that August before Francine and her family left for Spokane. But it was time enough for me to discover that Francine loved to do all kinds of crazy things I didn't even know I wanted to do, and would never have tried on my own. It seemed like she knew everything. She told me all about her very mysterious religion: Catholicism. She knew stories about sad girls that became saints because they suffered and were tortured but still refused to do any sins and died horrible deaths. She knew all about nuns, the scary, black-draped women that I remembered seeing when I was in the hospital back in California. She told about the terrible strictness and awful discipline in her school, which was for Catholic girls only. She was full of a lot of smart-sounding words and phrases like "pronto" and "ditto" and "Judas Priest!" that I filed in my memory to use as soon as possible. And she knew all about movies and movie stars, and what was going on in the place we'd left behind: Hollywood. She was wilder and braver than I was. Mom thought Mike was a nice little friend for Bob, but she wasn't thrilled with my new friend at all. I was enthralled. I thought she was perfect.

CHAPTER 15

Old Timers

I felt like I belonged in the Yaak School as much as anybody when I started fourth grade. This year, since we lived the farthest distance up the valley and had a car, it made sense for Mom to pick up all the other kids on the way to school.

We'd drop Dad off at the mill and pick up Jean and Carolyn Cummings and a couple of new kids from the mill, Kay Porter and her little brother, Billy. Then we'd stop and get the Chandler girls, Carol and Gail, who lived on a farm a short ways off the mill road. Including Mom and Bob, that made eight of us in the car. We sat in layers, Mom, Carol and Gail, with Bob on her lap in the front seat, and me, Jean, Carolyn and Kay with Billy on her lap in the back. Our little Ford—which Dad claimed might fall apart any time since there were bound to be consequences when a person took advantage of a car dealer the way he had by practically stealing the car—started up each morning like a champ. It could push through snow nearly as deep as the headlights and still keep chugging down the road.

Schoolwork was serious business, though, in fourth grade. I was one of the smart kids but I still had to work. In a small country school, I found out, the teacher has time to figure out what each student can do. If you're smart and having an easy time, she gives you harder work until you are struggling as hard as everybody else. She spends all her time making sure everyone is struggling.

My greatest beginning struggle that year was something I just couldn't seem to do: penmanship. I was left-handed.

We used the Palmer Method and each one of us had a penmanship book to practice in. The teacher would pass out the pens, which were plastic handles with grooves in the end, into which you fitted a metal tip. Then we each got a bottle of ink that fit into the hole in the upper corner of the desk. Then we would start, dipping and scrawling, making ovals and ripples and trying to make each circle and loop exactly as high as the lines in the book allowed, but no higher, and all perfectly formed and regular. When I tried to slant my writing to the right, my pen point snagged in the paper every time and I ended up with an ink blot and a hole. It was discouraging. The teacher had me try using my right hand. She was sure, she said, that if I practiced enough, I could make the change. I fought my way through weeks of right-handedness and felt completely clumsy. Finally I was told to go back to being a left-handed person if I wanted to. One day I noticed how Carol Chandler, two years ahead of me and the prettiest, liveliest girl in the school, held her pen—she was a lefty, too.

Alice Fix lived with her parents up the South Fork. That road was closed all winter, so Alice never came to school. She had waist-length hair and wore old-fashioned dresses. When we went up to visit, Alice was shy and hid in the barn until we were gone.

She curled her hand up and over the writing so she could get a better angle on the slant. Her circles and ripples, her handwriting, were beautiful. The Carol Method, I decided, might work for me. I tried it. It was awkward. The teacher gave me a look that said, "I told you so," so I went back to my scraping and scratching. Finally one day, as I worked along and my tired strokes began to sag from right to left, I discovered backhand. It felt natural. No snags! I could get near-perfect strokes with my pen. With the teacher rolling her eyes, I went about my penmanship business, circling and scrolling with the best of them. I had finally discovered the Doris Method, slanting leftward.

That winter, our second in the Yaak, came early. We got plenty of snow and cold early on, and it stayed.

But we were prepared for it. We were almost like the old timers now. We had plenty of wood and groceries to start off with. We had two vehicles, which helped a lot until we had to stop using the car because the snow was too deep and the plow couldn't keep up with it.

As soon as hunting season started that fall, Mom learned how to can venison. You needed a pressure canner, which she had, and you used a slab of bacon for one entire deer. She would cut the meat in chunks and brown it with pieces of bacon, add a little salt, pepper and garlic, and pack it in the jars. Once it was processed it kept all winter and was delicious and as tender as butter. One whole shelf in our bedroom was lined with jars of canned venison.

We went into the winter with thirteen chickens. Mac, in spite of everything we did, managed to get a few every now and then; a few just drifted off somewhere, probably snatched by coyotes. But the thirteen survivors, with tender care from Mom, laid a dozen eggs a day all winter long, even though sometimes they got so cold at night their poor combs would freeze. The frozen comb would crumble and fall off in pieces but it would eventually grow back all ruffly and odd-looking.

The rabbits were a different story. They multiplied so fast we quickly had a dozen hutches full. By fall we were running out of room but we had to wait until the weather was cold to do the butchering, so the meat would keep until we could get it to town.

The rabbits were a meat product. Dad had been telling us that all along. Rabbit stew. Fried rabbit. This was as much a part of ranch life as caring for the baby animals. But Dad was as grim-faced as anyone when the day came to do the awful business. Bob went from hutch to hutch and told them all goodbye.

Dad got us organized. He would do the hard part; the killing, out in the woodshed. He would do the gutting and skinning, too, and Mom would do the cutting up. I was to wash the pieces in cold water and then wrap them in butcher paper, two layers. Bob's job was to tape the packages closed and label them "Rabbit 10/50."

It took the entire weekend. We were quiet, like death, the whole time. Dad didn't want to talk about how he was killing the rabbits, but we had to know, so he told us; he hit them on the back of the head, right behind the ears, with a hammer and it killed them instantly. It didn't hurt them, he promised, it was too quick. And they didn't know what was coming because he took them one at a time, away from the others.

When it was over, we had three huge boxes of freezer-wrapped rabbit, chilling out in the cooler, ready to haul to town the next day. Bob and I went outside and looked at the long row of empty hutches.

That night after we were in bed I heard Dad say it was the worst job he had ever had to do in his life. No amount of money was worth that, he said. It was a nightmare. He hoped he would forget it eventually. It was going to take a while.

We thought we knew what to expect that winter, but after a while it seemed like there was so much snow that something must be wrong. Surely humans couldn't be expected to manage with such an awful amount of cold, heavy, white stuff to struggle through all the time. You couldn't get around in it; you couldn't see over it. You couldn't get it out of the way; there was no place to put it. It filled up too much of the world.

To make matters worse, Elmer Phillips was having problems with the bulldozer. So Casey Zimmerman, from the sawmill, did his best to try to keep the main road open, but it was too much for him. The mail couldn't get through regularly, either. We couldn't depend on being able to get groceries from town and were really, for the first time, relying on our stored-up food. Long about January, the mill closed. Then we had to face it: we were completely snowed in, and that was that.

No school again, is what it meant for me. I was pleased in a way. Of course it was fun, being home all the time in our cozy house, all four of us, snug as bugs in a rug. But part of me worried about what was going to happen when I finally had to go back to school. Mom had arranged earlier to get my books and some school supplies and it was agreed that I would study at home as best I could, until the roads were open. I worked half-heartedly some of the time, but somehow schoolwork didn't seem to matter when you were home all day. Mom was so glad to have company for Bob, she didn't care much about it either.

Dad brought a box of books down from the attic and started re-reading some of them. He said a few of those old books had been his when he was a kid and I might find something I liked if I looked through them.

The oldest books were obvious; they had broken backs, torn or missing covers and pages were gone out of some. I looked through *Robinson Crusoe*, *Kidnapped*, *Captains Courageous*. There was *The Warlord of Mars*, by Edgar Rice Burroughs, with the first thirty pages missing. I couldn't resist it, though, when my eyes fell on a description of Woola, the wonderful Martian dog. I read on, and was carried away with the adventures of the earthling, Jack Carson, with his marvelous, earthborn powers. Then I discovered the Jack Londons. These, I tried hard to read. An awful lot of what was there went completely over my head, but I got the main gist of the exciting parts. Dad said Jack London had the most marvelous sense of adventure. He read passages to us from *White Fang* and *The Call of the Wild.* Looking at the frozen world outside our windows, every bit of it rang true. Reading the tail of one worn jacket, I discovered Jack London's birthday was the same as mine, January twelfth! We were kindred spirits.

Mac became White Fang. I turned into Frona Welse, the "Daughter of the Snows." High adventure was my world, too, I decided. To heck with school. Up here in this country, school wasn't important anyway. Frona Welse had "nursed at the breast of nature." That's what I was doing. She could "swing clubs, and box, and fence…and swim, and make high dives, chin a bar twenty times, and walk on her hands." I had only just turned ten, but I was practically there already. I loved those Jack London books.

Besides hours of reading, Mom and Dad tried some paint-by-number pictures, and ended up with the giggles and used them for kindling. They tied dozens of flies and we played cards—toothpick poker—by the hour. Once we got the hang of it, Bob and I loved poker. Over the next several winters we won enough toothpicks back and forth to re-build a good-sized tree.

One winter the creek froze solid so we chopped ice and melted it for water. To our surprise, the melted ice water was full of tiny "wigglers." We strained it through a dishtowel and Dad put drops of bleach in each bucketful so it would be safe to drink.

A few gray days we went out walking on the icy crust along the edge of the lake "to get our blood circulating," Dad said. We trudged past all the silent trees, feeling like intruders in the midst of an army of sleeping, shrouded giants.

We invented new things to do with food—food we had on hand. Mom and Dad were creative in the sandwich area. Dad concocted his famous scrambled-egg-and-mustard-wich. Mom had three favorites: strawberry jam and bacon on toast, peanut butter and onion, and crushed pineapple and grated cheddar. After that last one, Bob and I decided Mom was a little nuts when it came to sandwiches; our main favorite food was canned soup. We mixed flavors, split pea with chicken noodle, or tomato and cream of mushroom. Sometimes we poured the broth off vegetable beef soup and heated the leavings with butter and ate them with a fork. It's amazing how interesting *nothing* can be, when your choices are really limited.

Dad took up fudge-making. He had a ferocious sweet tooth, and with seventy miles between him and the nearest Hershey bar, he was desperate. We all knew Dad was no expert in the kitchen, but this wasn't cooking, he said, it was chemistry. He had a book on chemistry in his box and he read all about sugar crystallization, suspensions, super-saturated solutions. He scoured every cookbook in the house. He experimented for hours and we were just as happy with the failures as the successes; it was all sweet, chocolatey goo to us.

Somehow, in spite of the unplowed roads, news still traveled up and down the valley. We heard reports of a cougar. Della Cummings was up near Shultzes' on a rare day when the main road was open for a few hours, and a huge lion jumped across the road right in front of her car. Gus and Rosy said they were hearing lion screams nearly every night, and then "something" got one of their calves.

The lion hunters from Libby were sent for, and they decided our place was the likeliest spot to set up their camp. Mom and Dad didn't know quite what to make of that. Here we had been, taking our leisurely walks around the lake, feeling perfectly safe, for weeks.

Well, don't do it anymore, the lion hunters said. Stay close to home. They would try to get rid of the troublesome animal.

They brought dogs to hunt with, but the dogs couldn't get around in the snow so they were left behind in the hunters' van all day. The hunters snowshoed off into the woods early every morning in the dark with their guns. They finally got the lion, a big female. They said it was probably safe for us to go walking outdoors in the daytime, as long as we all stayed bunched up together. We didn't go out at all, after that.

Another rumor we heard was pretty unbelievable. Reverend McCoy told it to us on one of his visits.

He still came around as often as possible. He said he had to keep coming, if only to visit his granddog. By then the entire valley had heard the horror stories about this pup of ours, but Reverend McCoy didn't care. He would cuddle Mac and fuss over him and Mac would prance and waggle like a favorite child. This irritated Dad no end, especially when Reverend McCoy hinted that if problems arose in a well-bred dog, it was nearly always the fault of the owner.

There were changes coming to the Yaak Valley, Reverend McCoy told us. They were going to put some kind of an Air Force installation on top of a mountain somewhere in the vicinity of the post office. It was supposed to keep the United States safe from an attack by the Russians. Imagine it, said Reverend McCoy, now the Communists had nuclear bombs.

Armageddon was upon us, he said.

So far it was all just a rumor, but you never knew. Rumors got started some how. And the real shame of it, Reverend McCoy went on, the real, dirty shame of the whole thing, was that just on the chance that one of our mountains was about to be taken over and desecrated by the United States Air Force, some fellow by the name of McCullom was going to open up a saloon in the valley! Not a church, oh no, of course not, never a church! Not even a grocery store! A saloon! Right across the road from the post office! It was just a dirty shame!

All worked up, Reverend McCoy went out and climbed into his tired old pickup. He drove off, determined to fight his way on up the valley in the snow, spreading word about the coming disaster. When he was gone, Mom said, "What do you think about all that, Dar? Is Russia that much of a threat?" "I don't know," said Dad. He looked thoughtful, even sad, I thought. They talked for quite a while about World War II and the Russians and I heard Dad say to Mom, "People never learn, do they?" I didn't care to listen. Although I thought Armageddon sounded pretty scary, the rest of this stuff may as well have been something out of *Mystery Theater* on the radio; it was that unreal. The Iron Curtain, the Cold War, Communism, the United States Air Force, were in some other world, not this one, and of no more interest to me than the weather in Timbuktu.

Within days the valley was on fire with the rumors.

An Air Force base? In this neck of the woods? Was it possible? What would it mean? What would it do to the valley? Which mountain were they talking about? And what was all this business about a bar?

To Reverend McCoy's dismay, most Yaakers thought having a bar in the valley wasn't such a bad idea.

CHAPTER 16

Zapped

In mid-February the snow let up for a while and word got out that the main road was open all the way to town. Everybody ordered groceries for the first time in weeks. Mom went berserk and sent in a list as long as her arm.

Dad had been working on a little project to pass the time. He had built a sled. Bob and I could play with it if we wanted to, he said, but he was making it plenty sturdy so it could be used to carry wood from the wood shed. As usual, it was put together out of whatever was lying around, and in Dad's style, was built to last. The sides and back were two-by-fours, two high, cut off in a sled-like curve in front. The bottom was stove pipe tin, neatly flattened out and nailed across the bottom and up the curved front. There was a brace across the middle to sit on. Finished, while not exactly sleek, it looked fairly streamlined. You could imagine riding it down a hill, lickety-split, gliding like a bar of soap over the snow. But you would be wrong. The "lead sled," or the "two-ton toboggan" as Dad called it, slid like a bag of gravel.

So, when the big mail day arrived and all the groceries were coming, it was Mom and Dad together who pulled the sled out to the mailbox to wait for the mail truck and haul home the boxes of groceries. They took Mac along and he followed them for a while but then circled off on some notion of his own and ended up back home again. Bob and I were waiting, bored and anxious for whatever goodies might be coming in the groceries. Of course, the mail truck was late. We got tired of waiting and decided to go outside.

It was one of those gray days when the sky came all the way down to the ground. Air and snow ran together and you couldn't see more than a few yards. But we didn't care; we had a pretty good snow fort—we'd become fort-builders by then—and we took candles out there and crackers and peanut butter and had a cozy picnic. Mac moved right in with us and stayed, as long as there was a picnic being had. Then he crawled out and started nosing around, like dogs do, wandering here and there.

Somehow in the frozen fog, a thick crust had formed on the snow. We noticed that Mac was walking around without sinking in. And he seemed to know, we noticed, just where the crust would support his weight and where it would not. It was uncanny, how dogs could sense things like that, sense all kinds of things humans couldn't. We decided to try out the crusted snow with our own weight. It held us too, as long as we stayed behind trusty Mac. We decided to follow Mac wherever he went, no matter what. It would be a good game, we decided.

We wandered for probably half an hour, the three of us, Bob and I crunching along on top of the frozen crust, our boots leaving only crumbled little dents on top of the snow. Mac meandered here and there, intent on some quest of his own. Who knew what mysterious dog-mission he might be on? He became White Fang, leading us across the frozen wastes. We didn't notice that in his travels, he was wandering ever closer to the lake.

We kept Conleys' cow one winter. Bob couldn't resist hanging around the cow. Bob kept trying to get a peek at the cow's cud. One day, Bob got too close, and the cow did a quick side-step. Bob tripped and fell, and the ornery cow loped right over the top of her, somehow managing to step only on a pinch of skin along Bob's ribs. In that terrifying minute, I discovered that I cared more about my pesty little sister than I'd ever suspected.

This year the lake was forbidden territory. The ice wasn't solid, Dad said, like the winter before. Temperatures had fluctuated too much, the ice heaved in places and there were big wet spots. There were air pockets out there, Dad said, where a person could fall right through. Dad, the worry wart. I told him that if I ever fell through, I would just climb back out again. It wouldn't be so hard. Dad asked me if I'd thought about my winter clothes; my boots and snow pants; how heavy did I think they'd be, soaking wet? And what would I do if I didn't come back up underneath the hole? That last possibility put some fear into me.

But sometimes neither dogs nor kids should be trusted. And that day

Bob and I were just following White Fang, wherever he went, no matter what. Even out onto the ice. Through slushy places, over cracks. Nothing happened. He wandered around in circles and back and forth, and we followed wherever our leader went, no matter what. It was perfectly safe. See? Dogs knew.

We lost track of where we were. All around us, above and underfoot, was nothing but gray and white, darker, lighter, smoother, bumpier. On we walked. It was like we were on the moon. White Fang turned into Woola the Martian dog, guiding us onward, through the fuzzy, moon-like air.

After a while I looked around and tried to figure out just how far out on the lake we'd come. I had no idea. You couldn't see twenty feet in any direction. And while we were trying to find ourselves out there, our trusty moon guide deserted us.

Dog-ears alert, Mac detected what we couldn't, familiar voices far out on the road. Mom and Dad were coming back, laughing and talking, huffing and puffing, pulling the heavy sled loaded with the boxes of groceries. Senses blazing, Mac shot away, disappearing like a wisp of smoke into the grayness. We called after him, but of course, being Mac, he kept on going. He flew the half-mile to Mom and Dad like a dart to a bull's eye, and settled in behind them to follow them home.

We'd been abandoned on the moon.

About then was when we heard the sound. It started from somewhere across the lake, raced toward us, and whizzed by, a sort of *cliggittycliggit-tycliggitty*, and disappeared in the distance. Bob said, "I felt something!" Her eyes were as big as saucers.

"That was a crack," I said, hardly breathing. We stood dead still.

From where we stood, we searched the snow for our tracks, any sign of tracks we'd made coming out: nothing. Gray, drifting cold; was all we could see.

Cliggittycliggittycliggittycliggitty!

"Let's get outa here!" I said. Bob was already running. Side by side, we made a beeline. For where, we didn't know. It went through my head that if we ran fast enough, we'd be lighter on the weak spots. We went straight through slushy places, dodged chunks of heaved-up ice. I tried not to think about thirty feet of water underneath us. And then flatness gave way to a sharp rise and we knew we had reached a bank, somewhere. It turned out we were on the wrong side of the creek, but we'd made it. We got home just as Mom and Dad came puffing into the yard with the sled, and with Mac trotting along behind them.

We didn't say a word about where we'd been. But the next day, in bright sun, there were our tracks, all over the lake. As if that wasn't enough, Mac decided to retrace the journey, sniffing all along the way.

Mom saw him out there and said, "Dar, look at that crazy dog. What's he doing way out there in the middle of the lake?" Dad went out to the edge of the ice to call him in. Bob and I sat in the bedroom and waited.

Dad was not a spanking dad. He didn't have to be. When he looked at us that day, grim-faced, and in a quiet voice said, "I can hardly believe you did such a foolish thing. We could have lost you both. I don't know when I've been so disappointed," it shook us to the depths of our souls.

Bob and I loved our knot-headed dog, all the same. But maybe it was inevitable that he would self-destruct. Later on that spring when the snow started to melt in the woods, he discovered a new joy: chasing deer. He'd take off early in the morning and be gone all day. Dad caught him at it a couple of times, once across the lake and once out on the main road. We suspected Mac actually caught a deer once; he came home covered in blood and with his tummy so full he could hardly walk. He didn't eat for four days.

But Yaakers won't put up with a dog that chases deer. One day at the saw mill a trucker muttered to Dad, "Dog that chases deer might catch a bullet." Other warnings came, from all sides. Then one day Mac just didn't come home. One day became four. We worried and tried to imagine what could have happened. Where was he? What trouble had he gotten into now? We asked around. No one knew a thing.

The spring weather was blustery with thunderstorms and cold rain. Bob and I were so upset that Dad took us out driving around for hours, looking for our poor dog in the rain. We finally gave up. We had no idea where to look. Another week went by.

In our hearts, I guess we all knew the sad truth: somebody had finally had enough of our delinquent dog and done away with him. But Bob came up with something better.

"I bet I know what happened to him," she said one day, grinning at the sheer poetry of it. "Maybe he got struck by lightning!"

Somehow, it didn't seem so bad. I could just see his shaggy yellow hulk, sitting on a hill somewhere, up against the sunset, tail curled around his feet.

Zap!

In a thundering flash he'd be gone. No more Mac. No more White Fang. No more Woola.

No more Lightning!

The spring breakup continued in earnest. Warm chinook winds ate snowdrifts overnight. Patches of weeds and grass showed up in the yard and out in the woods. The roads began their slow, muddy, thawing-out process.

People were getting stuck in mud holes all up and down the valley. Some of the holes were legendary. Soupy, three-foot-deep lakes of mud swallowed entire truckloads of gravel and were still soupy, three-foot-deep lakes of mud. In one hole, somebody threw in an old mattress and then tried to drive a pickup across before it sank. The mattress was never found and the pickup sat until June and had to be dug out with a front-end loader. Lots of people thought the breakup was worse than the snow. In a few places along the main road, temporary swaths were cut through the woods so vehicles could get around a really bad place.

With Jenny, we were among the few who could get through most of the time. Mom was an accomplished teamster by then so she started hauling all of the upper valley kids to school again. We bigger kids bundled up and rode in the back of the truck, standing up behind the cab as we churned through the rutty mess, sitting down only when Mom saw real trouble ahead, revved up the motor and shouted through her open window, "You kids better siddown!"

When we got to school, though, it was business as usual. Laurence and Billy, the other two fourth graders, both lived down near the school, so they had been there every day, studying away. Billy, who was now sitting behind me, had even found time to take the point of his compass and gouge a hole through the desk so he could surprise me with a poke in the shoulder blade every now and then. Once again, I wasn't too worried about catching up. But I hadn't figured on the multiplication tables.

My two classmates had been memorizing and reciting them every day, working their way up past the easy threes, through the fours, fives and sixes. They had been writing them out and having multiplication races up on the black board. I had hardly opened my arithmetic book all winter. Too late, I regretted the wasted time. Too many snow forts. Too much time following dogs on icy adventures. Too much Jack London.

For the first time in my life, I found out what it was like to be dumb in school. I was way behind and it was terrible. This wasn't me! How could I let Mom and Dad find out? They thought I was a whiz-kid!

Finally the teacher—we had gotten a new one during the winter, Mrs. Bloom—said she had to have a talk with Mom. The next week Mom came in after school. The kids who were waiting to ride home with us played around outside while I sat in the anteroom and listened while they talked about me.

Mom admitted right out that no, she was afraid we really hadn't worked very hard on school work. Who would have imagined we could be snowed in for three months? But I'd always been an *excellent* student. She was sure I could catch up.

Mrs. Bloom was a serious woman. There were no easy ways around Mrs. Bloom. As I sat there listening, I imagined that even the biggest boys sat up straight and listened whenever Mrs. Bloom did any scolding.

Maybe it would be best after all, she was saying, if Doris *repeated*—I heard the word and froze!—the fourth grade.

Mom took the suggestion perfectly calmly. In a completely normal voice she said she would talk to Dad. We all wanted what was best for me, after all. For my education.

To heck with my education! *Repeat* the fourth grade?! *Fail* the fourth grade?! Nobody could stand that! I had to pass to the fifth grade or else! Or die!

They talked it over for a while. I was an excellent reader, but the big obstacle was arithmetic, the multiplication tables. Mrs. Bloom said her fifth graders would have to be solid in multiplication through the twelves. They would be going on into long division. It was *imperative*, she said, that I have a good foundation in multiplication. Mom agreed. "I will discuss all this with my husband," she said.

I was beyond horrified. All the way home I sat in the back of the truck, tongue-tied with misery while the other kids screeched and giggled, bouncing on the bucking truck bed.

Later that night, Dad came in the bedroom and said we had to have a talk. He said he and Mom had been discussing my problems with school. I dreaded what he was about to say.

He said it looked to him like the multiplication tables were standing between me and the fifth grade.

Doomed, I agreed, "Yes. I guess they are."

"Well if that's all it is," he said, "let's get busy and learn them this weekend."

I stared at him. What did he think this was, whipping out a batch of fudge? A Cinch cake mix?

"It's only arithmetic!" he said.

We started Saturday morning at seven o'clock. I knew the two's and three's, sort of, up to ten. Right away Dad got a kick out of unveiling the wonder of the elevens to me. Think of it! Twenty-two, thirty-three, forty-four...it was wonderfully easy! Okay, next came the fours. These were harder, but still do-able, it was almost possible to picture the four-at-a-time leaps in your head.

Everybody could count by five, Dad pointed out, so the fives were fairly easy too. By two o'clock that afternoon, we started working on the sixes.

Dad hammered and drilled for the next day and a half. Mom and Bob waited on us hand and foot so we didn't have to stop. We carried on right through meals and until well after dark. I had some particular bugaboos: eight times nine, twelve times eleven, five times seven. Seven times eight was the worst.

Dad said, "Think, 'five-six,' and 'seven-eight.' Seven-times-eight-is-fifty-six."

That worked.

By Monday morning the weight of the world was off my shoulders. Hardly believing it, I discovered that my brain had actually been stretched around the entire, dreaded, one hundred and thirty-two combinations in the multiplication tables from two to twelve, in two days!

It didn't surprise Dad. After we'd done a final, entire run-through, he said nobody needed a whole year to learn the multiplication tables. That was malarkey. He couldn't imagine where some of these silly ideas came from. People built these things up in their minds.

Then he added, "I'm proud of you, Dee."

Open the window, I thought. I'm flying to school today.

Before the breakup was over, we had another casualty: Jenny. Our poor old truck was taking a beating, floundering through the mud, eleven miles each way, twice a day, to and from the school. One afternoon after we had dropped everybody off and were approaching Frenchman's meadow, where there was a notorious low spot with a bad mud hole, Mom tensed up and told Bob and me to get ready, she was going to have to really step on it to get across this next stretch. We braced ourselves and Mom speeded up to the maximum—30 miles an hour—and

During the spring breakup, the mail truck came up the valley early, while the road was still frozen. The mailman would stay overnight at Schultzes' so he could drive out on the frost the next morning.

we roared forward. But as we neared the meadow we saw there was a car up ahead, sitting in the middle of the mud hole. Mom let up on the gas and we saw it was Dorothy Cross, her car was stuck axle-deep. George Cash, a carpenter at the saw mill, was stuck in his pickup, up in front of her. He had been trying to pull her out. Most of the chain between them was buried in the mud.

We stopped short of the soft ruts at the near edge. George Cash climbed out of his truck and slogged over to us. It was plain he was glad to see us.

"Marilyn! By golly! You got a chain?"

Mom was prepared. "I think so."

We all got out and George dragged the chain out from underneath the seat of the truck. While Dorothy and Mom talked across the muddy space and Bob and I walked a log at the edge of the road, George got us hooked up to Dorothy's car and his own truck unhooked. When all was ready, Mom got back in the truck and started it up. In reverse, Jenny the Warhorse pulled like a locomotive.

Pretty soon we could see Dorothy's car began to lift and move forward, wheels churning. Slowly, as Mom backed the truck away, the car climbed out of the sticky hole. George unhooked the chain.

"Thanks, Marilyn!" Dorothy sang out, flashing a big wide smile through the window of her mud-caked car. "You know what? I've had enough of this! I'm staying home until it's over!"

George's pickup was in worse shape. He said he got dug in pretty deep, trying to pull Dorothy out. He waded in and fished his chain out of the mud and attached it to our chain.

"Okay, Marilyn, let's give 'er a try."

Later, Mom said she thought she'd felt the clutch slip, or something, during that pull. And maybe she'd smelled a little something odd. But once again, our amazing Jenny hauled the stuck pickup out of the muck. George disconnected the chains and piled them in muddy heaps, into the backs of each truck.

"Thanks again, Marilyn!" George said. He jumped back in his pickup and before we knew it, was off down the road.

"Humph," Mom said, watching him disappear in the rear view mirror. "You're welcome, George. Don't worry about us, we'll be fine."

We backed up about fifty yards so we could get another good run at the hole. Once we hit the ruts, it was like riding on a raft in rapids. We skidded and wallowed as we came to the mushy center. Mom tromped on the gas and Jenny roared and churned—we were up to our axles now—and we moved slower and slower until we were barely moving at all. Mom kept her foot to the floor. The engine rattled out a rough, jolting cough and for a sickening minute we thought the motor would die. But still we seemed to be moving, moving, a little more, and a little more, the big wheels chewing, finally they grabbed solid ground. We lurched forward and went fish-tailing across the slippery ruts on the other side of the hole. We'd made it. Good old Jenny!

But there was smoke in the air. It was rising from underneath the hood. Mom came to a stop on the dry road and shut the motor off. She said maybe we better get out. The three of us stood around, watching our smoking truck. Out loud, Mom went over the check list. Hers was pretty short. "The oil's okay, I know that. There's water in the radiator. Would a belt of some kind do that?"

She was asking me. I said, "I guess it's possible." Was it? I had no clue. "Should we lift up the hood?"

"Maybe."

We didn't know how.

The smoke seemed to be letting up anyway. And it was getting cold and starting to get dark. Gingerly, we all climbed back in, and Mom, teeth on edge, pressed the toe of her boot to the starter. The motor roared. What a relief! Everything seemed okay.

We drove the rest of the way home with no problem. Just a cloud of smoke rolling out behind us that you could see for a mile.

A few days later Dad said he thought the time had come to sell the truck. Maybe get a pickup. We would all miss our big old rig, we knew, but it would be nice to have a regular pickup that was easier to drive and didn't smell like gasoline. As we got more excited about a new pickup and Dad started talking about the business of trading in the truck, you could see a change beginning to come over him.

The Car Dealer Demon had begun to emerge.

It took four and a half gallons of oil to get Jenny into town. Dad drove, and we followed behind him in the car. Every few miles Dad would have to stop, raise the hood, and pour in another quart. But finally, exhaust billowing, we pulled up in front of the Chevrolet dealer in Libby. All squinty and demon-eyed, Dad disappeared into the sales office and stayed there for five hours. When he came out, we had a new buckskin-colored Chevy pickup, and the dealer had Jenny. Dad said he'd had to sweat over every penny with those crooks. Dishonest sonzabitches! Car dealers! He hated 'em!

Before leaving town we stopped at the Western Auto store and in a matter of minutes Dad came out with a pair of brand new bicycles for Bob and me. We went wild. I rode mine around the parking lot for a few minutes. It had been forever since I'd ridden a bike. I couldn't believe how much fun it was! Bob got on the back and I rode her around. I could hardly wait to get it home! Dad promised he would teach Bob to ride the very next weekend.

It was decided that I could ride home with Dad in the new pickup, to help keep an eye on the bicycles. The pickup was almost too clean. It smelled good. It had windshield wipers on both sides. It had a radio! And a heater! We could talk to each other without yelling, because the engine absolutely purred.

I could even hear the Car Dealer Demon chuckle softly to himself, as he pointed his crafty eyes up the road and we started for home.

CHAPTER 17

Summer
Shenanigans

As wonderful as our bicycles might have seemed at first, we quickly discovered that the Yaak Road was no substitute for pavement when it came to bike-riding. Sadly, the bikes were a short-lived experience, especially for Bob, and within weeks they had been hung on the back wall of the woodshed where they would be out of the way.

But two important things did happen for Bob and me that summer: we learned to swim and we learned to ride horses.

In early June, on sunny days, we put on our swimsuits and begged to go in the water: "It's June! June's summer!" Finally tired of arguing, Mom okayed wading, but only up to just above the knee. That was deep enough, she said, until we learned how to swim. Dad added that when we learned, we needed to learn correctly. Correctly or not, we wanted to learn right now.

One afternoon, Dad put on his suit and the three of us waded in. Dad stopped short, ankle-deep. "This water's like ice!" he said. "It makes your feet ache! How come you're out here in this?! It's too early!"

We didn't notice anything cold. "It's June!" we said, "we can't wait any longer."

It took him ages to get all the way in. "Just duck down, Dad, and get it over with!" we said. Finally, with a yelp, he did. It was the one and only time we ever saw him swim in our lake. He gave us the rest of our lessons from shore.

But that day he lasted long enough to show us the Australian crawl. We had to get the breathing technique down; that was going to take practice, he said. And the kick, that was important. He showed us how to reach straight out over our heads and take long, smooth strokes. It looked easy. I was excited. "Some day," I said, "I bet I'll be able to swim all the way across this lake."

Cautious as always, Dad told me not to get my hopes up. It had long been generally known that people in the Knowles family weren't good swimmers. We swam like rocks. We had no natural buoyancy, he explained. If we could manage at all, it was hard work. That's why good technique was so important.

This was discouraging to me. I wanted to be able to swim like a fish without putting forth a lot of effort. I even had a dream that this had come about, magically. Propelled by feet like an outboard motor and arms like windmills, I found myself knifing through the water like Buster Crabb. Then I woke up and discovered I was still a member of the Knowles family and swam like a rock.

But Bob and I spent entire days in the water. If our swimsuits were dry by bedtime we slept in them and were out in the water again before breakfast. We'd wade out to a trio of tree stumps that were submerged a couple of feet below the surface and then launch ourselves, paddling our feet and swinging our arms, flailing and splashing in what we thought was a pretty good imitation of Dad's technique.

Correctly or not, we learned. Pretty soon we were diving like dolphins and darting around under water and trying out fancy stuff like the Esther Williams Roll. Still, I discovered, Dad was right; swimming was hard work, at least for me. For her age, Bob was the better swimmer. I never could seem to get much distance before I ran out of wind. I realized that there were still times when I was the puny daughter. There was no possibility of my swimming across the lake any time soon.

The Conleys arrived for the summer and Mrs. Conley started bringing her kids over to swim with us. Mike became Bob's playmate and Francine and I took up where we had left off the year before, without missing a beat. We couldn't be together enough. We were after Mom and Mrs. Conley constantly, to drive us back and forth. After a few weeks of that, they let us sleep over at each others' houses.

Francine was a good swimmer—she'd had lots of lessons—and she was fearless in the water. The two of us drove Mom crazy. We rolled a log into the water and floated out from shore holding onto it. We floated all over the lake on that log, all summer long. "You girls get back in here!" Mom would shout, and we would paddle in a ways and then pretty soon we'd be back out there, way over our heads again.

In return for having the Conleys swim in our lake, Bob and I got to ride their horses. Mom figured we were in good hands over at the Conleys, with their nanny to help Mrs. Conley keep track of us all. The reality was, Mrs. Conley spent most of her time fishing and the nanny took care of the housework while the rest of us did pretty much as we pleased. Before long, Francine and I were riding all over the place on Roxy and Jasper, with Bob and Mike on behind us. We went down to Conleys' meadow and all along the river and up to Rosy Schultz's and back.

Dad came upon Mrs. Conley standing knee-deep in the river with a beer in one hand and her fishing pole in the other. She told him she was good for the whole day; she had one of her jeans pockets stuffed with grasshoppers and the other one stuffed with hellgrammites, and another beer stashed upstream.

Conleys' horses were gentle and old and did whatever we wanted. They tolerated all sorts of shenanigans. Francine would turn around so she and Mike were facing each other on Jasper's bare back; Jasper didn't care. Pretty soon Bob and I were doing the same thing, aboard Roxy. The horses knew the trails better than we did; it didn't matter if no one was steering.

You don't mess around with horses, though, without a mishap once in a while. Ornery Jasper, loaded with three kids, me, Francine and a visiting friend, made a quick swerve and raked us all off under a tree branch. One time when we were taking turns on Roxy, galloping in circles in Conleys' meadow, the saddle slipped with Bob. She slid right over with it, holding on for dear life and Roxy kept loping along with Bob riding out on her right side as if nothing was wrong. Finally Bob let loose and fell, and one of Roxy's hooves just missed her. It scared us all pea green. Another time, crossing the river, Pat's horse, Babe, decided she wanted to take a roll in the water, rider, saddle and all. Pat jumped off just in time, swearing a blue streak at her prize palomino.

Coming back from Rosy's one day, I was riding alone on Roxy and feeling pretty cocky. I had just discovered how to snap the reins. You laid the two leather straps together and held them in your hands, with your fists about six inches apart. Then you pushed your fists together, separating the straps and quickly jerked them back, *snapping* the two straps against each other. *Crack! Crack! Crack!* I thought I was so smart.

All of a sudden Roxy decided she didn't like that noise. She took off like a jackrabbit, throwing me backward out of the saddle. I came down on the skirt, behind the seat, with both feet out of the stirrups. I was able to reach the horn and hung on for all I was worth, but I couldn't get control of the reins to pull her in. I hollered, "Whoa!! Whoa!!" but it was useless. We came within sight of Conleys' barn and Roxy picked up speed. We had to make a sharp right turn to enter the gate, and the road was muddy. I was positive that crazy horse was going to slip trying to make the turn and dash me to pieces against the gate. I considered bailing off but couldn't seem to do a thing except hang on.

Somehow Roxy made the slippery turn without falling, slowed to a trot and stopped at the barn. Francine came trotting up behind on Jasper, laughing her head off. I tried not to look scared but it was no use.

All the same, I realized that riding horses was without a doubt the most fun I'd ever had.

Mom suspected that some of our horse adventures were wilder than she wanted them to be. She would shake her head and say she hoped we were careful, hoped Conleys' nanny was a responsible woman, hoped I kept an eye on my sister and that neither one of us did anything foolish. Of course not, we said. Mom said we'd better have a guardian angel up there somewhere, because she sure couldn't keep track of us every minute. She had too much work to do.

As time went on, Bob and I became pretty much obsessed with horseback riding. In fact, we were so obsessed, it turned us into criminals.

One day while Francine and I were paddling around the lake on our log, she told me that the whole Conley family had to go to Spokane for a week. Their hired man was taking the week off, too. Mrs. Conley hoped Bob and I could come over and feed the dog, cat and chickens, gather the eggs and water the horses, while they were gone. Sure we would, I said. And could we ride the horses, too? Francine answered, "I don't see why not."

Bob and I were wild about having an entire, heavenly week of unlimited, unshared use of the horses. We could hardly wait for the week to come. It did occur to us that Mom might not be thrilled about the idea. We had to get around that, somehow. The easiest thing of course, was not to say a word about it.

The day finally arrived. "Going riding today?" Mom asked when we appeared at the breakfast table in our Levis.

"Oh...well, I don't know," I lied. "I guess we'll go over to Conleys'. It seems too cold to swim."

Mom looked outside. The sky was cloudless; the air was still. Normally we would have been in the water already. "It's going to be *plenty* warm enough," she said.

Cool as ice, Bob announced, "All Conleys' horses are sick."

My mouth dropped open. I had to scrambled to cover such a whopper. "They have a...some kind of a bug horses get," I said, hoping that Mom, as she always claimed, knew next to nothing about horses. Then I kicked Bob under the table and we short-circuited breakfast and got on our way.

While we walked over to the Conley place we planned where we were going to ride on this, the first day of our seven-day riding binge. Today we would ride the river trail, we decided.

We fed Lassie and Calico and were on our way to the barn when we noticed a big padlock on the door of the tack room. Locked up inside were the saddles, the bridles, even the oats we always used to coax the horses near so we could catch them.

Everything else was wide open, both the front and back doors of the house, the chicken house was open of course, so we could get in there to feed and water the chickens. The barn door was standing open and there was the water bucket right next to the horse tank so we could water the horses.

But could we ride? Big no.

Boy, we were mad! We fiddled with the lock on the tack room door and tried to open the tack room window, which we knew had been kept propped open before, and was now closed tightly and locked. I could guess what had happened: when Mrs. Conley found out we were planning to ride the horses, she put her foot down. That tiny, irritating corner of my brain where I was just beginning to learn how to think like an adult, told me it was the only sensible thing for her to do.

But the disappointment was intolerable. And we had already begun the slide downward. Guilty already of the horse-flu fib, feeling wronged, we concocted a plan.

We'd borrow a couple of Dad's tools and remove one of the boards from the back wall of the tack room. Bob would squeeze through the opening and unlatch the window so I could climb in. We would get the saddles and bridles out through the window, and then ride all we wanted. At the end of the week, with the board nailed back into place, nobody would ever know. It was daring and dangerous. The perfect crime.

And it went off like clockwork. I used Dad's nail-puller and crow bar to remove a twelve-inch-wide by twenty-four-inch long piece from the rear wall of the tack room. Bob squeezed in and opened the window so I could get inside. We shoved the saddles through, then the bridles, then I handed Bob the coffee can with some oats, and off we went to the meadow. We caught Roxy and Jasper. That part was easy. I had saddled and bridled a horse only a few times by myself, but I managed just fine that day. I put one foot up on their bellies when I tightened the cinch, like I'd seen Francine's older sister do, so the saddles wouldn't have a chance of slipping. Then we rode those obliging animals for two whole hours, all over the meadow, along the trails in the woods and down to the river.

We rode every day that week; we actually got saddle sore. The last day we replaced every single thing, exactly as it had been. We even fluffed up the oats in the oat bin, so a few canfuls less wouldn't be noticed. We locked the window again and re-nailed the board in place, with the same rusty nails.

But it was a relief, once it was over. Guilt was eating away at us by the end of the week. It took us a while to shake off feeling sneaky and nervous. We were liars, robbers, horse thieves! And who could say we wouldn't somehow, someday, get caught?

Yet still, months later, whispering secretly across our dark bedroom about the Terrible Deed, we both allowed we would probably do it again if we had the chance.

Now that rabbits and chickens were in the past, Dad was examining the idea of raising fish in our lake. Earlier that spring, Elmer Phillips had taken us out on an egg-gathering trip at his lake, just to show us what it was all about.

We went along the edge of Phillips' lake in a flat-bottomed boat with a small motor. Elmer carried milk cans aboard to put all the fish eggs in. He had placed wooden traps in the gravel beds near the shore of the lake where he knew the trout would spawn. They could swim into the traps, but couldn't get out. There would sometimes be dozens of trout swimming around in each trap. He could tell the females because they would be deeper in the water, fanning their tails to make nests in the gravel for their eggs. The male fish stayed above them. After scooping up a male trout, Elmer would hold it carefully under the gills so as not to hurt it, and run his thumb and forefinger down the fish's belly to strip out the sperm, a white liquid called milt. He would catch the milt in a flat enamel pan like a pie tin. Then he would capture a female fish and strip the eggs out of her the same way, into the milt. He would put the eggs from several females into the milt from one male. Then he would swirl it all around and gently pour it all into the milk can. This would go on until the milk cans were full. Each time he finished at a trap, he would open it so the fish could get out.

This process went on for about a month every spring. Once they were gathered, the eggs went into the hatchery Elmer had built, down below the dam at the outlet of his lake. The hatchery was a series of wooden troughs with water running over them. When the eggs were all "eyed"—had started to turn into tiny fish called "fry"—Elmer and Alma packed them in ice and delivered them. At that time, Elmer was selling most of his eggs up in Canada.

With Elmer as his guide, Dad decided to begin the process of turning our lake into a fish farm. "We're on the right track now," he told Mom late one night, pacing around the kitchen, all stirred up after a visit with Elmer, "This is the opportunity we've been looking for. It makes sense. We'll be using the place for a purpose that suits it."

We wouldn't be a hatchery, raising eggs. We were going to buy fry from Elmer and raise them into full-sized fish—"table trout"—as they were called, to sell to restaurants. Phillipses had done that for years. Elmer told Dad it was a lot of work because you had to use gill nets to catch the fish, then you had to clean them and wash them and pack them in ice for delivery. And in order to do all that, you needed to have running water and be able to make ice. Phillipses had a waterwheel at the outlet of their lake, which gave them hydroelectric power. For us, a power-producing waterwheel would have to be located on our lake's inlet, somewhere along our creek.

In addition to electricity, Elmer said we would need a rearing pond for the fingerling fish. Big fish eat little fish, so fingerlings had to be kept in a place apart from the main lake until they were big enough to survive. Elmer and Dad had been outside that day, looking over our lake and all the surrounding area. They decided that the flat meadow just north and east of the house on the far side of the creek would be the best location for a pond. But it needed to be deeper. This could be accomplished by scooping out the bottom. All the dirt would then be used to make a dike to separate the pond from the main lake. It would be a big dike; big enough to drive across. Elmer said he could do it all with the bulldozer. He would put a culvert at the lowest point in the pond. Raising and lowering the level of the lake would allow water to flow in and out of the pond, through the culvert. So the water level in the pond could be regulated by controlling the level of the main lake, which was in turn, regulated by our creek.

The culvert would have a screen across it and when the fish were big enough, the screen would be removed, the level of the lake would be gradually lowered, and the fish would swim out of the pond through the culvert into the main lake.

I for one, got pretty bored with all the talk about a fish farm. It seemed like an endless, hopeless amount of work to me. I was not nearly as excited about raising fish now that I had lived on a lake full of them for almost two years and eaten countless numbers of them for dinner.

CHAPTER 18

All Things
Change

September came. At long last, Bob was in first grade. So was Gracie Cummings, her best friend in the world. And there was another little girl from the saw mill too, Myrna Buck. The three of them were a happy first grade class and the teacher loved them. And not only were there three new first-graders, that year, the little old Yaak School had grown to seventeen kids!

The rumor about the Air Force turned out to be true. There was going to be a military installation built on Hensley Hill, which was a mountain in about the middle of the valley, just north of the Yaak Post Office. There would be a "radome," a big white bubble, up on top of the mountain, that housed radar search equipment. The business about the saloon was true also; a man by the name of McCollum had started one, as suspected, right across the road from the post office. And probably because of Reverend McCoy's complaining to everybody up and down the valley, the saloon became known as the Dirty Shame.

Dad and Reverend McCoy sat at our kitchen table one night and worked over the subject for the umpteenth time:

"Is there no place for good, Christian people then, Darwin? Are we to find no peace, no freedom from corrupt society, anywhere on this earth?"

"My God, Mac, how could you ask for a more peaceful place than this? These are good people in this valley, church goers or not. They're not going to suddenly become evil because there's a saloon! There's no harm in a drink now and then, anyway."

"*Nor thieves, nor covetous, nor drunkards, nor revilers, nor extortioners, shall inherit the kingdom of God!*' said Reverend McCoy, "That's straight out of Paul's letter to the Corinthians! The Corinthians had saloons! They were nothing but trouble!"

"You're exaggerating this whole thing."

"It's a dangerous thing to underestimate Satan."

"It's a man trying to start a business."

"It's the Devil's work! How will you feel when the first drunkard drives his rig into that river and drowns! I'm not worried so much about my little flock. It's the others I'm worried about. Maybe you're immune from temptation, Darwin. But there are many who aren't!"

"Oh well, hell, I'm just a rum-soaked evolutionist, what would I know about right and wrong?"

"Those are your words, Darwin, not mine."

When it was over and Reverend McCoy was gone, Mom fixed Dad a hot rum toddy to cool him down.

Construction workers, working on the road up Hensley Hill, moved into the area. Between the school and the Dirty Shame, an area was cleared of trees for their trailers. Their children attended the Yaak school. In my grade, fifth, Billy Sims was gone, which nobody minded, but three new pupils had come. Joy of joys, two of them were girls! Donna Davis and Jayne Deyoe. Finally, girls my age!

I was fascinated by the way they dressed. Either I had gotten careless or they were very fussy. They were particular about every little thing like neatly turning down their socks and keeping their saddle shoes spotless and they wore little gold necklaces—a locket or a cross on a chain—and white lace-trimmed collars under their sweaters, and bright neck scarves to match their outfits. I started looking at clothes in the Sears catalog that I thought might make me look more like Donna and Jayne. Mom ordered me a few dresses and new shoes and socks, but made me promise that I would change my clothes after school every day if I wanted to wear such fussy things. Carrying in wood and filling kerosene lamps were not jobs to be done in clean white saddle shoes and dresses that had to be ironed.

In class, I had to seriously work to keep up with Donna Davis. It was no surprise when she became the teacher's pet. But I liked both Donna and Jayne so much it didn't matter.

Carl Cummings arranged for swings and a teeter-totter to be put up in the playground. With so many kids, we needed them. And at last we had enough kids to play work-up baseball with somebody to cover every position. The teacher had her hands full. The rule was finally made that nobody could go into the woods out of sight of the school house.

Before our family went into winter that year, we were blessed with a machine called a chainsaw. A two-man version was being used at the saw mill and Dad and Gib Hall arranged to use it for a couple of weekends. The amount of wood they cut was staggering. Dad hung the crosscut up in the wood shed and said, there it was going to stay. We had our whole winter's wood cut and hauled in, ready to split and stack in a matter of weeks.

Every time we went down to the post office, we could see more changes on Hensley Hill. The road to the top of the mountain would have seventeen switchbacks when it was finished. It was "a road-and-a-half," people said.

The Dirty Shame moved out of its temporary Quonset hut quarters and into a log cabin on the main road. Business boomed. Everybody stopped in at the Dirty Shame, coming home from town or whenever they went to the post office. Kids could go in too, so we did.

The bar was always cool and dark and smelled like beer. There were all kinds of nasty cartoons pinned up on the wall behind the bar and we kids would try to sneak up and read them, but couldn't get close long enough to see much. There was one cartoon that showed a tent in the woods labeled "Just Married." An elephant stood outside with his trunk reaching in through the tent door. The caption was, "Darling!" It was a few years before I figured that one out.

But the Community Hall was still the main social center of the valley. And the members of Reverend McCoy's church became its staunchest supporters.

All that winter, 1951-52, Mom drove the upper valley kids to school in our car. There were ten of us, plus Mom, so we had to ride in two layers again. The littler kids, Bob, Gracie, Myrna and Billy were on top, the rest of us were underneath. We sang the whole way and Mom harmonized with us. "Wait 'til the Sun Shines, Nelly," "Mocking Bird

Hill," "'Down By the Old Mill Stream." We thought the sounds that came from our lips and filled that car were absolutely gorgeous. We thought we ought to be on the radio.

When once in a while the car would go into a skid or fishtail on the icy road we would all squeal and hang onto each other until it was over. I felt perfectly safe, buried deep in the seat of the car, underneath the snow-suited body of another kid, with Mom at the wheel. It never once occurred to any of us that we might crash. Mom was sensible; she seldom went over twenty miles an hour, even when the road was bare and dry.

You never passed another car on the Yaak Road without stopping to visit for a few minutes; that slowed us down once in a while. But what everybody dreaded was meeting a logging truck. The road was so narrow, somebody always had to back up and get out of the way, and usually for the logging truck that was impossible. Once in a while we would meet one with our loaded "school bus." There we'd sit, nose to nose, while Mom got out and the truck driver got out and it was decided who had to back up to let the other guy pass. Mom always won. Ten kids was considered a tougher haul than a load of logs.

We were in the middle of a warm spell that winter, the January thaw. On January 12th, I turned eleven, and for once, with my chocolate birthday cake, we couldn't have ice cream because we had no ice to make it with. The creek was open and running, the lake was mushy and wet, and all the giant icicles that always hung on the eves of the house had melted. I settled for chocolate cake and…chocolate cake.

On her trips down to the school, Mom continued to visit Bea Harding. One day Bea told Mom that if the weather stayed nice, they wanted to butcher one of their pigs. She asked if we would be interested in half of it. Mom thought it was a great idea. We loved bacon and Mom was sure she could figure out how to cure the pork so it would keep. Bea said she wished they could butcher all five of those pigs. She said she was anxious to get rid of the damn things before one of them ate somebody.

It was decided that Dad, with his butchering experience, would do the butchering part of the job. My buddy Laurence, who at age eleven was already a crack shot and had even shot his own deer, was going to be the one to shoot the pig.

We got down to the Harding place early. Dad had his big cleaver and his meat saw and his knives all sharpened. Laurence had his gun out and loaded. Herschel and Bea were drinking coffee in the kitchen and discussing how to get the pig out of the pen, which was an enclosure inside the end of one of their barns. All five pigs were piglets when they were put in there and as they grew bigger and meaner, the wall of the pen, which was built of heavy logs just like the barn, was enlarged and reinforced. Now it was about four feet high and had no door. We all went out and looked at the situation.

When we made ice cream we broke large icicles off the eaves of the house, put the chunks in a feed sack, and pounded them to pieces with the flat of the axe.

If you shot a pig right there in the pen, Herschel said, the other pigs would eat him, or us, before we could get him out. But if you took out the pen wall, how would you contain the other four pigs?

Finally it was decided that a hole should be cut in the outside wall of the barn just big enough for one pig to crawl through. A gate would be rigged to be put into place as soon as a pig came through, so the other pigs couldn't get out. Laurence would be standing by with his gun to shoot the escaped pig in the head and kill him instantly.

It took Dad and Herschel over an hour to saw out the first log. Then the pigs kept poking their snouts out and snapping at the saw and trying to get out while Dad and Herschel sawed upward through the second log.

Finally, the second log was cut almost through on each side. When the last cuts were made and the second log removed, there would be a hole about two feet square. Dad said he didn't think it was going to be big enough. Herschel agreed. They were going to have to cut up through a third log. That would make the hole too big.

But it couldn't be helped. They left the second log in place and cut the third log nearly through on both sides. Then they hauled out an old barn door and stood it next to the opening, ready to be slid quickly into place as soon as the unlucky first pig came through the hole.

After all this, I came to the conclusion that even if Laurence was doing the shooting, I didn't think I wanted to see a pig get shot, even a man-eating pig. And Mom didn't want Bob to see it, for sure. She told Bea she was going to take us back up to the house. We would wait until we heard the gun go off and then we would come back out. We waited about a half hour. No shot came from the barn.

The next thing we knew, we heard Bea shouting, "Get outa there, dammit!" and all the canning jars on the front porch started rattling. Mom looked outside and said, "Good heavens, there's a pig on the porch!"

Actually, there were two pigs on the porch. And two more out in the yard. Dad and Laurence were down by the hole in the barn, holding the "gate" against the hole with their shoulders. They were having a hard time holding it there. Herschel had started up the tractor. He drove it toward the barn and ran it right up against the gate to hold it tight against the barn. He turned off the motor and left the tractor there. Laurence grabbed his rifle and the three of them started running toward the house.

The four escaped pigs were running all over the place and boy, was Bea mad! One pig headed directly for the chicken house. Bea grabbed a rake and chased it back into the yard. Chickens flew, squawking and scattering everywhere, and some of them landed up on the roof.

Laurence came around the corner of the house. He saw a pig and raised his rifle. Herschel shouted, "Not now!" so he lowered it. Herschel picked up a snow shovel. All four pigs ran into the chicken yard and started after the remaining chickens. Bea ran in the chicken house and came out with a coffee can full of wheat and dumped it out on the ground. The pigs ran to the wheat and Bea ducked back in the coop just in time.

For a few minutes the pigs were in one place. Everybody stood around looking pretty disgusted. Dad told Mom he'd never seen anything move as fast as those pigs. The first two shot through the hole in the barn like cannon balls, he said, right over the top of him and Herschel. The next two were out before anybody knew what had happened. They were barely able to get the gate in place in time to stop the last one. Bea just shook her head and kept on looking disgusted.

Dad and Herschel, with Mom, me and Laurence helping, moved some old sections of fence over and set them up in front of the chicken house, around the four escaped pigs. Meanwhile, Bea fed the pigs can after can of chicken feed so they would stay put. Then we had to catch all the chickens and lock them up in empty rabbit hutches to keep them away from the pigs, since the pigs, it appeared, were now going to live in the chicken house. The one lone pig, still in the barn, was the unlucky one. He was shot right there in the pen and hauled outside and butchered the next day. It was an exhausting weekend. Bea declared that after this, the other four pigs' days were numbered.

Once we had our half a pig, Mom decided to render out the lard. She piled big chunks of pig fat into a soup pot and put it on the back of the stove to melt. Before long the whole house was filled with a strong smell of hot pig. Bob and I thought it smelled pretty bad. "I know," said Mom, "but it makes wonderful pie crust."

She didn't look like she was enjoying the job too much and a little while later I heard an odd sound and there was Mom, throwing up into the kitchen sink.

Bob and I got all excited and wanted to make her go lie down but she shooed us outside and said she had work to do. We spent the sunny, windy afternoon on a teeter-totter Dad had set up for us—just a plank on a sawhorse—on a spot of bare ground that had melted through in the yard.

When we came in, the smell in the house was really strong. Mom had brought out the slop jar and set it on the floor next to the stove. Every few minutes she bent over and threw up into it. She threw up a lot over the next few days.

Then one February afternoon, she sat us down in the living room and told us the news. We had a new baby coming. It would be born sometime in October. She said she bet it was a boy, because she hadn't been this sick with either one of us.

We didn't know what to think. We said it would be fun to surprise Dad with the news. Mom smiled a crooked smile. "He knows," she said. "And he was surprised, all right. Even more surprised than I was."

CHAPTER 19

Little Miracles

Winter came back as it always does that time of year. And Dad did more than his usual amount of worrying. He and Mom had late night talks which I knew were serious, because they talked very quietly. I couldn't hear, no matter how hard I listened.

But Dad always said worrying was the first step to solving a problem. And the next thing we knew, he quit his job at the sawmill. He was going to go to work for the Air Force, up at the new radar station on Hensley Hill. He would be starting in April. It was a better job, he said. It paid more and right now we needed the income.

And there was still another worry. What if we got snowed in again? How would we get Mom to town in a hurry if we had to?

Dad sent a letter off to Bill Conley in Spokane and got a quick answer. Right away, we packed up the necessities and settled in over at the Conley place for the rest of the winter. Now we lived on the main Yaak Road where it was always plowed. We stayed there all through the spring and moved out just in time for the Conleys to move in for the summer.

Dad started his new job, working as a carpenter on the buildings at the radar station. The Air Force supplied him with insulated boots and a fur-trimmed parka for the weather up on Hensley Hill, where there were still several feet of snow and the wind blew a gale. In a few months he was promoted. A few months later, he became the civilian superintendent for the radar station. Mom said, "The cream always rises to the top." She was getting to be as round as an apple with our new baby.

Whenever the river rose in the spring, our lake would overflow. There was a low spot across the lake from the house where the water would spill out across our road, down a draw and back into the Yaak River. Dad tried to keep the overflow to a minimum by keeping the creek headgate partially closed. This cut back the amount of water coming into the lake. Still, "Little Yaak" as we called the wide, shallow overflow, ran for three or four weeks every spring.

It was running several inches deep over the road one day in late June when Mrs. Binder decided to walk over to visit Mom. Dad was driving home that afternoon and he came upon her, pretty much stranded out in the middle of the stream. She was dressed in her usual outfit, house dress, baggy sweater and tennis shoes. She had a huge box, almost as big as she was, balanced up on one shoulder. She was carrying a walking stick in her other hand and was perched precariously on a piece of driftwood in the deepest part of the water, obviously in a predicament. Dad drove ahead slowly into the water and stopped. He got out and waded over and held out his hands, first, for the box.

We spent a Christmas Eve with the Binders. August cooked a venison roast with garlic and bacon pushed into little slits in the meat. He sat next to the stove while it roasted, and peeked at it every now and then and adjusted the fire. They served sweet wine in little wineglasses and even gave some to me.

"Ach! No! No, no!" she said, following up with a menacing look and a bunch of chatter he couldn't understand. For sure, he could tell she did not want him to take the box.

He wasn't sure what he was supposed to do, but Mrs. Binder scolded and threatened him with her stick. Finally, after a lot more haranguing, he managed to figure out that she simply wanted him to steady her while she walked to the pickup, carrying the box herself. As they teetered along toward the truck she jabbered and raised her stick at him any time he made a move to steady the awkward box. When they got to the truck and he opened the door for her, she carried on something fierce until Dad finally stepped aside all together, bewildered. Carefully, she stepped forward and lowered the box onto the seat and closed the door.

Dad stood puzzling while Mrs. Binder chattered. Finally, he realized she now wanted him to load *her* into the *back* of the truck. Obediently, he waded over and lowered the tailgate and then waded back and helped her around and lifted her onto it. She set her stick down beside her, got a firm grip on the side of the truck and in a string of unintelligible words, made him know that he was now expected to get in and drive to the house. Dad said the only thing that was obvious was how astounded she was that one man could be so dense.

They stopped outside the house and Mrs. Binder resumed her chatter. As soon as Dad lifted her down from the truck she nudged him out of the way and marched around to the passenger door. Dad swooped quickly to open it so she could haul out the box. He stood back as she lifted it to her shoulder and stumped across the yard toward the house. Mom, who was by then, above all, pregnant, was standing on the porch waiting for her visitor.

The minute she laid eyes on Mom, Mrs. Binder turned into another person. The toothless grin that so few people ever saw, broke out all over her face and she cackled with glee at the sight of our ballooning mom. The two of them went on into the kitchen jabbering like a pair of magpies, Dad opening and closing doors and scooting kitchen chairs aside to make room for the precious box. Mrs. Binder placed it in the middle of the floor and like a magician preparing to bring forth a rabbit, rapped on the top of it with her stick. Mom of course, understood, and opened the box. Inside was a white wicker bassinet and, wrapped in tissue paper, a handmade baby quilt.

Mrs. Binder looked at Mom, and Mom looked at Mrs. Binder. And all the thoughts of all the years of all the mothers in the world passed between them. They bent together over the baby bed, Mom's dark pony tail brushing Mrs. Binder's puff of white frizz. The two of them made soft, clucking noises.

This was another language Dad didn't speak. He ducked outside and took refuge in the wood shed.

My expectant parents were taking no chances when it came to the birth of that baby. Labor Day weekend, almost a month before the baby was due, and just as Bob was having her seventh birthday and about to start second grade, she and Mom moved into town, Bonners Ferry, to stay at a boarding house across the street from the hospital. Bob would be missing the first month of school.

So Dad and I were home, batching again. This meant a truckload of egg-salad sandwiches. To console ourselves, we made and ate piles of another kind of sandwich, our favorite do-it-yourself cookie: chocolate frosted graham crackers.

We had an actual, paid, school bus driver in the Yaak Valley that year. The McCollums, who owned the Dirty Shame, had had to move out of the Yaak; Mrs. McCollum's lung problems couldn't take the rough winters. A man named Bill Kennedy became a partner in the bar and also took on the job of school bus driver. There weren't enough kids to justify an actual bus, but he bought a beautiful great big station wagon and there was plenty of room for all of us with only a couple of the little kids having to sit on laps.

I had to walk out our road to the main road to be picked up, and I had to get out there early, at 7:30 sharp, since we lived the farthest up the valley. Dad went to work even earlier and would be already gone, so I left the empty house and walked alone those September mornings. In the evenings, I was busy with school work—Mrs. Bloom was a pusher. And Donna Davis was hard to keep up with.

Our household lighting system had remained unchanged until that time, except that we had accumulated an unknown number of flashlights. Most of them didn't work. Or you couldn't find them. They got left out in the wood shed, left out in the car, left on, or once in a while somebody dropped one down the privy.

But the Coleman lantern hung on its hook in the kitchen, one of the two kerosene lamps stood on the table by Mom's wingback chair in the living room, and the other one was in Mom and Dad's bedroom. Bob and I were never allowed a kerosene lamp in our room. We never even asked. We were still a pretty rambunctious pair even at the ages of eleven and seven. Flashlights? We learned to do without them. In the summertime, we became so used to the privy we thought nothing of going out there in the dark with no light at all. Barefoot.

That September, while Mom and Bob were staying in town, Dad and his friend Bill Wickersham came home one day with a big, oily-looking motor in the back of the truck. They unloaded it into the chicken house.

The chicken house was, by then, empty of chickens. Throughout the summer there had been the usual unexplained disappearances and then some predator, probably a weasel, burrowed underneath the back wall and got four hens in one night. After that the egg-laying dropped off and one day Mom and Dede Hall decided that the best use of those last five hens was to process them in Mom's pressure-canner.

With all the talk about our upcoming fish business, Dad had started reading up on waterwheels and hydroelectric power and turbines and wiring, and had been bitten by the electricity bug. He developed an itch to do some dabbling.

Electric generators at that time—"light plants" as they were called— were so troublesome and unsatisfactory that generally nobody wasted time with them. And certainly, Dad admitted, this one was not the ultimate solution for us. But he had come across this very usable piece of equipment. And with the chicken house empty, we had the perfect place to set it up. He figured with an insulated building to shelter it from the weather, it might run just fine, even during the winter.

He cut a small chunk out of the log wall of the chicken house for an exhaust pipe. He ran wire overhead to the house and into the kitchen. A cord hung down from the middle of the kitchen ceiling with both a pull-chain socket for a light bulb and an electrical outlet you could plug into. Another wire went across to the living room and down to the floor in a corner near the front window, adding a second electric outlet. As simply as that, our house was wired for electricity.

Dad and Bill Wickersham worked on the motor for days; cleaned, scraped, oiled, tightened, tuned. Then one Saturday in late September, I heard the deep belch of an unfamiliar engine and a cloud of blue smoke blew up from the direction of the chicken house. The belch became a steady roar and the next thing I knew there was a real light bulb blazing away in our kitchen. Dad and Bill Wickersham celebrated the event with a concoction they called a "Rumble Seat"—rum and canned lemonade.

Four days later our new electrical system and everything else came to a standstill, when we got word via telephone and Rosy Shultz that Mom was in labor. Dad went straight into town and I spent the next few days doing laundry and ironing up at Rosy's.

It was a boy. Born October second. Dad had a name all picked out, a good, solid, manly name: Steven Michael. Once everyone was home again, the household and all the world revolved around our tiny new person.

Babies are work in any situation. Without indoor plumbing, without a washing machine or water heater, with not much space to spare in our little log house, our baby couldn't have caused more commotion if he had been a parade of elephants.

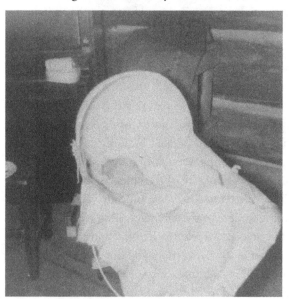

Steven Michael Knowles, new master of the household, in the bassinet from Mrs. Binder.

It seemed to Bob and me that both Mom and Dad were up all night taking care of the baby. In the daytime we all took care of the baby. Between bathing and changing and feeding and burping there was no time for anything else. Mom wasn't able to nurse him for very long. She said it was the same as with Bob and me: she lost her milk as soon as she got up and around. So right away there was a sterilizer full of bottles crowded onto the stove along with the usual dishpan full of dishes, tea kettle of water, and whatever food was being cooked. On top of that there was a wash-boiler full of diapers every few days. Mom soaked the diapers in a bucket of Purex water and then boiled them in Dreft to get them clean. Over the next months, we all washed diapers, hung out diapers, folded diapers, by the hundreds, maybe the thousands.

But he was worth it, our little Steven Michael, "Stevie-Mike" we called him. He had us mesmerized. Every move he made was amazing and adorable beyond words. And that's what we did in between changing him and feeding him and bathing him and rocking him and singing him to sleep; we sat and adored him.

Throughout all this, our experimental electrical system was working out very nicely. We began to get used to having electric light in our kitchen. And a light bulb in the kitchen was only the beginning.

One day Dad brought down a box of stuff from up in the attic, a collection of leftovers from California that were useless in Montana but had somehow survived the move. There was the Mix Master, beaters and all, on its white metal stand with the black revolving tray for the bowl. There was Dad's electric razor. There was a desk lamp. Down in the bottom, underneath a pair of ridiculous, fancy, George and Martha Washington figurines, and a treasured album of records by Dad's favorite soprano, Lily Pons, was a box of Christmas lights.

Later on that evening with the Mix Master at hand, Dad couldn't resist mixing up a batch of fudge. In recent months Dad's fudge had surpassed even his own expectations. We had all come to realize that Dad was a fudge genius. There were no chocolate chips, no marshmallows in Dad's version. His was fudge the old-fashioned way, made in a cast-iron frying pan using staples we bought once a year by the case and hundred-pound sack: sugar, canned milk, powdered cocoa. Dad brewed each batch like a scientist in a laboratory and lectured to us about the physics of evaporation, the effects of humidity, altitude, and so on. As the syrup cooked, blobs dropped in cold water were examined every few minutes. When the blob was the perfect consistency the pan was whisked off the stove and butter added. At a certain point in the cooling process you had to beat the mixture with a wooden spoon until it "lost its gloss." It was hard work. The scientific principle here, Dad would explain, had to do with incorporating air into the cooling candy to make it creamy but not sugary. An electric mixer would make all the difference he said, and by golly, it did. That night, with the light plant roaring away, turning the night air marvelously blue with exhaust, and our new baby basking in the light of an honest-to-goodness light bulb, we put away most of a batch of Dad's electrically aerified, miracle fudge.

You have to learn to do without conveniences like electricity, but all it takes is a nudge to get used to having them.

If she had a few spare minutes in the evenings, Mom started sitting in her wingback chair again to read, like she used to, back in California. The bright white light of the desk lamp on the table beside her was a far cry from the smoky orange of the kerosene lamp.

Dad picked up his electric razor and it was as if he had never been without it. Every morning he'd stand in front of the mirror in the kitchen with the razor plugged into the outlet on the bulb socket overhead, and whisk away his whiskers.

For all of us, the Mix Master was wonderful. We had fluffier mashed potatoes, quicker whipped cream, higher meringue pies and of course, fudge by the ton.

And then the weather changed.

The light plant began to give us trouble around Thanksgiving. I was the one who noticed the change, since it had become my chore to fill the tank with gas and start the motor every day around four o'clock when Bob and I got home from school.

At first, starting up the light plant had been fun. The engine fired right up and roared like thunder. The powerful motor shook the building and filled the yard with exhaust. And then the light would come on in the kitchen window and we were set for the evening with our wonderful electrical conveniences. Jerry-rigging was common in the Yaak, and Dad had rigged up a clever switch to turn on the motor, using a light bulb. He hooked up the connection from the battery to the light plant so that the circuit was interrupted by a light bulb. When you turned the bulb, tightening it into the socket, the bulb would light, completing the circuit from the battery to the motor, you pushed the starter button, and the engine started. That was all there was to it: Turn the bulb, push the button, noise, exhaust, power!

Then one day it took me three tries to get it started. The next day there was a cough and a puff of exhaust, but the motor kept dying. Dad took over the job. He tinkered around and managed to get it running most days, but in a short couple of weeks the light plant went from dependable to troublesome. We began to realize we couldn't count on it any more.

And the thing was, Bob and I *were* counting on it, a lot. We had decided that very first day, unpacking the collection of electrical leftovers from California, that this year we were going to have lights on the Christmas tree.

As the weeks passed and December loomed, the two of us became completely enthralled with the idea. We could hardly remember seeing a real, lighted Christmas tree, ourselves. And it was our baby brother's first Christmas! He had to have lights! As Christmas got closer, it was all we could think about.

But sure enough, when it was time to put up the tree, winter had settled in for good and the light plant had gone into hibernation. There it sat in the chicken house, as useless as the empty roosts in the corner.

Mom, even with baby Steve in one arm, was as much of a Christmas nut as ever. She untangled the box of Christmas lights and strung them on the tree anyway. "Just in case," she said. She didn't give up on things as easily as the rest of us.

As the days passed and the light plant refused to run no matter what Dad did to it, Mom gave Bob and me little reminders like, "Christmas is not just about lights on the tree you know," and "There are lots of other wonderful things to enjoy." Bob and I got the message: no lights, not this year.

The day before Christmas was gray and cold. The nighttime temperatures had been dropping below zero. We had presents wrapped, piles of cookies baked, school had been out for a week and forgotten. The tree was another one of Mom's masterpieces: tinsel garlands, scads of ornaments, box after box of icicles, the old-fashioned foil kind, hung one at a time on every needle, trailing straight down like real ice. It was such a beauty this year I thought, maybe we didn't need any old lights anyway.

But who was I kidding? Lights would be great. Bob and I were both grumpy and depressed about the whole thing.

Right after breakfast that morning Dad put on his jacket and hat and told me to fill and light the Coleman and follow him out to the chicken house. He brought out his tool box. He turned two of the nesting boxes on end for us to sit on.

I wanted to leap for joy. Dad the scientist, Dad the genius, Dad the magician, was going to fix the light plant! I sat there holding the handle of the lantern with a potholder, up close, so he could see to do his work. In the time that followed, he took every screw, wire, cap, filter, pipe and miscellaneous gizmo off that machine, cleaned, scraped, blew through, shook out and re-connected every one. He was meticulous, even for Dad. And every little while he'd stop and hold his hands over the lantern to warm them up and say, "Now try," and I'd reach up and turn the light bulb, and it would blink on. Then I'd push the starter button and the motor might give a shiver or sometimes even a cough, but that was all. Once it actually turned over a couple of times and out came a cloud of exhaust and we thought, Wow! Great! Here goes! But it died right away. It seemed like the light plant was having a good old time with us, laughing and blowing smoke out its exhaust pipe.

About two o'clock Mom came out and said it was too cold for us to be out there all day. We should come in the house. Don't let it ruin Christmas Eve, she said.

We were completely disgusted, hungry and cold. We'd done everything we could think of. We gave up and went in where it was warm.

The next thing we knew, Reverend McCoy came driving up in his pickup.

"Oh *no*," Bob and I groaned, "Not on Christmas Eve!"

But, in he came. He went to the bassinet and scooped up our baby like he was snatching up a rainbow with a dip-net. Mom, with her peculiar sense of humor, smiled like an angel and said, "Merry Christmas! How about a hot buttered rum?" Of course we all knew the answer to that, and "Oh golly, Marilyn, no thanks," Reverend McCoy said, "but I'd take a cup of hot chocolate if you've got one handy." And then sure enough, pretty soon he and Dad were going at it as usual, nose to nose across the kitchen table and putting away Christmas cookies by the plate load.

They regularly debated the age of the earth. "Six thousand years, Darwin!" Reverend McCoy insisted, "six thousand years! That's all there is to it." This argument drove Dad crazy.

"That's nonsense! Just look at the Grand Canyon for God's sake!"

"A patch of erosion from the Great Flood," explained Reverend McCoy, licking his fingers.

"A *patch* of erosion. Have you seen it? Geologists can read the layers of rock like a book! The Tapeats Sandstone is over five hundred *million* years old! Some of the youngest layers, the Kaibab Limestone, are two hundred and fifty *million* years old! The Vishnu Schist is two *thousand* million years old!"

"*Genesis Seven Twenty-Four!*" Reverend McCoy boomed out, in his awesome, God-in-the-clouds voice, "*And the waters prevailed upon the earth an hundred and fifty days!*"

Dad's boring geological theories could hardly compete with the Voice of God. And as soon as they wore out one argument they found another one. Reverend McCoy said the Lord was with him, in person, every minute of every day. Even rode around with him in his pickup. "I know it for a fact," he said. "Jesus himself kept me from going in the ditch this very afternoon on the way up here."

Dad's answer to that one was, "God gave people *brains* so they could keep *themselves* from going in the ditch!" Eventually Reverend McCoy always got back to his personal favorite, the End of the World.

"Darwin, these are the last days! If you would just sit down for once and study the book of Revelation you'd realize it! The signs are all there!"

And Dad often fell back on a personal favorite of his own: "Malarkey!"

That evening Mom interrupted. "Don't you think it's time the two of you simmered down?" she said. "It's Christmas Eve."

"And so it is," said Reverend McCoy, popping one last cookie in his mouth. He gave us the weather report, snow and gusting winds, and said he'd heard we had some packages come in at the post office that looked a lot like Christmas presents. Then, like always, he said, "Let us pray." So we did, and he left. Peace on Earth at last.

Mom and Dad decided to bundle up Stevie and make the trip to the post office before the bad weather set in. Bob and I, feeling a lot sorrier for ourselves than anybody ought to on Christmas Eve, were left with orders to fill the wood box. Later, when it was getting dark, we were sitting in the living room waiting for Mom and Dad to get home, and watching the Christmas tree.

It was just standing there in the corner like they do, an otherly sort of presence in a kid's Christmas-fired imagination, with all the sparkle and the smell and the little mysterious, unexplained flickerings. And I was starting to think maybe Christmas wouldn't be such a failure after all. And then Bob, whatever in the world got into her, came up with the idea that we ought to say a prayer to get the light plant fixed.

"Oh sure!" I said. "Never mind that Dad and I just spent the whole day out there. Sure, we'll just pray, like ol' Reverend McCoy, and poof! like magic, the light plant will work."

Bob was a lot like Mom. She didn't want to give up on things, either. And she could be a real smart-aleck for a seven-year-old. She got up and marched straight into the kitchen, got down on her knees in the middle of the floor, put her hands together, closed her eyes and started mumbling.

After a few seconds she opened her eyes and ordered me to set the egg timer. Like some kind of a robot, I obeyed. She clamped her eyes shut again and there she stayed, rooted like a stump. I couldn't believe it. Reverend McCoy had converted my sister!

Well, it was a long three minutes. It gave me time to think. Maybe it wouldn't be such a bad idea to give it a shot myself, just in case. It certainly couldn't hurt. After all, it was Christmas. In my head I framed up the words:

"Dear God."

Just then the timer went off and Bob jumped to her feet. We grabbed our jackets and headed for the chicken house with me in the lead. If any miracles were happening around our place, I was going to be there.

We got out there, bare-headed and panting puffs of pure frost. It was snowing again. And boy, was it cold.

I reached for the light bulb. "This is about the fiftieth time today, you know," I said.

Bob said, "Go ahead! Start it!"

I turned the bulb and it gave off its weak little glow. I pushed the button. And nothing happened.

But then, as if it had been kicked good and hard from behind, the motor coughed, shook itself and roared to life.

There we were, standing right next to the big dead beast, and all of a sudden it decided to start up and run! Outside, a giant cloud of exhaust spewed into the air, tumbling snowflakes backwards, up into the sky! The whole thing was impossible! We were more than startled, more than amazed. And this was more than just noise and smoke. This, I realized in one thunderstruck moment, was nothing less than the very voice and breath of God Almighty Himself, come down to earth in our chicken house!

For a minute we just stood there with our mouths open. My knees were shaking, I know that. The floor was shaking. For all I knew, the earth was shaking.

Our profound wonderment didn't last long, though. Seconds later Bob and I were making tracks back up the path to the house without even a backward glance at The Presence in the chicken house. I dove under the Christmas tree and groped around in the dark corner for the wire with the electric outlet. Then I scrambled around trying to find the plug on the string of lights. I bumped an ornament and it broke on the floor. Bob was screeching, "Plug 'em in! Plug 'em in!" I had pine needles in my eyes. I was inhaling tinsel. Where was the plug? I fumbled a minute...Bingo!

Color shot in every direction. Fireworks, frozen in mid-air, filling the room, spilling out the windows and all across the snow in the yard. Christmas lights!

In a snowbound valley hidden away from the world by miles of mountains, who could imagine it? Christmas lights, in such a place! Where no one had ever seen them before.

Now, I thought, now, this is Christmas! Straight from God! Glory and Hallelujah!

The headlights of the pickup popped into sight just then, across the lake. They hovered along for a short ways, the truck bumping over the snowy road and then stopped. Of course, Mom and Dad had spotted the lights. We could just imagine what they were saying! All of a sudden the truck started moving again at a pretty good pace, up the road to the house.

They came barreling into the yard and there was a lot of shouting and carrying on as we tumbled, baby, packages and all, into the house. Bob and I herded everybody right on into the living room to get a good close look at the tree. We knew our baby brother had to be wonderstruck at the sight.

Dad was looking puzzled though, and all he could say was, "What'd you kids do? What did you do?"

Finally, the commotion died down and I knew it was time to explain. I wasn't sure how to begin. How was I going to tell my dad that a real, Reverend McCoy–style miracle had come to pass?

I just plowed in. "We prayed, Dad," I said. "Bob did mostly. We prayed for the light plant to be fixed, and poof! It was. God answered our prayer." There. It was out.

Dad looked doubtful. I waited for my sister's testimony. "Tell him, Bob," I said. I knew I needed somebody to back me up. Instead, Bob threw in a monkey wrench.

"No sir!" she said, "I said my prayer to Santa Claus! Santa fixed the light plant! Not God!" And she looked at me like I was the traitor.

Theology is a hazy business for kids. And for Bob and me, raised in the Religion of Common Sense by a hardheaded evolutionist, Reverend McCoy's persistent visits and scary apocalyptic warnings had only maintained the confusion. To top it off, even at eleven years of age, I still, in our isolated world, hung onto the tiniest wisp of faith in a deity that wore a red suit and flew a sleigh. So, okay, was it Santa Claus then? Or God? Or Dad? Or had that crazy motor somehow unkinked a glitch in its innards all by itself?

Who knew?

These were questions that would bother me for a long time, although one was resolved the following summer when Francine Conley set Bob and me both straight, once and for all on Santa Claus.

But Dad was going to get to the bottom of things then and there. "Well somebody sure did something!" he announced, and he reached for his coat which was still covered with live snowflakes. And then he reached for the door.

He had barely touched the doorknob when suddenly there was a loud *whump!* and you could almost feel the house hunker down like it always did in a bad storm. The next instant the door blew open with a crash and the howling blizzard that had been brewing all afternoon roared full force right into the kitchen. It took Dad and Mom both to get the door closed. We looked at the thermometer. The temperature had fallen eight degrees in about that many minutes. You could barely hear the roar of the light plant over the wind.

Mom said, "Dar, don't go out there now," and Dad stood there staring out into the storm, puzzling, analyzing, trying to figure out what could have happened.

He finally shrugged off his coat, and I could see he was baffled. Dad, the man who had the answer to every question, was completely perplexed by this one.

Mom said, "Well! It's Christmas Eve, everybody!" It was plain she thought the whole thing was marvelous, however it had come about. And, hilarious! She handed Dad a hot buttered rum and said, "I'll be anxious to hear how you explain this to Reverend McCoy!"

We had lights the next morning, too. With snow drifted nearly to the eaves of the chicken house, the crazy light plant started right up again the next day. Dad just shook his head and said it was the damnedest thing he'd ever seen.

But sometime well before spring Dad and Bill Wickersham took the light plant out for good and hauled it away. We just couldn't depend on it. Mom, determined optimist that she was, went ahead with her own plans: she got three dozen brand new baby chicks from Reverend McCoy and kept them in a box next to the kitchen stove, waiting for spring.

º

Dad's Fudge

In order to make a good batch of fudge, you ought to understand the scientific principles involved.

—Dar Knowles

Rounded 1/4 cup butter (rounded like a muffin)
Rounded 1/2 cup cocoa
3 cups sugar
3/4 cup canned milk mixed with 3/4 cup water
1/16 teaspoon cream of tartar dissolved in a few drops water (measure out a level 1/4 teaspoon, then use a knife to divide into 4 equal parts in the measuring spoon. Each part equals 1/16th teaspoon.)
dash of salt
1-1/2 teaspoons vanilla

Measure out all your ingredients first. In a cast iron frying pan over a medium fire, melt the butter then add the cocoa. Stir well using a wooden spoon. Stir in the sugar. If it wants to boil already, your fire is too hot. Slide the pan away from the firebox to a slightly cooler part of the stove. Next, start stirring in the milk, a bit at a time. Finally, add the cream of tartar. Keep stirring with the bowl of the spoon flat against the bottom of the pan. You can feel the grains of sugar under the spoon. Stir until the mixture comes to a boil and the sugar is dissolved. Then stop stirring or the sugar might crystallize.

When the liquid is mixed into the sugar, most of the sugar crystals dissolve, or fall into tiny particles and seem to become liquid themselves. As long as the solution is cool, not all of the sugar will dissolve in this amount of liquid because there isn't room for it. This is called a saturated solution. Heating makes the molecules in the solution move faster and get farther apart so more of them can dissolve. As the syrup gets hotter, more sugar dissolves, and it becomes a super-saturated solution. But sugar in this form is unstable—it always wants to go back to its original, sugary state.

Sugar, as we know it, has another name: sucrose. A grain of sugar is a sucrose crystal and is made up of two smaller kinds of sugar molecules fitted tightly together, fructose and glucose. Each sucrose crystal is like an ice crystal in a way. When one forms, it tends to grab onto any dissolved sucrose right next to it and turn it into crystals. Then all of a sudden they all grab onto each other and make a whole mass of crystals. This can happen in a matter of seconds and your whole batch of fudge will be grainy because it's turned back into sugar. That's where the cream of tartar comes in. Cream of tartar contains tartaric acid. It breaks the sucrose molecules apart into the two kinds of smaller sugar molecules and, once they're separated, they aren't so apt to turn back into crystals. Still, disturbing the syrup in this form might make it crystallize anyway, so be careful not to stir it.

Once it's boiling, wait for the syrup to cook. Don't let it burn. Keep the pan wherever the stove's just hot enough to maintain your boil.

What makes this stuff turn into candy?

As it boils, some of the water molecules evaporate; they are released into the air. As that happens, there's less water, yet the same amount of sugar in the solution, so the syrup is getting more concentrated, more super-saturated. Once a fudge syrup has evaporated to about 80% sugar, cooled as a super-saturated solution, then stirred rapidly so the sugar crystals remain tiny when they re-form, it will end up with a smooth, fudge-y consistency.

Put a little cold water into a cup, then take a clean spoon and dip out a little dab of the syrup from the middle of the pan. Dribble it into the water and see if it clings together. Usually it doesn't, the first time. Let it cook a little longer, just a few minutes, then try again. As soon as the syrup stays together in a soft blob and you can pick it up in your fingers and roll it around, it's done. Take the pan off the stove and set it aside to cool. Don't stir—you can set off crystal formation. You want it to just sit there and cool down as a super-saturated solution.

After about an hour, check to see if you can slide your hand under the pan and hold it there. If it feels comfortably warm, it's ready to beat. Put in the salt and vanilla and start your beating. Beat hard and fast. You want to incorporate air into the syrup and, the faster you beat, the smaller those sugar crystals will be when they are cool enough to re-form. If you get tired and want to hand it off to somebody else, keep the spoon going while you make the change, because if you stop beating, large sugar crystals can form instantly, and there goes the whole batch.

When the fudge starts to lose its gloss and look creamy, it's ready to spread out onto a buttered dish. Let it cool completely before you slice it.

༜

CHAPTER 20

School Rules and
the Magic of Twelve

The Yaak school system was in a muddle that year, 1952-53. To start with, we got another new teacher. Mrs. Bloom decided to leave because of the difficult road conditions in the winter. So it was decided that our new teacher, Mrs. Bemis, should have living quarters nearer to the school. Carl Cummings donated one of the mill cabins for a teacherage and moved it over on skids and put it right next to the school. No sooner had Mrs. Bemis settled in, than the construction workers finished their road work on Hensley Hill and left the Yaak Valley. Gone were my girl classmates, Jayne and Donna, and one of the fourth graders, Patti Lindner.

Then Reverend McCoy's church decided to open up a school of its own. All the Adventist kids left the Yaak School and went to their new church school. The Adventist school was held in a little building up our way, near the Upper Ford Ranger Station and not far from the sawmill. And because it was handy, all the people at the sawmill who had children, decided to send them to the church school, too. That ended Mr. Kennedy's job as bus driver, since there weren't enough students in the public school for him to haul.

So, with no school bus, and the church school only a few miles from our house, Mom and Dad put their heads together and decided that Bob and I should go there, too. This brought the number of students remaining in the Yaak public school down to two. That meant it was in danger of being closed.

At the Adventist school we had religion classes every day and Bob and I decided we needed to know more about this End Of The World business. All the kids were talking about it. We told Dad it sounded pretty scary. Seriously, didn't he think we ought to be paying more attention to The Signs? We wanted to go along, didn't we, when everyone was Lifted Up? Before long Mom and Dad put their heads together again and decided that Bob and I should return to the public school.

So, we went back to riding the eleven miles down the valley, this time with Dad. He had to be at work at the radar station at seven-thirty, which was way too early for school. But we were allowed to wait in the warm little living room of the teacherage until the Harding boys came up the hill from their place and school could start. For part of that year, five of us, me, Bob, Laurence and Gary Harding and a new little boy named Jack Neal, made up the entire student body of the Yaak School.

The teeter-totter holds all Yaak school's students; (from left) Laurence Harding, Bob, Jack Neal, Dee, Mrs. Beamis (teacher), and Gary Harding.

It was a strange time. We rattled around in the school room. We didn't bother dressing up for school; Bob and I started wearing our jeans, just like the boys. Mom said she always would rather see us in dresses, but she had to admit, long pants were a lot more practical and easier to care for.

We didn't keep a regular school schedule and some days the teacher spent the entire day reading to us. At recess it was hardly worth going outside; what can you do with only five kids? Playing "Three Flies Up," with Gary doing most of the batting and the rest of us chasing after the ball, was about it. Gary and Laurence usually walked down the hill to their house for lunch and that left Bob, me and Jack with the teacher for an entire lunch hour. Some days the four of us, including Mrs. Bemis, played Sorry or Parcheesi, or Bob and I sat on the floor and played jacks.

But Mrs. Bemis was determined that our little school not be ignored. For Christmas, she wrote a play and a school song and with Mom helping out with the harmony, we entertained the entire Community Hall with Christmas carols and the silly play, starring Jack Neal and the Harding boys. At the end of the show we sang our new School Song, to the tune, more or less, of the chorus of *Jingle Bells*:

> *Yaak School, Yaak School,*
> *District twenty-four.*
> *We wish you'd take these old, cold seats*
> *and wrack your brains once mo-ore!*
>
> *Yaak School, Yaak School.*
> *Give us your attention, please!*
> *We're on the map, we're here to stay,*
> *One, two, three, four, Wy-ay-ay-kay.*

Then, for the big finish, we all shouted the school cheer: "One! Two! Three! Four! Wy! Ay! Ay! Kay! YAAK......YAAAYYY!!"

I turned twelve that twelfth of January. Twelve. It was the magic age I'd been waiting for. Nan Bobbsey seemed always to be twelve. Bobby Benson, my radio hero of the B-Bar-B Ranch, was twelve. Twelve wasn't a little kid anymore. For my birthday we had plenty of ice and therefore plenty of ice cream and I had a four-layer cake. Bob and I rearranged our bedroom. I told her since we were both getting older, we each needed our privacy. So we put our dressers back-to-back in between our beds. It was a little more like having your own room. Against the wall at the foot of my bed, I set myself up a little wash stand using the old footlocker from up in the attic, which I stood on end. I covered it with one of Mom's old bridge-table cloths and was given a wash basin and soap dish, plus a mirror to hang on the wall. I got books for presents from Mom, *Anne of Green Gables* and *Little Women*. Dad gave me a pair of small-sized snowshoes he had gotten from Julius. They used to be Mrs. Binder's, Dad said, but she hadn't used them in years. Bob gave me new wool socks for my eternally cold feet. Right behind my birthday was Dad's, on February 11. He turned thirty-seven. He said that made him fifty-seven in Yaak years.

With my new snowshoes, I went out for walks with Dad. Mostly, we just snowshoed through the woods together. I always had an awful time keeping up with him, but I was getting better, faster, longer-winded. Not many lectures happened. It was a time for walking. But once in a while Dad would say, "Stop a minute." And we would halt where we stood and behold. It might be the afternoon sun, pink on the looming shoulder of Mt. Henry. It might be ice-lace threading across an open patch of ripples on snowbound Koo Koo Creek. Or snowflakes falling in clumps on our sleeves. Or a rabbit, on snowshoes much smaller than mine.

These were the things, Dad told me, these "exquisitely intricate things" that made him believe in God. Not words in a book. Did I know, he said, that there were actually people who thought that all of this, all these marvelous things in this world, were an accident? How ridiculous could you get?!

And that was why it was so silly, he said, to talk about the world ending. Why on earth would God end the world when he was right here in the middle of it? We weren't arithmetic problems on a blackboard that could be erased like some kind of mistake. We were God's work. And God wasn't finished. And he sure as hell wasn't going to quit on us now.

We spent one day in the meadows between our place and Conley's, without snowshoes, walking all over on a thick crust on top of four feet of snow. It was like a wood floor. On the way home we came to the place we called Garrigus Meadow. From there was a clear, open stretch along the river to the mouth of our creek. Dad walked a little faster, so I speeded up. Then he walked a little faster, so I speeded up. And then I saw the grin on his face and we both speeded up, and pretty soon we were wide-open striding, Groucho Marx–ing together, side by side across that meadow, breathless, laughing like a couple of nuts as we tried to out-walk each other, and boy, were we making time!

I'd never seen a "silver thaw" before. Afterwards, everybody talked about it like it was one of the wonders of the world.

It was a weekend in late February. We were still buried in snow, a couple of feet at least. Then one day it warmed up to fifty degrees and rained. That night, with everything slushy and well soaked, the weather cleared and the temperature dropped to fourteen.

The next morning every surface under the sky, down to the tiniest pine needle, was coated with ice. The first rays of the sun flashed brilliant fingers across the snow's icy crust. All around the house, arm-thick icicles hung from the eves, glowing ice-blue and sun-red.

Before long Dad half walked, half slid outside, and busied himself in the wood shed. It was my day to walk over to the Binders to get our weekly gallon of milk. I discovered I could walk on the crunchy crust, so, silver thaw or not, I was headed over to the Binders.

In the bright sun, the temperature was on the way up again. As I left the yard, out of habit, I turned around and looked back. It was a dazzling sight. The willows along the creek had become colossal, shimmering bouquets of ice. In the woods behind the house, the trees sparkled like blown glass. And almost before I could see it all, the crystal world was melting. I could hear the trees dripping, ice was falling in pieces, shattering into fragments and sliding on crusted snow. At that moment, age twelve, I heard a voice in my head. It said, "Remember."

I couldn't tear my eyes away. The willows, the house, the trees, all seemed to be ice and fire together, melting under the sun.

The rest of that winter, Bob and I missed school off and on because as always, snow plowing was up to whoever had the time and equipment. Sometimes nobody did. Dad had to stay overnight at work, often for a week at a time because he couldn't be sure about getting back and forth. Sometime in midwinter, more people came to work at the radar station and a few of them had children. My two girl classmates were replaced by a couple of boys, Jimmy Chappell and Chuck Ross. Then the church school ran out of money and had to close. All the church school students came back to the old Yaak school again. The number of students grew to eighteen, the most anybody could remember. Mr. Kennedy got his job back as school bus driver.

Mr. Kennedy's job wasn't easy. But he made it harder because he was gruff and never talked to any of us. We were pretty sure he didn't like kids, so we weren't very nice to him either. We sang a lot, like we'd always done while we rode along and somehow a song evolved, to the tune of "On Top of Old Smokey." It started out, "On top of old baaaldy, all covered with scaaabs..." Nobody actually *said* it was about Mr. Kennedy, but he did happen to be bald. Lucky for him, we could never come up with a second line that rhymed, so the song died after a few weeks.

Mr. Kennedy drove a little faster than Mom. We slid off the road into the snow bank every once in a while. But every kid on the bus was used to those little winter accidents. It was just something that happened on the Yaak Road: you slid into the snowbank, dug out, and went on.

The Yaak Road got so bad one spring that people started running out of necessities. The Air Force base arranged for a helicopter to fly to the Yaak Post Office and drop off supplies.

One day on the way to school, near Earl Stratton's place, we started down a hill a little too fast. Mr. Kennedy touched the brakes and we went into a skid. Not a fast skid, more of an out-of-control, slow-motion slide down the hill at an odd angle. Coming down the other side of the hill toward us was an empty logging truck doing exactly the same thing. We all saw what was going to happen. Nothing could stop it. Big red letters, MACK, loomed in front of us. We hit, and heard a shrill *ka-squiiiinnnchhh!* as the fender of the truck caught the hood of the station wagon and peeled it back over the top of us like a piece of tin foil. We came to a stop with the black hulk of the truck tire pressed against our door. Everybody was shaken up and a few of the kids had bloody noses, but nobody got hurt. The truck didn't have a mark on it.

Earl Stratton hauled us all to school in his pickup—the four littlest kids crammed in the front seat and the rest of us in the back. The new station wagon was towed into town to be fixed, and Mr. Kennedy borrowed another station wagon to use in the meantime.

Less than a week later, in the borrowed station wagon, we collided with Reverend McCoy as he was pulling onto the main road in front of the Community Hall. Nobody was hurt this time either. But both rigs had dented front bumpers and smashed headlights.

By then Mr. Kennedy's own station wagon was fixed as good as new. We rode in it for one day. Then when he came to pick us up the next morning, the shiny new hood was all dented up again. He had hit a deer the night before, on his way home.

It was simply too hilarious to ignore. And we didn't; we were merciless. All the way to school there were jokes, with crashing noises, about running into trees, running into people, running into animals:

"Look out!! There's a mail box!! AAAGGGHHH!!"

"Look out!! There's an elephant!! AAAGGGHHH!!

When Bob and I got home that night, in stitches with the tale about the latest accident, Mom said it was high time somebody checked into Mr. Kennedy's driving. But it didn't matter, because right after that, he quit his job as school bus driver and went back to just running the Dirty Shame.

So then it was every man for himself, getting to school. We managed until the spring breakup came. Then, without Jenny, Bob and I and most of the other kids in the upper valley, were stuck at home.

This time the Air Force came to the rescue. For two weeks, a weapons carrier, a four-wheel-drive military truck with a canvas-covered bed with lots of room for passengers, came up the valley to each house, and picked us up. Everybody got to sit under cover, comfortable and out of the wind, while the tough vehicle wallowed right through the mud holes and got us to school and home again.

It was no wonder then, with such a disorganized school-year, that a problem developed. We discovered that Bob, my smarty-pants sister, nearly at the end of her second year of school, could hardly read a word.

I was oblivious to this and happy to keep her enslaved as she had been for so long, still perfectly willing to brush my hair, make my bed, anything, for an hour with Little Lulu or Mary Jane and Sniffles or the *everlasting* Bobbsey Twins. But Mom was shocked the first time Bob brought home her reading book so she could practice. They struggled for two hours and Bob was terrible. Mom and Dad both went down to the school to have a talk with Mrs. Bemis.

Mrs. Bemis said she hadn't noticed until recently how far behind Barbara was. She'd been wracking her brain to figure out what the problem was. Could it be this new teaching technique, Sight Reading? Sight Reading was the modern approach. Phonics was out, and words were memorized using flash cards. It was supposed to be a superior method.

On the way home in the car we heard what Dad thought about all this:

"No *phonics*?! How can anybody read without phonics?! Whoever heard of such a thing?! What do they think we are, Chinese?! Why do they think we have an alphabet?! Who comes up with all this malarkey, anyway?! No daughter of mine is going to be used for some silly experiment!"

Beside me in the back seat, Bob leaned over and whispered, "What's a phonic?"

I answered, "I bet you're going to find out."

That weekend, Dad and Bob holed up in our bedroom and started with the vowels. By Saturday afternoon they were doing consonants, by Sunday noon, combinations of consonants. Then, the exceptions: Laugh. Walk. Enough and stuff. Kite and flight.

"*Europe*," I put in.

At the end of the weekend Bob could sound out any word a third-grader might happen to run into. My slave was free.

CHAPTER 21

The Mystery Dog

The ghost town of Sylvanite was way down at the other end of the valley from us. There wasn't much left of the old mining town. The Morning Glory Mine was a collection of rusting metal shacks climbing the hillside on the north side of the road. Not far away, on the south side, was the skeleton of an old lodge—Buckhorn Lodge. I was fascinated by it because it had a pair of real saloon doors on the front. I always wanted to stop and see it when we drove past, but we were either in a hurry to get to town or trying to make it home after a long day, so we never stopped. I never got to see if the doors would actually swing back and forth like they do in the movies. Just at the edge of Sylvanite, was the Grush place, literally on the Yaak Road, the house on one side, the barn on the other.

Gene Grush and his wife were early homesteaders in the Yaak. They had a gas pump at their place and cabins for rent. One day late that spring, Mrs. Grush went down to clean up after some guests had checked out, and she found a thirsty, starving, frantic dog trying to claw its way out through the door. It had been trapped in the cabin for two days. We heard through the Grapevine that Mrs. Grush was trying to find a home for the abandoned dog. The spring breakup was over by then and the road was dry. Mom, Steve, Bob and I were headed into town. We decided to stop by and see the dog.

She was a medium-sized, curly brown and black, spaniel type. She wasn't a puppy but she seemed young, maybe around a year old. She was graceful and well-mannered and had eyes like molasses. "Probably part Brittany spaniel," Mom said, reaching down to smooth the dog's silky coat while we all stood there, falling in love. Mom found a telltale scar on her tummy. "Look here," she said, "she's been spayed."

Mrs. Grush said she had written a card to the people who left her behind but received no reply. How someone could go off and leave such a lovely dog was anybody's guess. She was ours if we wanted her. Boy, did we!

We picked her up on the way home from town. We had a name picked out: "Flossie." It was Bob's idea.

It took Flossie a little while to get used to us. Right away, we found out we mustn't ever leave her in the house alone; she couldn't stand it. So most of the time she rode along with us wherever we went and was perfectly happy to wait in the pickup or the car. She was pretty much everything our poor old Mac wasn't. She hated cows. She would bristle and burst out the door barking and have them on the run before any of us knew the herd was in the area. If there were coyotes howling she posted herself out by the wood shed and stood there, silent and all business. Our new second batch of chickens were now running loose in the yard, but she ignored them. Flossie ate dog food, period.

How on earth could anyone go off and leave such a lovely dog? We never stopped wondering about it.

And then one day, she disappeared.

We called and called at dinner time. She had always come right away. We searched the place. In near dark, Bob and I walked all the way up the creek to the river, calling. Dad drove up and down the road, head out the window, calling.

None of us wanted to stop looking, but it got too dark to see. We finally gave up and went to bed sometime after midnight. Nobody got much sleep.

The next morning there she was, lying on the porch watching over the place as if nothing had happened. We covered her with hugs and she must have wondered what the heck all the fuss was about. But all the next week she was gone every night and sometimes during the day. We tried to watch her to see where she was going but she would slip away and disappear before anyone realized it. Flossie had obviously been spayed; the telltale scar was plain, right there on her tummy. Even so, by then, the possibility of a litter of puppies had occurred to all of us.

One Saturday Bob and I were home alone for the afternoon and we began to hear small sounds, high-pitched, mewling noises coming from underneath the house, beneath the floor of the closet in the corner of Mom and Dad's bedroom.

We had to get under there. The foundation of the house was tightly-packed rocks and at that end of the house, the bottom-most log was less than a foot above the ground. But at the far end, underneath our bedroom, the foundation was several inches higher and mid-way along the wall there was a narrow opening. If we removed just one more rock we would have a hole big enough to crawl through. I used a crowbar and pried it out.

We dug out every flashlight in the house and after switching batteries around, got a couple of them to work. Then, flat on our stomachs, we inched our way through the opening. Once we were under there, I could see it was going to be a long, dark crawl to the opposite end of the house. I wasn't crazy about spiders and tried not to think about what might be hanging from the floorboards just above our heads. Bob didn't seem to care. She took off on hands and knees. I followed.

The ground rose as we went along, so there was less and less room overhead. Midway across, we came to a stout log stringer. It nearly touched the ground and ran the full length of the house, supporting the floor. Seeing this, I was ready to give up on the whole idea. But Bob was determined to get to the cute little noises at the far end of the house. She worked her way along the log, looking for a space high enough to squeeze under it. When she was almost all the way to the front of the house, she found a place to wiggle underneath, lying on her back. Try as I might, I couldn't begin to squeeze under there. So I waited where I was, following the beam of her flashlight as she belly-crawled toward the far corner. All of a sudden I heard a clunk and her light went out. "Shoot," she said, "I dropped it. Now it won't come back on." I tried to shine my light over to her but it wouldn't reach.

"Maybe you better come back out," I said, liking where we were, less and less by the minute. "Dad'll figure out a better way."

"I want to see what it is!" she said, and I could hear her moving further away. Finally she called out, "I'm here," in a flat, muffled voice, sounding about a mile away.

"Can you see what it is?"

"No. They're all…oh!" She sounded scared. "There's a whole *nest* of…something! I dunno! What if it's pack rats?!"

That did it for me. I was creeped out. I yelled, "Bob! Come on! You get away from there! Right now!" I heard her yell back, "Okay! I'm coming!" I turned around to look for the daylight opening. It seemed very far away.

Just then the hole in the rock foundation went black. For a panicky instant I felt doomed, trapped, like I had to stand up and push the floor of the house off the top of me or die. Then suddenly Flossie appeared, right next to me. And there was the hole, open again. I grabbed onto the dog and was able to swallow my craziness. "Flossie!" I said, "What're you doing under here?" Panting lightly, Flossie moved past me, wriggled underneath the log stringer and headed directly toward the corner where Bob was. Seconds later Bob sang out, "It *is* puppies! Oh Flossie! Good dog!"

One at a time, with Flossie closely supervising, we brought out all seven puppies. Bob crawled tirelessly back and forth and handed them one at a time, under the stringer to me. We made a bed for them in the kitchen. Flossie didn't mind. Bob was beside herself. I was just glad it was over.

"I guess that explains why they left her behind," said Mom, looking over the seven little Flossies in their box later that day. "Someone didn't want to deal with a litter of puppies. But why would she choose such an awful place to have them? And what do you suppose made that scar on her stomach?" Those were mysteries about our dog that were never solved. A couple of months later we took the whole litter to the Community Hall and to Bob's disappointment and Mom's relief, every one was adopted.

CHAPTER 22

Four Jacks

In London, England on June 2, 1953, a new queen, Elizabeth II of England, was crowned. What I knew of this event came from a coloring book Mom bought for me with pictures of the coronation. It was a fairy tale, complete with coach, castle and crown.

In the real world, our world, on June 2, the Air Force sent Dad to Spokane for a week of meetings. Mom and Steve went along. Bob and I still had a few days of school left so we stayed with Jack and Dorothy Cross.

It was interesting, being at the Crosses'. They lived on the Yaak River at a place known as "Two-Jacks." On the main road next to their mailbox was a sign that said "Two Jacks Cabins" and Jack Cross did indeed have two cabins on the river which he rented out to fishermen.

The Cross place was on a slow-moving section of the river where the water was deep and clear. Bob and I loved to go fishing there with Jack, who had practically grown up in the Yaak and knew millions of fishing secrets. We would drift slowly along in his boat and watch the trout way down below us. They would come two and three at a time, nibbling at our bait—canned corn—and then all of a sudden—whup! You had one!

There was a bridge across the river there called the "Two Jacks Bridge" and an old homestead on the far side, the Smoot place. Mr. Smoot was one of the men who organized the Yaak residents to build the Community Hall back in 1925. After the Smoots, Jack West and his son, Jack Jr., lived there. They were the "two Jacks" that gave the place its name. A number of others had lived there after that, but the old house, which was set low and close to the water, had been empty for years when Bob and I first explored it. It was an unusual house in the Yaak because although it was built of logs, it was painted white. It had big windows and a homey-looking porch facing the river. As nice as it looked though, Jack Cross told us the house flooded nearly every spring and that was why so many people got tired of trying to live there.

Dorothy and Jack Cross could haul their water from out on the bridge. There was a pulley and a rope out in the middle where the river water was deepest and ice cold. You would clip on a bucket, lower it to the water, then pull it up, brim full. It was a novelty for us, and Bob and I argued over who was going to get to haul up the next bucketful of water for Dorothy.

South of Crosses' place about a mile and a half as the crow flies, was Helmer's Lake. Bob and I loved it up there. We'd been up there twice the previous summer, hiking with Dad and Jack. You had to know where you were going, to find the Helmer's Lake trail. To get there, you crossed the Two Jacks Bridge and then followed an old road past the Smoot place to another deserted homestead, the Lang place. Up in the woods behind the Lang place, you watched for a narrow little trail that took off through the trees. It led southward to Vinal Creek and from there on up to the lake.

The lake itself was down in the bottom of a deep, thumb-print canyon with the trail running around the canyon-side about halfway up. You could start a rock rolling from up on the trail and watch it tumble faster and faster until it finally plunged into the water. A lonely old house overlooked the lake, with an odd little lookout tower perched on its roof and a rickety stairway that wound up inside of it. The walls of the house were papered with old newspapers from the 1920's. It was said Old Man Helmer was buried somewhere near the house and we'd looked around for the grave. We never found it. But if a ghost ever haunted anyplace, Old Man Helmer's ghost lurked in that tower. To Bob and me, Helmer's Lake was one of Dad's Jack London novels come to life: dangerous, spectacular, *The Call of the Wild*. It was irresistible. We were dying to get back up there.

Hiking up to Helmer's Lake was the first thing we thought of when we found out we were staying with the Crosses. Then Dad, the everlasting worrier, reminded us that on that trail you had to wade across Vinal Creek. This was early June and the creeks were still high and therefore dangerous. He told us to forget about hiking up to Helmer's Lake. This time of year it was out of the question. Boy, did we get tired of all that worrying!

That particular week, Saturday night was Community Hall night, so Jack and Dorothy were going up to the hall for most of the day to clean, sweep out the privies, haul in wood and water, and start the fires in the stoves. Mom and Dad were expected back sometime that afternoon and planned to pick us up wherever we might be, at Crosses' or at the Community Hall. After breakfast that morning, Jack and Dorothy got ready to go up to the hall. They asked us if we wanted to go along or stay home. We guessed we'd rather stay home. As soon as they left, we looked at each other: we were both thinking the same thing.

We could be up at the lake in no time, and back before anyone missed us.

We wrapped up some graham crackers in waxed paper—Dorothy was generous with graham crackers—and set out. Crossing the bridge, I pointed out to Bob that although the river was still high with runoff, the Smoot house wasn't the least bit flooded this year. That, right there, proved Vinal Creek couldn't be *too* high, either. And within minutes we were following the old road behind the Lang Place. There we stopped to count the coffee cans. The last residents, a couple by the name of Weideman, had disposed of coffee cans by turning them upside down over fence posts; we counted fifty-seven cans. Then we went into the woods behind the house and after some searching around, found the trail, a narrow path nearly overgrown with Oregon grape and pine grass. Pretty soon we were climbing up the hillside through a thick growth of lodgepole pine, toward Vinal Creek.

I have to admit, I was uneasy when the first sounds of noisy water came echoing down to us through the trees. When we reached the creek, we were shocked. Dad had been right. Vinal Creek, normally three or four feet across, was several feet outside its banks and carrying a huge amount of water. It was unbelievable. Last summer in August, we had tiptoed across on little stepping stones and hardly gotten our feet wet.

So much for this idea, we decided.

But Helmer's Lake, *The Call of the Wild* was unrelenting. We hung around the creek bank, threw rocks and dipped our feet in the icy pools along the edge and grew accustomed to the spectacle and roar of the water. We took daring leaps out onto the sunny tops of boulders and stood in the midst of the swirling current. We noticed all the logs, jammed every which-way in the creek.

Maybe we could find a good one, a good safe one, to get across on if we looked.

We started walking up and down the bank. I found a couple of places where logs were entangled, solidly spanning the creek. It looked like it would be simple to get across, so I climbed around and tried, but the water rushing so close underneath, made me uneasy. I knew Bob wouldn't like it either. So we kept looking. And somehow, in the midst of all that searching, I made up my mind: one way or another, we were going to get across that creek.

Finally we came to a good-sized tree that had tipped over, roots and all, and was hanging across the creek about four feet above the water. The green branches were thick and perfect for steadying yourself as you walked across. You hardly minded the water racing under you.

The top of the tree hung in mid-air a few feet above the ground on the far side. Once we got over there, it was an easy jump to the ground. Suddenly there we were, across the creek, safe and sound.

I was pretty proud of us. We hadn't given up, by golly. And we'd found a perfectly safe way to get across. Dad would be amazed. We'd been completely careful. After all, we were Yaakers.

Hell, I was twelve.

We had to climb over and scramble through a wide swath of windfall to get back up to the trail, but pretty soon we were on our way again. And we were so busy patting ourselves on the back as we hiked along, that we broke the Second Rule of Julius without even thinking about it: we walked away from our log bridge in the middle of all that tangle of windfall, without once looking back. Without bothering to give it a second glance.

Near its end, Vinal Creek trail goes up over a rise and suddenly you are standing with the lake about a hundred yards below you, down in a heavily timbered canyon. All you can see at first is a dark sparkle of water far below, through the trees. There is a wonderful echo from there and Bob and I exchanged hellos with it for a while. We rolled rocks and logs down the steep sides of the canyon and watched them splash into the water below us.

The trail circles around toward the abandoned house on the far side of the canyon rim. There we continued our search for a sign of the lost grave of Simon Helmer. Then we tramped around in the old house and climbed the dilapidated stairs into the tower. We ate our graham crackers up there, while a breeze drifted in and out of the empty window frames and ruffled the surface of the lake and the peeling newspaper on the walls. We thought up creepy stories about the ghost of Old Man Helmer. We imagined him weaving in and out of the tower windows at night, all black and rotted with fiery eyes, then ran down the stairs and outside, screaming like banshees. Then we decided to go down to the water, a pretty good downhill climb, for a quick skinny-dip.

It was even colder than our lake and very different on the bottom. Two steps from shore, you were in water over your head. I told Bob she better stay close to the bank.

Bob splashed around and I did cannonballs off a rock at the water's edge. But before we knew it, trees were shading the water and the air had turned cool. I realized all of a sudden that the time had gotten away from us.

I got cross when Bob wouldn't hurry up and get out of the water. It took her forever to get dressed. We were really going to get it, I told her, if we didn't get home *pronto*.

We climbed back up the steep canyon. It seemed twice as far going up. We headed back along the trail, glad it was mostly downhill. I said I guessed if we hurried we might have a chance to make it back before Jack and Dorothy got home.

June days are long in Montana. And I was surprised when I saw how low the sun was, as we came out of the trees. It was late. We were in trouble, no doubt about it. Ahead of us, we could hear the roar of the creek. When we got there, we were in for another mean surprise: we couldn't find our fallen tree.

We were tired, and climbing back over all that windfall seemed impossibly hard. We climbed all over the place but nothing looked familiar. Why hadn't we looked back and picked out a landmark? How could we have been so dumb? From this side of the creek, all we could see were acres of tangled logs.

Could it have been *upstream*? Could we be confused? People in the woods got confused when they were tired, we knew that. And tired, we were.

So we climbed back over to the trail and looked upstream. Which of course, was a waste of time. There was very little windfall there, so we realized it couldn't be right. We went back down and tried wading out in the shallows of the creek to peer across, hoping to see the base of our uprooted tree on the far side. All I could see was that our sunny June day was just about gone. Long shadows filled the woods and darkness had settled in the tangles of willow and brush along the creek. In the water, the eddying pools looked black and deep. I gave up worrying about what Dorothy and Jack were going to think, or worse, what a mess of trouble we were going to be in with Mom and Dad. I knew I needed to be worried about only one thing: how in the world were we going to get back across this creek?

And that's when I remembered with a sickish feeling in my stomach, that we'd broken the First Rule of Julius, too. Not a soul knew where we were.

We decided we had to try wading across. The ford was where the trail crossed. Maybe if we hung onto each other we could hold each other up in the current. We found the place, and from this side, the water there seemed shallower. I took Bob's hand and started in. It was freezing! I got in up to about my knees with the current rushing hard against my legs. I wasn't sure Bob was heavy enough to stand up in it.

After a few more steps I was in thigh-deep and not very steady on my feet. I couldn't see the bottom and the water moved so fast the rocks tumbled around wherever I stepped. Bob couldn't do this. Not a chance. "Go back!" I hollered, and we went back to the bank.

Bob turned around and glared at me with her hands on her hips.

"We can't get back across!" she announced, like she just discovered America. "This was your stupid idea!"

"I know!" I answered. "Just let me think a minute."

I hated how dark it was getting. Also, for some senseless reason, I hated all that rushing water in the dark. It seemed more treacherous and bigger, like a monster pouring out of the mountains.

But I knew what we needed to do. And I hated that worse than anything. "Bob," I said, "you're going to have to stay here."

Her face changed. She wasn't mad now, she was scared, so I jabbered on, trying to convince her without sounding panicky. "I have to get across and go home and get Dad! You know that's what he would tell us to do. You can't get across in that water, it's too swift!"

I knew it would be awful to stay there alone in the dark. But for once, Bob didn't argue. She knew as well as I did, it was the only thing we could do.

We found a huge, tall spruce tree right by the trail and not far from the creek. It had lots of thick branches spreading all the way to the ground and you couldn't possibly miss it, even in the dark. Bob crawled back underneath it and sat down. I said she had to promise she would wait there, without moving an inch, until Dad came to get her.

"He'll be here as quick as he can," I said. "And you know how fast he can walk!" All she said was, "Okay," but she sounded little and miserable. I hated leaving her there, under that tree.

I headed back to the creek with all kinds of things racing through my head: Is this how kids drown, doing stuff like this? What if I can't make it? Would anybody find us way up here? Dad is just going to die! Being scared is the worst thing there is. That Jack London stuff is malarkey!

I found a place where there were logs hanging down into the water from both sides of the creek. The water looked deep out in the middle. But I thought if I could make it out to the end of one log, I might be able to grab across to the log on the other side. I started across and was waist deep in no time. The cold was even worse than the current. I thought I could probably make it across okay, as long as I didn't fall. My shirt caught on a twig and I glanced backward toward the shore. There stood Bob.

"Go back!" I shouted. I screamed, "Damn it, go back! Damn you, Bob! You promised!"

Just then, if my hand hadn't caught hold of a sturdy branch underneath the water, I would have gone down. I would have gone head first and been swept under the log in front of me. I froze and braced myself. I realized I had to pay attention here, or else.

I reached across and caught the end of the log sticking out from the other side. I knew I'd made it then. I grabbed on, and hauled myself along the log and stumbled numb-footed up onto the bank. I turned around and saw Bob, still standing there. She looked like she'd shrunk down to about half her normal size, over there all by herself. I shouted as loud as I could, "You can't make it! Don't try!" I shook my head and waved my arms, motioning her away. "Go get under the tree! We'll come right back!"

I had no idea if she heard me or not, but while I stood there, I bent over and picked up a big rock. I hefted it, made ready to heave it at her if she made a move toward the creek. Finally, she turned away. I saw her walk back up the bank and she disappeared in the dark woods. I knew she was crying.

I waited a few more minutes, watched for her, didn't see her. Then I ran. Numb legs and all, I ran for all I was worth. "God! Don't let her try it!" I said out loud. My voice stayed in my ears after the roar of the water was gone. I could hear myself; I sounded exactly like what I was—a scared little girl.

There was still enough light to make out the trail and I kept on running, down the mountainside, around the Lang homestead, across the meadow to the Jack West place, across the bridge and finally, to Crosses' house.

The house was dark. There was nobody home.

I started to cry. I couldn't help it. I couldn't believe there was no one home. I went inside and when I saw the clock I was shocked. It was twenty minutes to ten! Of course there was nobody home! They were out looking for us!

I wasn't sure how to use one of the Yaak telephones, but Crosses had one. I didn't care who answered, I just needed somebody. I picked up the receiver and turned the crank three or four times and nothing happened. I cranked it again and shouted, "Hello! Hello!" into the crazy thing, but still, nobody answered. And then it struck me that nobody was going to answer. The ranger station was closed and probably everybody else in the valley was at the Community Hall.

Bob couldn't stay up there much longer. I knew her! She'd get tired of waiting and try to wade that creek. Should I go back? I guessed I had to! I'd leave a note and go back. Somebody would come.

I didn't know it then, but it was one of those perverse sets of circumstances that allow things to go perfectly wrong. Jack and Dorothy came home that afternoon planning to have an early dinner before the Community Hall meeting. When Bob and I weren't there, they figured Mom and Dad had come by and picked us up. They never dreamed we would go off on our own. At the same time, Mom and Dad were delayed getting back from Spokane. Until they walked into the Community Hall about nine-thirty that night, expecting to find us there with Jack and Dorothy, nobody even missed us.

I knew I would need a flashlight to find the trail. I started looking for one. I wonder how many hours people spent in the Yaak Valley in those days, looking for flashlights in the dark? I spent an age rummaging around in a kind of panic, through Dorothy's kitchen and bedroom drawers. Finally I realized I couldn't see, and lit a kerosene lamp. Then I continued to rake through cupboards. Finally I gave up on the flashlight. I'd just have to get back up to Vinal Creek without one. I began a wild search for a pencil and piece of paper to write a note.

My plan was crazy. I would have certainly gotten lost in the dark, up in the woods behind the old Lang place, trying to find that wisp of a trail. But some poor old worn-out guardian angel, if there are such beings, must have decided Bob and I could use some help, because all kinds of confusion filled my head and it slowed me down even more. It took me forever just to find a pencil in Dorothy's kitchen. Finally, I wrote a note, big letters, HELMERS LAKE TRAIL—STRANDED AT VINAL CREEK. Before I could get it situated underneath the lamp on the kitchen table, two sets of headlights were coming down the road. Weak-kneed with relief, I went out and stood in the driveway.

Our car was first. Mom jumped out and said, "Where on earth have you kids been?! You scared everybody to death!"

I hated to tell them. I hated even more to tell them how bad it really was.

I'm not sure exactly what went on then, in those next frantic minutes. Dorothy was apologizing over and over to Mom. Jack Cross, looking older than ever and very worried, said, "Dar, I'm afraid I'll slow you down if I try to go." Dorothy lit a kerosene lantern and gave it to Dad saying, "It's full." Mom had to go in the bedroom to take care of Steve, who was crying up a storm. Then all of a sudden, Dad and I were striding—he was striding, I was full out running to keep up with him—back up the trail toward Vinal Creek. Dad was mad. His jaw was set tight and he didn't say a word. He wouldn't have taken me along at all, except that I needed to show him where Bob was. All I could think was, *Please don't let Bob try to cross that creek.*

When we heard the sound of the water ahead of us, I got up the nerve to speak.

"There's a big spruce tree on the other side of the creek," I said, puffing for breath. "That's where I told her to stay."

I had hoped for a reply; I was disappointed. We just kept on going, our footsteps pounding as fast as we could travel, up the trail. We got to the creek and I felt a rush of relief when I saw the top of the big spruce. There it was, sticking up against the night sky. I pointed it out. "There. That's the tree where she is."

Dad was looking at the water.

He said, "God in heaven, Dee, what were you thinking?"

In the flood of light from the lantern, the fearful look on his face nearly knocked me off my feet.

I swear, that water was higher than it had been earlier that day. We never would have crossed it if it had been so wild and rushing as it looked to me then. We walked down to the edge and Dad handed me the lantern.

Without any hesitation at all, he stepped out into the dark water. He was waist deep in the middle and grabbed a bunch of partly-submerged willows to steady himself, then staggered on across. I held the lantern up as high as I could, but he disappeared on the other side. All I could see was black, roaring water. I stood there an endless time.

All of a sudden they came out of the dark, Dad, with Bob piggyback on his shoulders. They stopped at the edge of the water. Dad had a heavy branch in one hand and he poked it into the creek bottom to steady himself as he picked his way back across. Bob held on for dear life around his neck.

I was crying again, sobbing with relief, I guess. Dad took the lantern from me and we started back down the trail. We walked a ways with Bob still up on Dad's back, hugging him around his neck and patting his chest now and then. I was pushing tears out of my eyes with both hands so I could see to walk. After a while, Dad let Bob down. She was feeling pretty happy about how things had turned out. She started telling all about how we'd looked and looked for that darned old foot log but couldn't find it, no matter what. Finally Dad said in a strained voice, "Bob, I don't want to talk about it now."

When we got to the Lang homestead, Dad set down the lantern and we stopped to rest. After a minute he came over to me and put his arms around me. He held onto me tight, for a long time.

There was no place, no place else in the whole world I wanted to be.

CHAPTER 23

Guns, Horses
and Movie Stars

For Francine and me, everything was perfect that summer of 1953. We were old enough to go all over on the horses. We rode up to the Canadian border to see the forty-foot clearing. There it was, a swath through the timber that looked as if it had been cut with a giant lawn mower. It ran up and over mountains in a perfectly straight line, as far east and west as you could see. About a dozen times, we rode back and forth between the two countries:

"Now we're in Canada!"

"Now we're in America!"

"Now we're in Canada again!"

In between horseback rides, we'd swim in the lake. We had a new boat to row around in. Dad had ordered it from the catalog back in the fall. It came, dozens of pieces of wood in a box, and he had put it together over the winter with lots of wood glue, filler and elbow grease. He painted it green and christened it "Half-Pint." It was intended for fishing but as long as we wore our life jackets we could row it wherever we wanted. Sometimes we just drifted, letting the breeze carry us. We loved the far side of the lake where the water was shaded by a stand of lodgepole. Pink "water lilies," as we called them, floated in the shallows.

Then we'd be back on the horses or over at Conleys' again, sitting up in their barn talking about boys and sex. Francine filled me in on all the bits and pieces I'd heard at school. I discovered most of it was actually *true!*

Between us, Bob and me, and the Conley kids, we must have made a million trips back and forth from our place to theirs. If we were on foot, we always went the back way: up along our creek to the river, then along the river past the old Hoskins and Benefield places, through a section of woods to Conleys' meadow, then up the meadow road to their house. Francine and I grew so familiar with that mile-and-a-half walk that both of us could make the trip alone after dark and not think a thing about it.

My friend, Laurence Harding who had his very own hunting rifle, had taken me shooting a couple of times, unbeknownst to either of our parents. I became fascinated when I looked through the scope sight of his gun. All you had to do was put those cross hairs on the target and squeeze. It wasn't hard! We threw a cocoa can out in their lake and waited until it drifted way out, about a hundred yards, then we took turns shooting. He sank it of course, with one shot, but I came near to hitting it; we saw it move in the water.

Pat Conley was fourteen that summer, and also had her own .22 rifle. Just to be ornery, she decided to give me and not her "spoiled" sister, Francine, shooting lessons. Pat's gun had a peep sight and was harder to aim than a scope. But we practiced for hours, lining cans up on the fence rail, and shot box after box of shells, until I could hit every can all the way across without a miss. Eventually Pat gave in and allowed Francine to join us. We all went gopher hunting in Conleys' meadow. The gopher holes were dangerous for the horses, so Mr. Conley said to get rid of every single critter if we could. We shot gophers for two days, taking turns. We sang the awful song, "Great Green Gobs of Greasy Grimy Gopher Guts" as we carried the dead critters by the tails and put them in piles for the coyotes to eat.

Finally, after hours of safety lectures, Dad gave in and took me out shooting with his .22. I was used to hearing about gun safety all the time, since we had guns in our house—everyone in the Yaak did. But Dad went over everything with me all over again, about what you did and didn't do with a gun. You never ran, or climbed a fence with a gun, you set the gun through the fence on the ground and then you climbed over. You always kept a gun pointed toward the sky and the safety on unless you were ready to aim at your target. And the main thing to remember, Dad preached, over and over, was that there was *no such thing as an unloaded gun!*

"But what if—"

"No such thing!"

"Even when—"

"No...such...thing, Dee! Period!"

We went walking out over our own meadow and I eliminated a dozen or so of our gophers in short order, proud of my shooting skill. There was no doubt about it, Dad said, I was a pretty good shot. But when I asked if I could go out shooting by myself he said there would still be several hundred gophers out there when I was another year older.

The northeast end of the Yaak Road went up the East Fork of the Yaak River and finally came out at Rexford. This section of the road was called "Dodge Summit." We had come into the Yaak Valley that first time from Canada, over Dodge Summit. It was said you weren't a real Yaaker until you had driven over Dodge Summit in the wintertime.

The East Fork of the Yaak was one of the earliest parts of the valley to be settled. That's where the Phillipses lived and also the movie stars, the McIntires.

That summer we became acquainted with Big John Phalen. In a valley that was already full of unusual people, Big John stood out. He worked for John McIntire and Jeanette Nolan, taking care of their place up on Basin Creek whenever they were in Hollywood making movies. He was a great, big, rosy-faced man with a full white beard and head of hair. He came as close to looking like Santa Claus as any human ever could.

John McIntire came to the Community Hall one Saturday night. We had a square dance caller up from Troy, so everyone was dancing. Francine and I were partners and McIntire was in our square. I was nervous when I had to dance with him. He was tall; I mainly remember his belt buckle.

Big John drove all over the valley in his old army jeep, Florabelle. And, like the Binders, he might just show up at your house anytime for a visit. He liked whiskey and once the Dirty Shame was up and running, he started going down there to "socialize." Sometimes he socialized so much that he had to pull off on the side of the road on the way home and sleep out the night in his jeep. He did that summer and winter and didn't seem bothered a bit by the cold. He came to our house one day when Francine was there and took the two of us for a ride in Florabelle. We went careening up and down the West Fork road and over to the sawmill and back. Honestly, I was glad when it was over. It was worse than a runaway horse.

Mom, Bob, Stevie and I went up to see Big John one day because he'd been sick. Dede Hall was with us. John's cabin on Basin Creek was perched on a hill above the creek. Like Crosses, he had a pulley arrangement to get his water, but his was even more fun because the bucket sailed down out of sight when you sent it to the creek. You could hear it splash into the water and then you could pull it up. John had a dog named "Dog." When he called him, he'd say, "Where's Dog?" and Dog would come. While we were there visiting, Dede asked John if he was planning on coming to the Community Hall on Saturday night. John answered, "I guess I'll hafta turn m' shirt inside out and come." Bob and I thought he was hilarious.

While we were all there visiting, Jeanette Nolan herself came riding down the Mount Henry trail on her horse. She was dressed in buckskin from head to foot and her black hair was pulled back in a clip at the back of her neck. I really did think she looked like a star in a movie, then and there. Again, I noticed her beautiful smile. She reached down and took Steve from Mom and sat him up on her horse in front of her. She fussed over him and called him a sweet little lamb. That day the sun set on the heroine of my childhood, Cousin Anne. For a long time afterward, I thought if I ever could be like somebody else, I wanted to be like Jeanette Nolan.

CHAPTER 24

The Curious and
The Curiouser

Some odd things happened that fall. The first was the Yaak Post Office closing. After thirty-three years, Icie Betzer was retiring. On the thirtieth of September, 1953, she took down the U.S. Post Office sign. All our mail would be routed through Troy and our new address would be, "Route 1, Troy, Montana." The ladies in the valley put on a huge party at the Community Hall for Icie. Mom was on the decorating committee and made four lemon meringue pies for the occasion. Icie got a corsage made of pansies and the governor sent her a special award for all her years of service. It was the end of an era, Mom said.

And at the Community Hall that night, there were some strange happenings. They were never fully explained to Bob and me. All we heard was that a disagreement arose over how much coffee was to be used in the big, Community-sized coffee pots. Alma Phillips was heard to exclaim, "I've been making coffee in these pots for fifteen years!"

A while later, in the hubbub and confusion in the kitchen, it was discovered that somehow all four of Mom's lemon meringue pies, lined up with the other desserts on the back table beside the roaring cookstove, had somehow gotten coffee spilled all over them. They were ruined and had to be thrown out. Alma Phillips, sweet as pie herself, said, "Oh, Marilyn, what a shame! Well, we had too many desserts anyway."

Later, sometime during the ceremony for Icie, the entire platter of Alma Phillips' famous fried chicken disappeared. Alma was shocked. Everyone else was mystified.

That night, driving home, Dad kept looking across the car at Mom, then chuckling and shaking his head. Mom was staring straight ahead, into the night.

Figuring we were asleep and not wanting to wake us, Dad asked in his quietest voice, "What did you do with it?"

Mom shrugged her shoulders.

After a few minutes Dad said, ever so quietly, "Dump it in the fire?" and Mom fell into a fit of stifled giggles. Months later, an empty platter was found in the Community Hall, on the floor underneath the cookstove.

Another odd thing was *really* odd. Almost too odd to talk about.

One night, in the middle of the night, an Air Force pickup came driving into our yard. Dad heard the motor and was out of bed right away. Before he could get his pants on, someone was knocking at the door.

We heard a short, hushed conversation in the kitchen, and minutes later, as soon as Dad could get the rest of his clothes on, he drove off with the person in the pickup.

We had a party at our house for the air force base personnel. There were several couples, some of their names being Oschner, Hoabie, Jablonski, Norton, and Torgarson. A few of the men were musicians and one, Woody Woodruff, was a wonderful singer. They crowded into our tiny living room and played for us.

The next morning, when we got to school, the news had spread like wildfire:

A flying saucer had landed up at the radar site!

Of course, nobody believed it. But everybody was talking about it. Gradually, as various Air Force personnel stopped by the Dirty Shame, information leaked into the Grapevine.

The airmen that were on duty that night, up on top of the mountain—nobody was sure just who they were—had seen a brightly-lit object come down out of nowhere, hover over a nearby hill, drift closer and closer to them, and then land, not far from the radome, the bubble-like structure that housed the radar apparatus. Being a military installation, there were weapons available, so the men got rifles and went out toward the thing. It was saucer-shaped. Lights pulsed all around the rim. Suddenly, without knowing why, the men dropped their rifles and ran back to their building. Soon after, the lights on the "saucer" grew very bright and it lifted off and "jack-rabbited" across the mountaintops and eventually disappeared from sight.

Had they picked it up on the radar? No one knew. How many people had seen it? That was unclear. What was the official word on what it was? That was also unclear.

Bob and I figured we had a direct route to inside information. But Dad used his favorite word, "malarkey" and told us just to forget about it.

"Forget about it?! How can we forget about a thing like that? One of the kids in school saw a movie in town, *Invaders from Mars*. What if Martians are coming here? Are there really such things as flying saucers?!"

Dad told us we needed to calm down. Sometimes people misunderstood what they saw. That's what probably happened at the base, he said. Maybe somebody'd spent too much time at the Dirty Shame. No. There were no flying saucers from Mars.

"Then why do we need an Air Force base in the Yaak?"

"To warn the country in case of an attack."

"What kind of an attack?"

Dad looked irritated. He was tired of this conversation. But he sat down and looked long at the two of us. Finally he said, "The world is changing. There are dangerous weapons now, that enable one country to do a great amount of damage to another. So we have to protect ourselves." He said it again: "The world is changing. It always will be."

"What countries?"

"Russia. The United States. But," he said, getting up from his chair, "most certainly not Mars."

I didn't know what to think. Sometimes it seemed like Armageddon was the least of our problems.

Chapter 25

On Top of
the World

Summer, 1954. I was thirteen and invincible and healthy as a horse. I started out by winning the battle of the gophers. I was allowed to take the .22 out at last, and with my head drilled full of "be careful"s, I stalked around in our meadow after the umpteen jillion gophers that inhabited it. Our new rearing pond was going to flood the whole area anyway, Dad said, so I might as well have at 'em. And I did; I was an absolute deadeye. Piles of gophers were left behind for coyotes. Like rabbits, dozens more appeared, and within days, they too, were coyote food.

Then I attacked the lake.

Countless times, kids, visitors, relatives and friends had asked if I'd swum across it yet. Not if I *could* swim across it, or if I *wanted to*, but just if I had. As if it would be so *easy*! As if, well, I lived there and swam all the time, so why hadn't I swum across it yet? It made me furious. The summer before, Francine had dared me to try. She followed beside me in the boat. Using a combination of the Australian crawl and my own brand of breast-stroke/dog-paddle, I worked my way to the middle. I stopped, and treading water long enough to reconnoiter, had to admit that it was farther than I thought. Even Francine's "Humph!" couldn't get me going enough to make it across. I finally had to grab onto the rope trailing off the back of the boat and allow her to tow me in.

This year was different. Bob was my tender. And we both knew I was going to make it, even before I started. "I want to go straight across the middle," I said to her, "so keep me on course." She did. And I did. Right straight across, without stopping. I touched bottom and stood up on the rocky, opposite shore thinking, *Now!* Just let somebody ask me. I can say, "Yeah, you bet I have! I swam across it on July tenth, nineteen fifty-four!"

Bob the smart-aleck asked if I wanted to ride back, or was I planning to swim?

I was on top of the world.

I had my friend Francine to pal around with and there were a couple of new boys staying in a cabin in our end of the valley that we thought were pretty interesting. Pat Conley, up to her usual mean tricks with her sister, allowed me—*me!*—to ride her precious Babe. One day after Elmer Phillips was all finished bull-dozing our new rearing pond and building the dike across our meadow, I galloped Pat's gorgeous palomino all the way across the dike. Blue water, blue sky, the perfect horse, the perfect place, the perfect day. It really was, without a doubt, the most fun I'd ever had.

I was only vaguely aware that, all summer long, Dad was struggling with his major project. After all the hours of reading and research about waterwheels and electricity and the raising of wild trout for commercial use, the real work had begun. Dad and Elmer used a transit to do some measuring across the new rearing pond area and along the creek. Then, for days, Dad stood out on the new dike as it grew, yard by yard across our meadow. Dad had his clipboard, Elmer was on the bulldozer, the two of them shouted back and forth over the noise of the engine. Later, while Elmer continued work on the dike, Dad started the process of hand-digging the new, short spillway that would divert water from the creek over a six-foot waterfall and then into the lake, instead of down the original, gradually-sloping channel past the house. Eventually, the waterfall would drive the waterwheel to make electricity for our fish operation and, hopefully, for our house. Dad lined the new spillway with heavy timbers and put in a head-gate to control the flow out of the creek. Then he installed a second head-gate on the main creek so he could completely divert the water over the new spillway whenever he wanted to. Finally, he built a wheelhouse to shelter the whole works. Like everything else Dad built, it was made to last. It had a sturdy wood floor with an opening beneath the flume for the water to fall through. The water would drop from the end of the flume over the waterwheel, then down through the opening in the floor and out along the base of the dike for about fifty feet, where it would empty into the lake. All of this turned out to be "one miserable son of a bitch of a job," according to Dad. Over and over, he marveled at how Henry Binder had accomplished the feat of widening the entire creek by hand, all the way to the river, all those years ago.

In the course of his project Dad had taken various cups and glasses out with him to dip up a cool drink from the creek whenever he needed to. He had managed to lose or break quite a few. Finally he discovered a particular cup that hung nicely on a twig on a nearby pine tree and it lasted longer than most, before it too, disappeared, probably underneath the growing pile of rocks next to the new wheelhouse. Someday an archaeologist exploring the Yaak Valley will come across a silver baby cup with my name on it, and wonder how the heck it got there.

Of course, once the rest of us were able to see that Dad's grand vision was actually coming together, we got all excited, especially about the prospect of electricity. But Dad said, first things first. First, we had to get the rearing pond filled and allow the water to settle so we would be ready for the fry—the tiny trout hatchlings—when Elmer was ready to plant them.

CHAPTER 26

Gathering
Clouds

Mom had her own struggle going that summer. She had a couple of difficult projects. I was one of them. She seemed to be after me constantly. If I wasn't spending too much time with Francine, I was spending too much time with my nose in a book. My jeans and shoes were sloppy. My hair was a disgrace; I needed a permanent. My table manners were appalling; I ate like a lumberjack. For that, I had my pat comeback: "I'm as hungry as a lumberjack!"

One night in bed I overheard her complaining to Dad.

"It's just a shame when the most important thing in the world to a girl of that age is how good a shot she is with a twenty-two! She's getting rough around the edges. They both are. And of all things, she refuses to wear a bra!"

Mom's other struggle began as she watched the early stages of Dad's waterwheel project. He was working too hard out there, she said, and she decided she couldn't stand it. She had an idea there might be an easier way.

Over the past couple of years some of the Yaak residents had tossed around the idea of getting an electric power line put into the valley. Mom and a group of her friends got together in Mrs. Grush's kitchen and decided to give the project a try. They composed a letter to Senator Mike Mansfield asking for help and advice. The senator responded, writing a nice personal note of encouragement to each one of the ladies. On his advice they set out to circulate a petition among the valley residents, asking every family to contribute ten dollars and sign up for the service. According to information from the Rural Electric Association, if the Yaak Air Force Base would sign on, the project would surely go ahead. But even without the base, if enough residents signed up, it would still be feasible to bring power to the valley.

All fired up, Mom and her friends went out with copies of the petition and large manila envelopes to hold all the money. Mom ended up with a single ten-dollar bill to show for her efforts. "It's fine the way it is," was the opinion of many of the Yaakers.

The Air Force base passed. It had its own power plant.

Of the people Mom contacted, Julius Binder alone said he wouldn't mind having an electric light in his cabin, and had pulled out his wallet and given her a ten.

She was flabbergasted. "Doesn't anybody want things to be a little bit *easier?*" she said. "You'd think they'd want to see some *progress* once in a while!"

Late one night I overheard this kitchen conversation:

"Well as far as I know, all the Yaak kids board in town."

"But she seems…so young for that."

"Well it's still more than a year away. But, yes, you're right, she does."

"How often do you think we can get her home?"

"Whenever there's a ride, I guess. We'll go and get her as often as we can. Depends on the roads."

"I can't imagine her living away from home."

"Isn't there some kind of an academy somewhere?"

"Yes. Gary Harding is going to the Adventist academy at Spangle, Washington. But that's so far away!"

Either the conversation ended there, or I stopped listening.

In late July, we began to hear about forest fires up in Canada. The air became hazy with smoke. Some days the sun was a blood-red ball in a brown sky.

The ranger from Sylvanite came by one afternoon and told Mom we needed to keep an eye on the situation in our end of the valley. If ever we saw flames on the mountains to the north, Lick Mountain or Bonnet Top, we needed to "get the aitch outa here, as fast as you can." But a few nights later we heard that the fires were all under control, and we didn't have to worry. We sat on the porch and watched the sun go down, still blood red in the smoky air. And there were sure a lot of gnats around, Mom remarked, so we went inside.

When it was dark, and the Coleman was blazing away in the kitchen and we were starting to think about bed, Mom stared suddenly at the kitchen window and said, "Oh my God. Look!"

There were gnats, millions, probably billions of gnats, covering the window. A solid swarm, inches thick, moved like a piece of wool against the glass. Almost immediately, we noticed there were swarms flying around inside the house, all around the lamps. "Close the windows!" Mom hollered, and we all hurried to do it. Gnats were streaming in through the screens. Too late, we saw that the house was full. There were clouds, swarms, everywhere.

"Oh...Oh God!" said Mom. Her voice was frantic. She flailed at gnats in her face and stumbled to a chair, reaching out for Stevie and pulling him to her. She huddled over him.

We all knew Mom didn't mind a few bugs; none of us did, but this made your hair stand on end.

"Blow out the lamps," Dad ordered, moving quickly to turn off the Coleman. I hustled into the living room and bedroom and blew those out, too. You couldn't avoid inhaling bugs. It was horrible.

"It's the forest fires," Dad said, bending over Mom in her huddle. "Bugs are trying to get out of the—*pfooh!*—smoke."

Dad stumbled off through the buggy darkness and came back with a blanket. He waved it up and down and then let it settle over Mom and Steve. Then we stood there in the dark, breathing through our hands, not sure what to do. Mom wiggled and brushed at bugs underneath the blanket. Stevie, buried under there with her, said, "Bugs, bugs, bugs!" and we all had to laugh, even Mom. Bob and I pulled chairs over and sat alongside them. We pulled our shirttails up over our mouths and noses to breathe.

Dad took the Coleman down from its hook and carried it outside, away from the house. He re-lit it and left it on the ground, way out near the creek. He came back in, waving great clouds of bugs out of the way as he moved, and left the kitchen door standing open. He was covered in bugs. They were in his hair, down his neck, everywhere, you could see them shining in the light from the lantern in the yard. I helped him brush off. We watched as a thick cloud grew around the lamp, obscuring the bright white mantles. The air in the house got better.

Steve was wriggling on Mom's lap and Dad was standing over her. "Okay, Butch?" he said. She nodded weakly, still huddled, and he sat down beside her in the dark kitchen. "God almighty," he said, and I agreed. That many bugs would give anybody the creeps. But I couldn't help feeling surprised that such a little thing, harmless, tiny gnats, bothered Mom, *my* mom, so much.

After a while, through her hands and from underneath the blanket, Mom murmured something I didn't want to hear.

"I don't know about this anymore, Dar. I just don't know."

In the early daylight, about five, I woke up to the sound of Mom and Dad brushing and sweeping up piles of gnat bodies. The window sills were two inches deep in gnats. All the furniture, our beds, blankets, even—Yuck!—our pillows, were covered with dead gnats. We spent all day cleaning. It would be weeks before we stopped finding remnants of the gnat plague.

By the month of August, Dad was ready to put his plans into action. The meadow that was to become the rearing pond had been scraped out clean. The bottom was hard-packed clay, sloping gradually toward the dike that separated it from the main lake. The dike had been raised and graded and was wide enough to drive a car across and had a culvert in place, connecting the pond area with the lake.

Elmer had spent several more days with the tractor, working on our road out where the lake overflowed every spring. The road bed was now several feet higher so the lake would no longer overflow, but could be contained at a new, higher level. Dad went up to the main head-gate on the river and, for the first time since we had lived there, opened it wide, to allow the maximum amount of water to come down our creek. Our babbling little creek became a millrace.

We all went out to watch when Dad was ready to open the new spillway into the wheelhouse. One at a time, he pried up the thick planks of the head-gate that held back the water. After the first two, a sheet of water slid over the dry surface of the new flume and then—*ploppety-plop*—fell the six feet from the end of the flume through the hole in the floor of the wheel house to the dry dirt below. Dad got another plank pried up and another six inches of water slid through the gate. The last plank came up, the flume filled, and within seconds we had a full-fledged waterfall pounding down through the wheelhouse. From there the water flowed along the base of the dike and into the lake. In the original creek bed, the water level dropped to a narrow trickle. There would be just enough water left flowing there to keep the kitchen pump going, Dad said. We would need all the flow possible through the wheelhouse in order to power a waterwheel.

Dad stood back and was pleased with the whole thing. Our waterfall was sufficient to produce power. The flow into the lake was almost double what it had been. Soon the lake would rise and water would flow through the cul-vert into the rearing pond. So far, every-thing was working as planned.

Mom, Bob and I were fascinated by these new attrac-tions for about a week, but then they became less inter-esting as things like that, even water-falls, always do. We were anxious to get on with the project. Dad watched and measured daily to see how the level of the lake was rising. First things first, he reminded us.

Stevie, Dee, Flossie, and Bob during their last days in the Yaak, at the Crosses' cabin.

Long story short: the rearing pond didn't fill. Even after three weeks of wide-open flow, the water only lapped at the lower lip of the new culvert. There, mysteriously, the level of the lake stopped rising. It was higher than anyone had ever seen it, but it had to rise another four feet, Dad figured, before the pond would fill and become deep enough. He put stakes in the ground at different locations to mark the water line, and checked them daily. To his amazement, some days the level actually dropped.

He was dumbfounded. He couldn't sleep. He paced and grumbled. Measured. Brought Elmer down to look; Elmer was just as puzzled. Daily, Dad walked up the creek, armed with his rifle and a pitchfork, to remove any sign of a beaver dam or a "damn beaver." The creek continued to run wide open. Still, the water level of the lake stayed the same. The rearing pond was nothing but a shallow mud-puddle.

In a frustrated outburst, Dad said, "God almighty, what am I going to have to do, divert the whole damn river?"

One day, August and Julius came over. August's back had been giving him trouble lately, so they drove Julius's pickup. Instead of coming to the door, the two men ambled across the front yard and down to the edge of the lake. They stood there together, talking, August gesturing out over the water with his pipe, Julius standing and listening, as usual, lean Levi-legs spread apart, hands on his hips. Dad went down to talk with them.

"So, you gonna fill 'im up, dere, Darwin," said August, poking his pipe at the lake.

Dad shook his head to show how exasperated he'd become lately, and said, "Well, yes, I'm sure trying to."

August looked thoughtful for a minute and then he said, "You tink maybe ve got somehow a flow, from your lake to mine?

Dad stared at his two neighbors. "What do you mean?" he said.

Julius said, "Our lake is about to flood out the ice-house and the garden. Ve nefer seen it so high, even in the spring."

Dad climbed into Binders' pickup and rode home with them. He came back about an hour later. When he came in the house, his underbite jaw was tight and there were deep creases across his forehead.

"*Binders'* lake is rising!" he announced to all of us. He shook his head as if to clear his brain. "Can you believe it? They've just about lost their ice house! There must be an underground outlet in our lake that is filling theirs! What in the hell can anybody do about a crazy thing like that?!"

The answer was, nothing. No one, not even Elmer Phillips, knew what to do about an underground outlet somewhere in the bottom of a lake. Dad went up to the river and closed down the headgate so the flow in our creek returned to its earlier level. Sure enough, in two weeks' time, Binder's lake went down. Their icehouse was safe. Their garden, high and dry once again.

A short time later, Dad diverted the creek back into its old bed and the new channel and the wheelhouse were abandoned. Without the added flow there wasn't enough water power to run a waterwheel, he explained to us. It seemed we were not destined to have electricity. And we were not going to become a trout farm, either.

CHAPTER 27

Odds and Ends

I didn't allow these things to affect me very much. I wasn't really inter-ested. I wanted to ride, swim, target practice, sit by myself up in the now silent wheelhouse where I wouldn't be bothered, and read.

School started. Eighth grade. We were the big kids now. Best at everything in the classroom and on the playground. For me, life was absolutely as it should be, complete with a boyfriend; Laurence and I were bona fide boyfriend and girlfriend now. Near his place there is a tamarack with a heart carved into the bark with LH + DK inside it. We kissed some. Anything more, and I panicked. But we would just keep on growing up together, I assumed irrationally, forever.

At home, Mom put me in charge of things once in a while so she and Dad could get away together. I didn't mind. It wasn't my first choice, but if I had to, I could potty my brother and get him to eat better than Mom could, I could keep my sister in line most of the time, split wood and handle the wood stoves, cook, haul water, do whatever else was needed, even drive the pickup down to get gas if the roads were dry. I didn't know about the rest of my family, but I was sure what was best for me was right here, right now, and from now on. I was in my element.

I paid as little attention as possible to the frustrations of my parents. They seemed silly. Mom got an insane yen for avocados. She wrote to both grocery stores in Troy and was terribly disappointed when they couldn't send some. She said, what was she going to have to do, drive all the way to Spokane? Dad spent every single Monday night fighting with our stubborn old battery radio, trying to tune in *The Voice of Firestone*. The reception was always terrible, of course, and you would have thought hearing Richard Tucker sing "Vesti La Giubba" was a major world event and we were the only people on earth missing it.

With electricity gone from the horizon, Mom went out and bought a gas-powered washing machine. The motor was nearly as loud as our old light plant. But the clothes agitated clean, and there was an honest-to-goodness wringer to feed them through. It saved an enormous amount of work. It sat outside on the back porch in between uses. Of course, as soon as the weather got cold, it wouldn't start, so it was back to the boiler and plunger and wringing by hand for the winter.

Then Mom jumped with both feet into a new development in the valley, the Pinetoppers Women's Club. She helped make the hand-printed handbooks and took on the job of club treasurer. There were close to thirty members. They met monthly for a potluck lunch and did needlework projects. They always had a discussion topic like "My Favorite Casserole" or "My Pet Peeve." Mom and Dede Hall organized a Labor Day picnic at our place. Mom got ice from Binders' ice house and made

As her clothing shows, Mom truly wasn't prepared for this surprise birthday party. She's seated in her wingback chair, and Stevie is in the foreground. From left, seated: Marge Beck, Rosy Shultz, Mom, Vera Vandervere, unknown, Dede Hall, Jerry Hall; standing, Ruth Norton, Dorothy Cross, Rosie Sandborn, Alma Philips.

homemade ice cream for the whole group. Pretty soon, though, she had to admit, Pinetoppers was too much work and she didn't have the time.

During hunting season that fall, Mom and Dad went out together one Saturday. They were strolling along a deer trail up behind the place known then as "the Carlton Place," where Dede and Gib Hall lived. It was across the river from the Upper Ford Ranger Station and had once been owned by Carlton E. Morse, the man who wrote *One Man's Family* for the radio.

They hadn't started seriously hunting. They weren't expecting any deer that close to the main road. But all at once, a black bear rose up out of the trees on the hillside in front of them.

Bears were unusual in the Yaak at that time. For years, old timers had considered bears purely a nuisance and shot them whenever possible. The homesteaders had done a good job of clearing them out of the valley by the early Fifties.

But the woods are still the woods, and it was fall, and there, definitely, about thirty feet up the trail, was a bear. Mom and Dad stopped dead in their tracks, not quite sure what to do.

The bear decided. The people were too close; it was a reflex. He dropped to all fours and started toward them.

Dad raised his gun. That, too, was a reflex. He fired. The bear stopped as if he had suddenly changed his mind. He lay slowly down in the trail as if he had decided to take a nap instead.

Mom and Dad stayed where they were, half expecting the bear to rise to his feet again. They were sure he couldn't have been killed so easily.

After a while, with Mom holding aim on the bear, Dad approached, cautiously. Finally he was standing right over the animal. There was no blood. No sign of a wound. It was eerie. In a quiet voice, Dad said, "Watch him, Tweet. I'm not sure about this." He picked up a stick and poked at the black heap. Nothing moved.

After several minutes and more poking, Dad was convinced the animal was dead, he just wasn't sure how or why. Finally, he noticed something odd about one eye. He looked close and saw that one eye was gone, and in its place was a black, bloodless hole.

ご

"Good shot," said Julius, looking over the shaggy black heap in the back of our pickup. "Sure. You can dress 'im out. I'll help. But you nefer gonna eat 'im, you know, ven you see 'im dressed out."

They did the job in the woodshed and Julius was right. Grisly as it sounds, a skinned-out bear looks very much human. It was so horrible, Mom said, it would give us all nightmares. So we didn't eat the bear meat, we gave it all away. But we did render out the lard and it made wonderful pie crust. Dad had the hide made into a rug; teeth, claws, everything. Once the two little fake glass eyes were in place, you couldn't even tell which one had taken the bullet.

That year we had more than the usual number of coyotes. They were probably drawn to our place by all my piles of gophers, and as the snow got deeper, the coyotes got bolder. They started playing a deadly little game with our dog. With the pack waiting in the trees, one coyote would come prancing out on the snow in plain sight and kick up a howl. Even coyote-proof Flossie was fascinated. The coyote would rear up on its hind legs and wave its front paws in the air, *ki-yi-ing* playfully. If Flossie was out in the yard, she would whine and prance with excitement. We mentioned this to Julius and he warned us to keep Flossie inside at night and not let her venture out into the woods. He said the coyotes would actually attack and eat her. He knew of people who had lost dogs that way.

Midwinter that year, Mom and Dad took Steve and went to town for the weekend and left Bob and me home. By then, Bob and I were quite the self-sufficient pair, the two of us. We knew how to bank the fire in the heater stove at night, how to work all the dampers and drafts in both the stoves. We had been brainwashed into being scared stiff of anything that might cause a fire so we handled the lamps with enormous care. We could both split wood and I was perfectly capable of taking the axe down to the creek, chopping a hole in the ice and hauling in a day's worth of water.

That weekend the coyotes came around in broad daylight, and the prancing decoy tried his tricks in a new spot, right across the creek from the house, up on the edge of the snow-covered dike. Flossie whined constantly.

"I'm going to solve this problem once and for all," I crowed, and brought out my .22. Steadying it against the side of the open doorway, I took aim and shot. We saw something red fly up from the snow. Instantly, the coyote dropped, disappearing from sight behind the dike. "I hit him!" I yelled. "Did you see that?! I got the bugger, by golly!" Bob let out a cheer.

A day later when Dad went with us to look for the body, all that was left was bloody snow and lots of tracks. He'd been eaten by the others, no doubt. It was entirely satisfying.

See, you had a problem, you solved it, no more problem.

Later on that winter, Dad and I went hunting. This time it was a serious trip. We needed meat. We both knew I was ready for this. I was armed with "Iron Mike," Dad's best deer rifle, a .32 Winchester Special with a peep sight. I'd been target practicing; I was deadly.

We went early, in the dark, drove for about a half hour, and then parked the pickup in a wide spot and set out through the woods in deep snow. With barely enough light to see, Dad led the way and soon we were walking easily and silently along a deer trail that followed an old logging road. After about a quarter mile, we left the trail and waded through the snow a short way into the trees. Ahead was a meadow where the gray shapes were already gathered, browsing on willows. Dad motioned me to use a nearby tree as a rest. I took aim.

And I aimed.

And aimed.

"Shoot," Dad whispered.

"Shoot, Dee," he said again. This was serious business going on here. But I couldn't. I don't know why. I just couldn't.

Heaven knows, I'd seen enough deer killed by then. I'd shot enough other things. But then and there, I couldn't shoot a deer myself.

Was I afraid I would miss? No. I knew I wouldn't. Was it because this wasn't a game? Maybe. I'd been upped a level and if you killed food, you were an adult. Was that it?

Whatever the reason, Dad finally got tired of waiting, raised his own rifle, his old M-1, and fired. We dragged the deer home on the snow and neither of us said much. I never knew if he understood what went on that day any better than I did. He teased me once in a while about "buck fever" but he wasn't serious. It remains one of those questions about what happens inside your head when you're halfway between being a kid and growing up, that you never quite understand.

Eighth Grade Graduation was at the Community Hall and everyone in the valley attended. I wore my graduation dress, a pale blue nylon, embossed with white flowers, a flowered tiara in my hair and my first pair of high shoes, white wedgie sandals with tiny rhinestones on the toes. And nylons, of course. And my new watch, my graduation gift, a delicate circle of white gold on my wrist.

We had printed programs, run off at the school on the mimeograph machine. The four of us, the Class of '55, sat side by side facing the audience with the podium in front of us. I was valedictorian and had rehearsed my speech carefully, but was scared half out of my wits. How I got through it, I'll never know. A lady from the Air Force base with a beautiful voice sang "You'll Never Walk Alone." Carl Cummings, head of the school board, handed out our diplomas.

Afterwards, when everyone was cleaning up, our rambunctious little Steve, wearing a cowboy hat, was running loose all over the hall with a knot of little kids. Bob was sticking close to Gracie Cummings. I went around with my parents, accepting congratulations and, along with Mom and Dad, saying our good-byes to everybody. Before the end of the month, we would be moving away.

I'd gotten used to the idea over the past few months. We all had. It wasn't easy. I'd heard all the reasons, cried, even threatened to run away once, but I didn't mean it. I'd begun to realize I was wrong. This wasn't a place for Bob and me to become adults. It had been a wonderful adventure but the wide world was out there. We had our educations to think about. Mom and Dad had come down to earth. They weren't kids anymore. The valley was changing. Of course the important thing was that we all be together, wherever we were. After lying awake for months worrying about boarding school, I especially agreed with this last point. I might be able to run our home in the Yaak all by myself, but the thought of leaving it behind and going away to high school, scared my socks off.

Mom was hugging with all her friends and Dad was shaking hands around. Alma Phillips and Mom did their duty and hugged each other. No problem there, saying goodbye.

Dee and Bob, in 1955, at the kitchen doorway.

All the kids promised to write letters. I promised back. Laurence and I promised. We would see each other soon, was what we said. I wasn't grieving any more. I was ready to get on with it.

We had sold the place easily, to a man by the name of Besley. He came around one day after the deal was closed to look things over. He climbed out of his big black pickup wearing a pistol in a fancy leather holster. He never moseyed around much in these hills, he said, without his little buddy strapped on his hip. He had big plans for this place. He was going to turn it into a dude ranch. Horses. Cabins. First thing he was going to do was stain the house barn-red so it looked like a real log cabin. Then he was going to log off all them damn tamaracks behind the house before they fell on it. Lotta lumber in there.

Mom's mouth dropped open. Fortunately she managed to close it, she told us later, before she actually called him a jackass.

He wanted possession of the place right away, so we were going to have to move out sooner than we expected. Within days Mom arranged to sell or give away most of our furniture—even though it had taken a beating over the past six years. Mr. Besley had said if we wanted to leave anything behind he would be happy to take it off our hands. Mom told him there was a folding bathtub in the attic that we would be happy to leave for him.

Actually, we weren't taking much with us at all. We were leaving the old Victrola and all the scratchy records behind. And the kerosene lamps, of course. The footlocker. The wash boiler. Dad said when it came to the kitchen table, we had no choice, the house must have been built around it.

With her two hands, Mom smoothed the wings of her old chair, as if to put it to rest after such a long, crazy flight. We left it sitting alone in the corner of the living room.

We stayed in Crosses' cabin at Two Jacks for the last few weeks. Bob and I made one last trip with Dad, up to Helmer's Lake.

And one morning, almost before we knew it, we were driving down the Yaak Road for the last time. Dad was in high spirits. His job with the Air Force was promising. They were transferring us to a base in Spokane, where he would eventually become Chief of Civil Engineering. We would be city-dwellers and have a normal life again.

Mom and Bob and I talked about all the things we'd been missing and Steve had never known: A refrigerator topped the list. Television. A bathroom, with a tub! Movies. A grocery store. For me, high school loomed ahead, huge.

Nobody said a word about what we were leaving behind.

When we got to Highway 2, Dad stopped and we all looked back at the Yaak Road. Our friend, our enemy. Savior and deathtrap. Would any of us miss it?

Hell, no.

We turned left, toward Troy. Dad said there was a place he wanted to see. The Forest Service had recently set aside an area along the river and he wanted to stop there for a minute. It was now or never, he said.

We drove a short way to where the highway crossed the Yaak River. We crossed the bridge and pulled over to the side of the road. Dad got out, so we all followed, Flossie too, but we were impatient now; we were anxious to get on with the trip. Dad picked his way along a trail beside the river with us behind him. Somewhere not too far ahead, we knew by the deep, resonant roar, was the Kootenai River.

We came to an opening in the willows, beneath a stand of tall cedar trees. The Kootenai slid by, a great sweep of turquoise water. A sheer rock cliff rose out of the water on the far side. Here also, was the end of the Yaak River.

The Yaak shot its arrow straight into the Kootenai, the current reaching across to the cliff on the far side. There the arrow was halted by the solid rock. Beneath the cliff the two rivers boiled in a roaring jumble of whirlpools. Over time, the rock face had been hollowed away by the converging currents. The crossing water curved upstream, searching another way. At the edge of the swirling eddy, the Yaak's circling current was caught again, subsumed and swept downstream by the Kootenai.

The early sun was beating on our backs as we stood there, watching the rivers converge.

"Just something I wanted us all to see," said Dad, "before we go."

Epilogue

Anna and August Binder lived in the Yaak until the end of their lives. Anna died in 1957 at the age of eighty-three and is buried at Boyd Hill Cemetery in the Upper Yaak Valley. August died in 1962 at age eighty-six and is buried beside his wife. Julius had "Mother" and "Father" put on their headstones. After their deaths the Binder homestead was sold and eventually became a guest ranch.

Julius Binder moved to Troy after his parents were gone and lived in a cabin in the woods just outside of town until near the end of his life. He died in 1990 at age eighty-four and is buried at Boyd Hill Cemetery.

Rosy Shultz was killed in December of 1960 when she and Gus hit a patch of ice and went off Stonechest Grade in their pickup. She was sixty-seven. She is buried at La Crosse, Wisconsin. Gus was killed not quite a year later, when his pickup went off the Yaak Road in almost the same place. He was sixty-seven. Gus is buried at Boyd Hill Cemetery.

Alma and Elmer Phillips lost their son Gerald when he was killed driving a logging truck on Moyie grade near Bonners Ferry. They sold their place in the Yaak and moved to the Washington coast and later, to Coeur d'Alene, Idaho, where they spent the rest of their lives. Their lake is now named "Lake Okaga" and is still privately owned.

John McIntire and Jeanette Nolan continued their busy careers as actors in movies and on television. John became the wagon master, the lead role, on the television series *Wagon Train* in 1961. He died in 1991. Jeanette made her final screen appearance in the movie *The Horse*

Whisperer. She died in 1998. Their daughter Holly still owns their ranch and Florabelle is parked in a shed near Big John's cabin.

The Cummings Sawmill on the West Fork burned in the late 1950's. The mill pond is still there and you can find pieces of the old mill if you know where to look. The Cummings girls now live in Oregon with their families.

Gary Harding became a doctor. He and his wife live on the original Harding property in the Yaak. Laurence spends summer vacations there with his family.

Francine Conley became a registered nurse and later, a nun. She did not stay in the convent but continued her nursing career. She was killed in a bicycle accident in Honolulu, Hawaii sometime in the 1980's.

After leaving the Yaak Valley, Dar and Marilyn Knowles lived in Spokane, Washington and Tillamook, Salem, and Bend, Oregon. Dar died in 1986, a much-loved father and grandfather. Marilyn still lives in Bend, in a log cabin.

Doris, "Dee," the author of this book, went to nursing school, graduating with Francine Conley. She and her husband visit the Yaak whenever they can.

Barbara, "Bob," became a pharmacist and married her high school sweetheart, Bruce Anderson. Bruce, a chemical engineer, had a job that took the two of them all over the world. They lived in England, France, India and Singapore. Bob's health failed after two bouts with cancer and she died in India in 2006 at the age of sixty.

Steve is a business owner and hobby gunsmith in Bend, Oregon, where he lives with his wife, Linda. They love listening to Mom reminisce about the Yaak.

The cabin and lake property once owned by the Knowles family is well cared for and enjoyed by a retired couple from Washington state. The lake still has a subterranean outlet and the fishing is still good.

Dar and Marilyn Knowles on the front porch, about to be joined by Stevie.

About the Author

Doris Knowles Pulis was born in California and spent her early childhood in the Yaak Valley in Montana. She later went to school in Spokane, Washington, and became a Registered Nurse, a profession she practiced for twenty years. She met her husband, Cal Pulis, in 1962 while they were both still in school and working at American Lake Veterans Hospital in Washington State. They lived in Montana's Bitterroot Valley for twenty-five years, where they raised Christmas trees. They reside in Bend, Oregon, and have two children, Anne and Chris, and one grandchild.